W9-BFK-626

THE SOURCEBOOK OF ARCHITECTURAL & INTERIOR ART 17

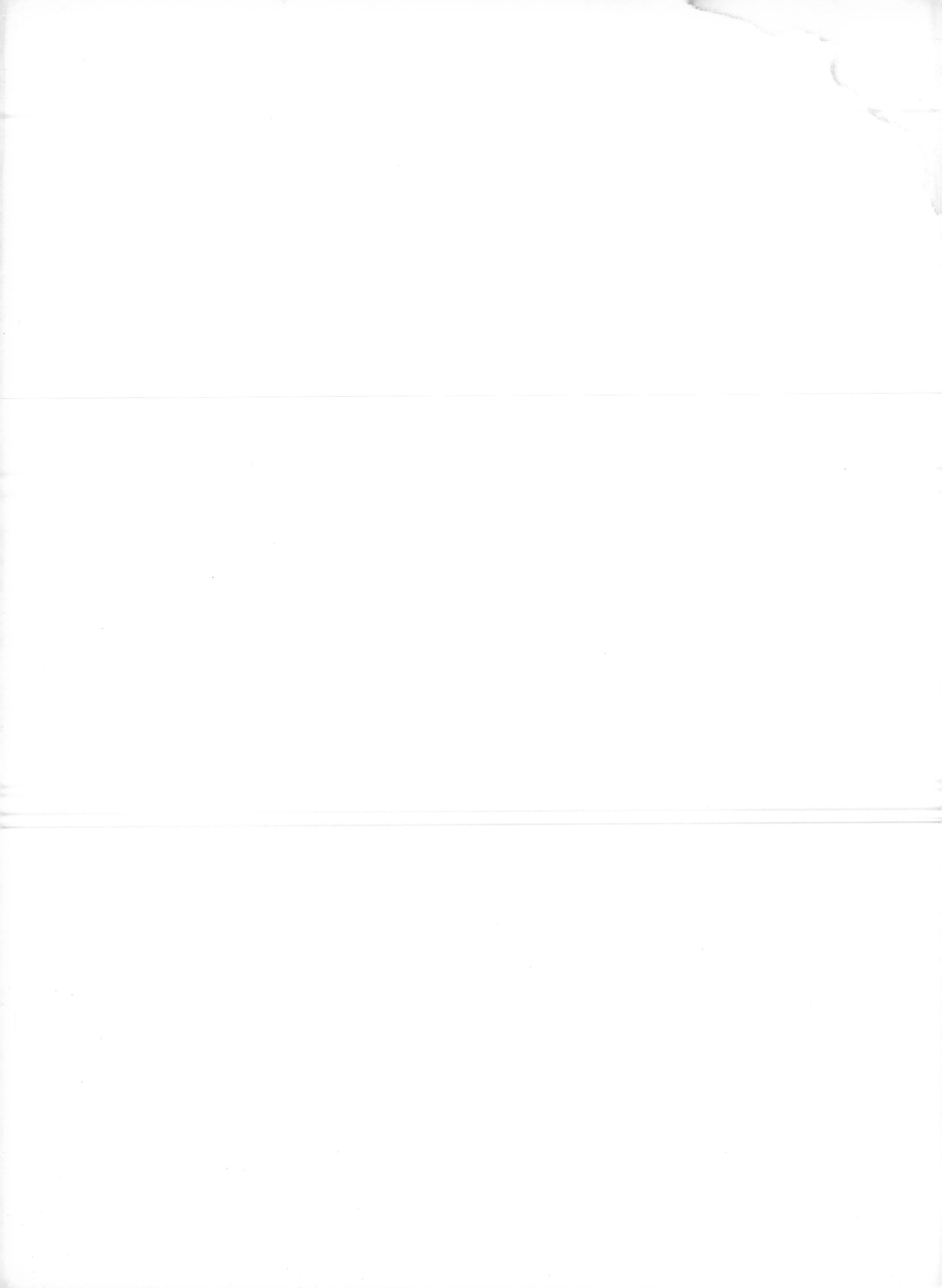

THE SOURCEBOOK OF ARCHITECTURAL & INTERIOR ART 17

GUILD Sourcebooks
Madison, Wisconsin
USA

THE SOURCEBOOK OF ARCHITECTURAL & INTERIOR ART 17

PUBLISHER
GUILD Sourcebooks
An imprint of GUILD, LLC
931 E. Main Street
Madison, Wisconsin 53703
TEL 608-257-2590 • TEL 877-284-8453

ADMINISTRATION
Toni Sikes, CEO and Founder
Reed McMillan, Vice President of Sales
Jeanne Gohlke, Administrative Assistant

DESIGN, PRODUCTION AND EDITORIAL
Georgene Pomplun, Art Director
Bob Johnston, Production Artist
Katie Kazan, Chief Editorial Officer
Jill Schaefer, Editorial/Production Coordinator
Sarah Streed, Writer (Interviews)

ARTIST CONSULTANTS
Nicole Carroll • Carol Chapin • Carla Dillman
Lori Dumm • Amy Lambright • Laura Marth

ISBN (hardcover) 1-880140-48-9 • ISBN (softcover) 1-880140-47-0

Printed in China

Cover art: Paul Housberg, Peninsula Hotel, Chicago, Illinois, 2001, fused/cast glass, 12' x 9'.
Photograph by Jon Miller © Hedrich-Blessing.

Page 5: Binh Pho, *Dynasty,* 2001, sycamore, dye and acrylic, 14" x 10"Dia. Photograph by Binh Pho.

On a Mission

For almost two decades, we've been on a mission. GUILD sourcebooks — annual explorations into the world of commissioned art — have introduced design and art professionals to the artists who turn dreams into reality. We have watched beginning relationships grow into exhilarating collaborations, and we've been on hand to celebrate the results. It's a happy day in the GUILD offices when we see photos of completed commission projects. ■ Each GUILD sourcebook takes almost a year to produce. We work hard to put this multitude of resources under one cover — all with one goal in mind: to make you aware of some remarkable artistic possibilities. ■ One look through these pages should convince you that these possibilities are virtually unlimited. From that point on, it's up to you. Call or e-mail an artist and explore their versatile talents one-on-one. Or take GUILD sourcebooks with you to client meetings (a sure-fire way to convince a client to include art in your project). ■ Better yet, just sit with the book for a while — and dream. Let the work in these pages be a launching pad for your imagination. ■ However or whenever you put GUILD sourcebooks to their intended use, we hope they become an essential tool to help you realize your vision of buildings, interior spaces and public environments that enliven, stimulate and give context to our lives. ■ When that happens, our mission is accomplished.

Toni Sikes
Publisher and Founder
GUILD Sourcebooks

Table of Contents

Table of Contents

FEATURED ARTISTS

Turn the page for a listing of featured artists.

SECTIONS

Artists by Section

Architectural Ceramics, Mosaics & Wall Reliefs

Architectural Metal

Architectural Glass

Architectural Elements

Atrium Sculpture

Artists by Section

Representational Sculpture

Non-Representational Sculpture

Public Art

Artists by Section

Liturgical Art

Furniture & Objects

Lighting

Murals & Trompe L'Oeil

Paintings, Prints & Drawings

Artists by Section

Fine Art Photography

Art for the Wall: Mixed Media

Art for the Wall: Paper

Art for the Wall: Fiber

Using the Sourcebook

The Sourcebook of Architectural & Interior Art 17 is designed specifically for individuals and trade professionals seeking artists to create large- or small-scale commissioned artwork. In addition to each artist's display of images, listings in the back of the book describe the artist's range of work, commissions and recent projects. These listings are organized in alphabetical order by the heading on each artist's page. They contain all the information necessary to contact the artist about your project, thus making the sourcebook a unique direct-call resource.

PRODUCT SEARCH

If you already know what type of work your project calls for, a search by section will help you find results quickly. Artists in the sourcebook are arranged in sections covering work as varied as large-scale glass in the Architectural Glass section to art quilts and tapestries in Art for the Wall: Fiber. Check the Table of Contents for a list of sections.

When paging through a particular section, keep in mind that the photos presented on each of the artists' pages are representative of the work that they do, not the full extent of their capabilities. If you like an artist's style but are interested in having him or her take on a different type of project than the ones pictured, contact the artist and see if it's a good fit. Likewise, you can broaden your searches to several different sections to find an even wider variety of choices. If you are searching for freestanding sculpture, for example, you might want to look through not only the Representational Sculpture and Non-Representational Sculpture sections, but the Public Art section as well.

ARTIST SEARCH

If you know the name of the artist you want to work with, you can easily search using the Artist Information section or the Index of Artists and Companies, both found in the gray pages at the back of the sourcebook. The Artist Information section provides a wealth of detail about each artist, including the materials and techniques they use, examples of their commissions and collections, and publications that feature photographs of their artwork (including previous GUILD sourcebooks). Both the Artist Information section and the Index of Artists and Companies include page references, so you can easily locate the artist's full-color page in the book.

Want to know more about an artist's work? Don't hesitate to call the artist directly for more information.

LOCATION SEARCH

Looking for an artist in your area or another particular region? The Location Index is an invaluable tool for such searches. Located in the back of the book, this index can help you find artists from across the United States, Canada and abroad.

INSPIRATIONAL BROWSING

Even if you don't have a specific project in mind, *The Sourcebook of Architectural & Interior Art 17* will prove a valuable tool. It can be taken to client meetings to show a world of possibilities, browsed through for future inspiration and used to see the newest projects of artists you've collaborated with in the past.

Sculptural installation by Archie Held Studio. *See page 133.*

The Commission Process

The nearly 250 artists featured in *The Sourcebook of Architectural & Interior Art 17* represent a remarkable spectrum of artistic talent and vision. Whether you're looking for a large-scale public sculpture or a residential accessory, this book can put you directly in touch with highly qualified artists throughout North America. Any one of these artists can be commissioned to create a unique work of art — but with so many exceptional artists to choose from, finding the right one for your specific project can be a challenge. Once the artist has been selected, careful planning and communication can help ensure a great outcome.

Having watched art commissions unfold since the first GUILD sourcebook was published in 1986, we can suggest steps to ensure successful partnerships between artists and trade professionals. We especially want to reassure those who have been reluctant to try such a collaboration because of questions about how the process works.

This article is a how-to guide to the art commissioning process. It suggests strategies to help the selection and hiring processes go smoothly and discusses advantages of including the artist in the design team, and doing so early in the process. Finally, it describes the full spectrum of services now offered through "GUILDtrade," our resource division specifically for architects, interior designers and art consultants. For more on GUILD's expanded services to trade professionals, turn to page 21.

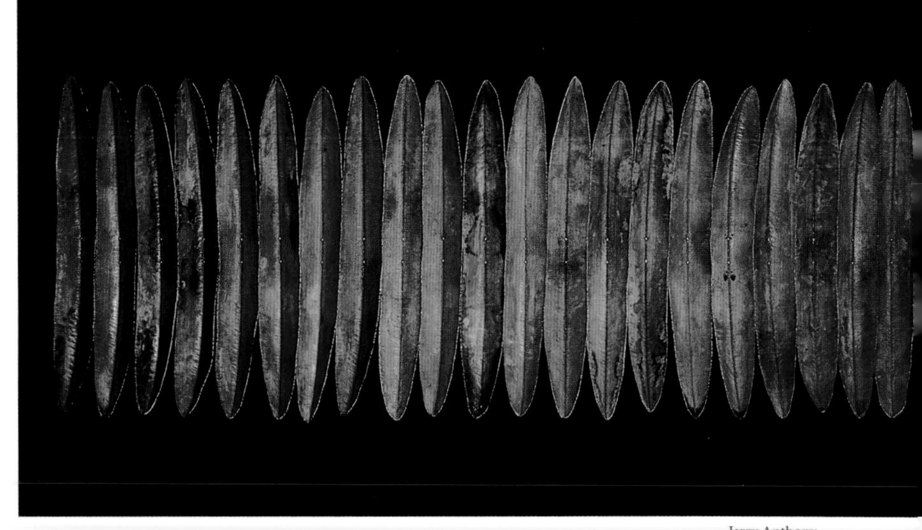

Jerry Anthony

FINDING THE ARTIST

By far the most important step in a successful commission is choosing the right artist for your particular project and budget. This choice is the decision from which all others will flow, so it's worth investing time and energy in the selection process and seasoning the search with both wild artistic hopes and hard-nosed realism. The right choices at this early stage will make things go more smoothly later on.

Some clients will want to help select and work with the artist. Others will want only minimal involvement, leaving most of the decision-making to the design team. Regardless of who makes the decisions, there are several ways to find the right artist. Obviously, we recommend browsing through *The Sourcebook of Architectural & Interior Art 17.* Every artist featured on these pages is actively seeking commission projects; that's why they're included in the book. Many of these artists already have strong track records of working with designers, architects and art consultants; you will gain from their professionalism and experience. Others are newer in their field; their determination to prove themselves can fuel an exciting and successful collaboration.

The Trade Sales Consultants at GUILDtrade are another unique resource for trade professionals seeking artists for specific projects. Our consultants are trained to discuss your project with you, determine your art requirements and suggest artists who can fulfill your particular design needs. If the project is a large one, they can guide you through a request-for-proposal (RFP) process that can draw responses from all over the continent. Your RFP can also be posted online through our "Post a Project" feature (see page 21). Post a Project allows you to broadcast your RFP to our list of nearly a thousand juried artists and invite them to respond to your call. A GUILDtrade staff member can be a great ally both when seeking an artist and when steering your way through a commission project.

NARROWING THE FIELD

Once your "A-list" is narrowed down to two or three names, it's time to schedule meetings, either face-to-face (for local artists) or by phone. During these discussions, try to determine the artist's interest in your project, and pay attention to your own comfort level with the artist. Try to find out if the chemistry is right — whether you have the basis to build a working relationship. This is also the time to confirm that the artist has the necessary skills to undertake your project. Be thorough and specific when asking questions. Is the artist excited about the project? What does he or she see as the most important issues or considerations? Will your needs be a major or minor concern? Evaluate the artist's style, approach and personality.

If it feels like you might have trouble working together, take heed. But if all goes well and it feels like a good fit, ask for a list of references. These are important calls; don't neglect to make them! Ask about the artist's work habits, communication style and, of course, the success of the artwork. You should also ask whether the project was delivered on time and within budget. If you like what you hear, you'll be one important step closer to hiring your artist.

EXPECT PROFESSIONALISM

If this is an expensive or complicated project, you may want to request preliminary designs. Since most artists charge a design fee whether or not they're ultimately hired for the project, start by asking for sketches from your top candidate. If you're unhappy with the designs submitted, you can go to your second choice. But if the design is what you'd hoped for, it's time to finalize your working agreement with this artist.

As you discuss contract details, be resolved that silence is not golden and ignorance is not bliss! Be frank. Discuss the budget and timetable, and tell the artist what you expect. Now is the time for possible misunderstandings to be brought up and resolved — not later, after the work is half done and deadlines loom.

WORKING WITH AN ART CONSULTANT

As your project gains definition, you'll need to pay attention to its technical aspects, including building codes, lighting specifications, and details related to zoning and installation. Most designers find the artist's knowledge and understanding of materials, code, safety and engineering complete and reassuring.

However, complex projects may warrant hiring a consultant to help with these details, as well as the initial selection of art and artists. Make sure the consultant is sophisticated and experienced enough to provide real guidance with your project. This means the ability to help negotiate the technical aspects of a very specific contract, including issues like installation, insurance, storage, transportation and engineering costs.

PUTTING IT IN WRITING

It is a truism in any kind of business that it is much cheaper to get the lawyers involved at the beginning of a process rather than after something goes wrong. A signed contract or letter of agreement commits the artist to completing his or her work on time and to specifications. It also assures the artist that he or she will get paid the right amount at the right time. That just about eliminates the biggest conflicts that can arise.

Contracts should be specific to the job. Customarily, artists are responsible for design, production, shipping and installation. If someone else is to be responsible for installation, be sure you specify who will coordinate and pay for it: if not the artist, it's usually the client. With a large project, it's helpful to identify the tasks that, if delayed for any reason, would set back completion of the project. These should be discussed up front to assure that both parties agree on requirements and expectations.

Most trade professionals recognize that adequate compensation for the artists is in their best interest, as it assures the type and level of service needed to fulfill their expectations. The more skill you need and the more complex the project, the more you should budget for the artist's work and services.

Above left: copper wall sculpture by Linda M. Leviton. *See page 279.*

PAYMENT SCHEDULE

Payments are usually tied to specific milestones in the process. These serve as check points and assure that work is progressing in a satisfactory manner, on time and on budget. Payment is customarily made in three stages, although this certainly depends on the circumstances, scope and complexity of the project.

The first payment is usually made when the contract is signed. It covers the artist's time and creativity in developing a detailed design specific to your needs. You can expect to go through several rounds of trial and error in the design process, but at the end of this stage you will have detailed drawings (and, for three-dimensional work, a maquette, or model) that everyone agrees upon. The cost of the maquette and the design time are usually factored into the artist's fee.

The second payment is generally set for a point midway through the project and is for work completed to date. If the materials are expensive, the client may be asked to advance money at this stage to cover costs. If the commission is canceled during this period, the artist keeps the money already paid for work performed.

Final payment is usually due when the work is installed. If the piece is finished on time but the building or project is delayed, the artist is customarily paid on delivery, but still has the obligation to oversee installation.

You will find that most artists keep tabs on the project budget. Be sure that the project scope does not deviate from what was agreed upon at the outset. If the scope changes, amend the agreement to reflect the changes.

THE ARTIST AS DESIGNER

We should say up front that not every artist charges a design fee. Some consider preliminary sketches a part of their marketing effort and figure they will be compensated for their time by the client once the project is approved. But it's more common for an artist to require a design fee of 5% to 10% of the final project budget. In some cases, especially when the artist has considerable experience and a strong reputation in a specialized area, the design fee may be as high as 25% of the project budget; this is most common when an artist is hired to envision specific solutions to complicated architectural problems. Obviously, in this kind of situation the artist is not merely asked to supply a product, but also to contribute a significant part of the design solution; here, the artist's ideas and experience are as important as his or her tangible work.

A few points about design are worth highlighting here:

1. Design Ideas Are the Artist's Property

It should go without saying that it is highly unethical, as well as possibly illegal, to take an artist's designs — even very preliminary or non-site-specific sketches — and use them without the artist's permission. Some artists may include specific language about ownership of ideas, models, sketches, etc., in their contracts or letters of agreement. Even if an artist does not use a written agreement, be sure you are clear at the outset about what you are paying for and what rights the artist retains.

2. Respect the Artist's Ideas and Vision

When you hire a doctor, you want a thoughtful, intelligent diagnosis, not just a course of treatment. The same should be true when you hire an artist to work with a design team. Most GUILD artists have become successful through many years of experience, and because of their excellence in both technique and aesthetic imagination. Take advantage of that experience and expertise fully by bringing the artist into the project early, and by asking him or her for ideas.

3. Keep the Artist Informed of Changes

Tell the artist about changes — even seemingly minor details — which may have a significant impact on the project design. If the artist is working as a member of the design team, it's easier to include him or her in the ongoing dialog about the overall project.

4. Consider a Separate Design Budget for Your Project

A design budget is particularly helpful when you:

- want to get lots of ideas from an artist;
- need site-specific ideas that involve significant research;
- require a formal presentation with finished drawings, blueprints or maquettes.

To evaluate designs for a project from several artists, consider a competition with a small design fee for each artist.

It comes down to an issue of professionalism. Artists have the technical skills to do wonderful and amazing things with simple materials. But they also have sophisticated conceptual and design talents. By being willing to pay for these talents, trade professionals add vision and variety to their creative products. In such a partnership, both parties gain, and the ultimate result is a client who is delighted by the outcome of the collaboration.

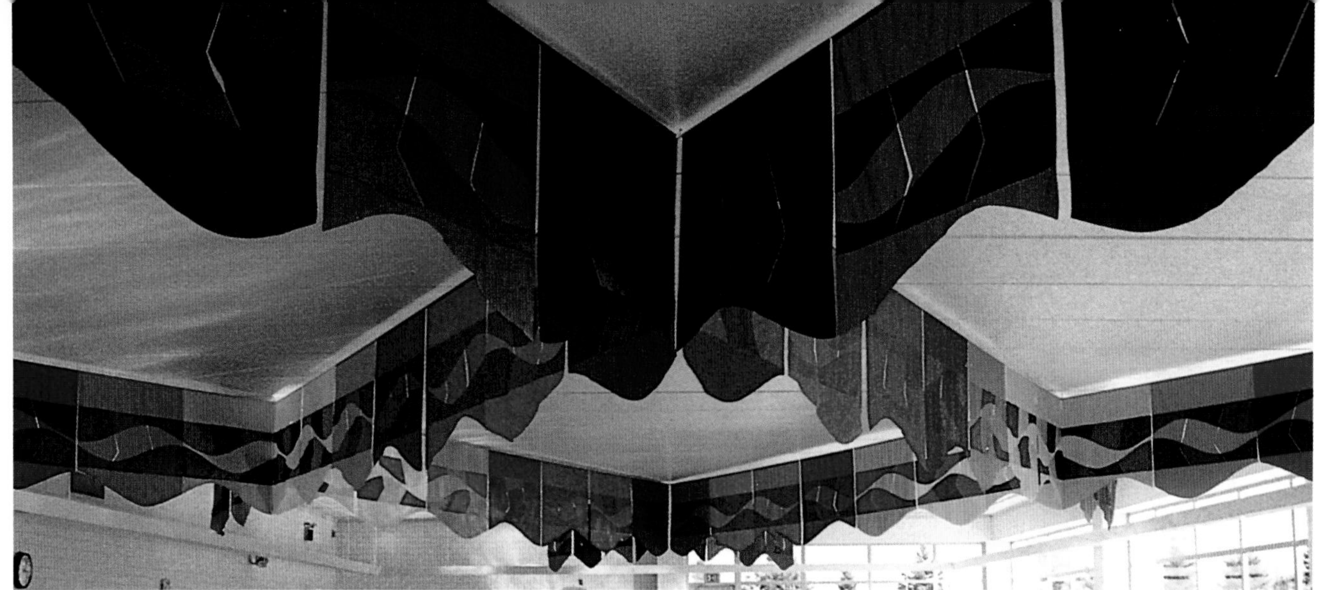

A COLLABORATIVE ATMOSPHERE

With most commission projects, it's best to bring the artist into the process at about the same time you hire a general contractor. By involving the artist at this early stage, the space will be designed with the art in mind, and the art will be designed to enhance the space. As a result, there will be no unpleasant surprises about size or suitability of artwork. Furthermore, when art is planned for early on and is a line item in the budget, it's far less likely to be cut at the end of the project, when money is running low.

Early inclusion of the artist also helps ensure that the collaborative effort will flow smoothly throughout all phases of the project. If the artist is respected as part of the team, his or her work can benefit the project's overall design.

Naturally, the scope of the project will determine the number of players to be involved with the artist. How will decisions be made? Who is the artist's primary liaison? Will a single person sign off on designs and recommendations? Are committees necessary? It's important that all individuals understand both their own responsibilities and the responsibilities of their collaborators.

SEEK TWO-WAY UNDERSTANDING

Be sure the artist understands the technical requirements of the job, including traffic flow in the space, the intended use of the space, the building structure, maintenance, lighting and environmental concerns. By doing this, you ensure that the artist's knowledge, experience and skills inform the project.

Keep the artist apprised of any changes that will affect the work in progress. Did you find a certain material you specified unavailable and replace it with something else? Did the available space become bigger or smaller? These changes could have a profound impact on an artist's planning and work. If the artist works as a member of the design team, it's easier to include him or her in the loop.

At the same time, the artist should let you know of any special requirements his or her work will place on the space. Is it especially heavy? Does it need to be mounted in a specific way? Must it be protected from theft or vandalism? What kind of lighting is best? You may need to budget funds for these kinds of installation expenses.

Most artists experienced with commissioned projects factor the expense of a continuing design dialog into their fee. There is an unfortunate belief harbored by some trade professionals (and yes, artists too) that a willingness to develop and adapt a design based on discussions with the client or design team somehow indicates a lack of commitment or creativity. On the contrary. The ability to modify design or execution without compromising artistic quality is a mark of professionalism. We recommend looking for this quality in the artist you choose, and then respecting it by treating the artist as a partner in any decisions that will affect his or her work.

Of course, part of working together is making clear who is responsible for what. Since few designers and architects (and even fewer contractors) are used to working with artists, the relationship is ripe for misunderstanding. Without constant communication, things can easily fall through the cracks.

Above: banners by Judy Dioszegi. *See page 94.*

FORGING A PARTNERSHIP

The partnership between artists and trade professionals is an old and honorable one. Many venerable blueprints indicate, for example, an architect's detail for a ceiling with the scrawled note: "Finish ceiling in this manner." The assumption, of course, is that the artisan working on the ceiling has both the technical mastery and the aesthetic skill to create a whole expanse of space based on a detail sketched by the architect's pen.

The artists whose work fills these pages — and with whom we work every day at GUILD — are capable of interactive relationships like those described here. We're delighted to see increasing numbers of trade professionals include artists on their design teams. After seeing the arts separated from architectural and interior design for too many years, we're happy to be part of a renewed interest in collaboration.

COMMISSION GUIDELINES

• Contact GUILDtrade for assistance in recommending artists or posting your project.

• Bring the artist into the project as early as possible.

• Be as specific as possible about the scope and range of the project, even in early meetings before the artist is selected.

• Be honest and realistic when discussing deadlines, responsibilities and specific project requirements — and expect the same from the artist. Don't avoid discussing the areas where there seem to be questions.

• For larger projects, use specific milestones to assure continuing consensus on project scope and budget. It may also be necessary to make adjustments at these points.

• Choose an artist based on a solid portfolio of previous work and excellent references from other trade professionals. And remember that it's less risky to use an artist who has worked on projects that are similar in size and scope, who can handle the demands of your specific job.

• Consider hiring an art consultant if the commission is particularly large or complex. The consultant should help with complicated contract arrangements, and should make certain that communication between artists and support staff (including subcontractors and engineers) is thoroughly understood.

• Trust your instincts when choosing an artist. Like selecting an advertising agency or an architect, choosing an artist is based partly on chemistry. You need to like the work and respect the artist, and you also need to be able to work together comfortably.

Photo: William A. Porter, San Francisco, CA

GUILDtrade

A COLLECTION OF SERVICES FOR THE TRADE PROFESSIONAL

The Sourcebook of Architectural & Interior Art 17 is only one of several tools for trade professionals available through GUILD. Since 1986, GUILD sourcebooks have introduced architects, interior designers and art consultants to top artists. More recently, GUILDtrade has expanded on the basic functions of our sourcebooks through a series of companion services for trade professionals. These services are found under the umbrella of GUILDtrade's "Trade Resource Program."

THE GUILD SOURCEBOOK ONLINE

The hallmark of our Trade Resource Program is the "GUILD Sourcebook Online." Created in response to the growing number of trade professionals who use the Internet to source products and services, the online sourcebook provides quick and easy access to our comprehensive artist listings. Visit www.guildtrade.com to browse the GUILD Sourcebook Online. For more about this exceptional resource, turn the page.

POST A PROJECT

"Post a Project" is a great complement to GUILD's online sourcebook. This feature allows trade professionals to broadcast descriptions of their upcoming projects to GUILD's database of commissionable artists, and is equally useful for large RFPs or small design accessories. New Post a Project listings are e-mailed promptly; individual artists respond to projects that match their abilities and interests. Post a Project is an efficient and effective way to broadcast a general call for artists and ideas.

CONTACT THE ARTIST

Once you've perused the sourcebook and found an artist you'd like to consider for a project, fill out the electronic "Request Commission Information" form linked to that artist's online page. This form captures basic information about your project, enabling the artist to respond with insights and possible solutions. These responses are a good way to gauge an artist's initial interest and suitability.

TRADE SALES CONSULTANTS

Perhaps the most valuable service offered by GUILDtrade is the personal assistance of our experienced staff. Our "Trade Sales Consultants" are available via e-mail or phone to make art recommendations and offer expert advice. Simply give our knowledgeable staff an idea of your art needs, and they'll put together a comprehensive portfolio of recommendations, available in electronic or printed versions. Call 1-877-565-2002 during business hours to speak with a consultant.

Glass installation by Sandra C.Q. Bergér. *See page 51.*

Sourcebook Online

A GUIDE FOR THE DESIGN PROFESSIONAL

The Internet is a tool of endless potential; it allows us to research and purchase everything from wedding rings to t-shirts to automobiles. For design professionals seeking just the right artists for their high-end projects, GUILD has harnessed this potential in the GUILD Sourcebook Online — an ingenious complement to GUILD's paper-and-ink sourcebooks.

A TERRIFIC NEW RESOURCE

Visit the Sourcebook Online anytime. Just drop by www.guildtrade.com and click on the sourcebook link. You'll agree: the Sourcebook Online is a wellspring of ideas, inspiration and information for you and your clients. Best of all, it's a free resource for all design professionals.

BROWSING THE SOURCEBOOK ONLINE

There are three ways to browse within the Sourcebook Online: by category, product or artist name. Category listings match the section headings in the sourcebook while product listings allow you to focus on more specific types of work. Product groupings are varied and enticing. They include armoires, bannisters and railings, bars, beds, benches, cabinets, CD holders, ceramic wall reliefs, chairs, children's furniture, clocks, coffee tables, credenzas and buffets, desks, dining tables, doors, dressers, fences, fiber wall hangings, finials, fireplace screens and accessories, fireplaces/mantles, fountains, furnishings, gates, lamps and sconces, light fixtures, lighting installations, metal wall hangings, mixed media wall hangings, mobiles, mosaics, murals and tromp l'oeil, paintings, prints and drawings, panels and screens, paper wall hangings, photography, screens and panels, sculpture, shelves and shelving units, side tables, stools, tabletops and countertops, textiles, tile murals, tiles, wall reliefs, walls and ceilings, waterfalls and windows.

CONTACTING THE ARTIST

The Sourcebook Online enables you to be in touch with an artist with a click of your mouse. Simply fill out the online Artist Contact form linked to the top of each web page, and GUILDtrade will contact the artist on your behalf.

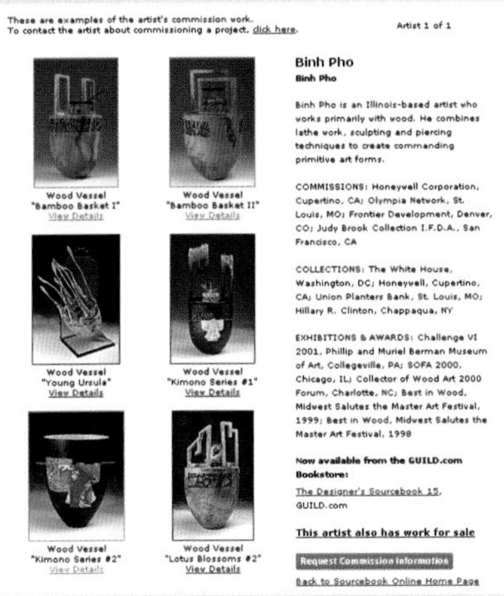

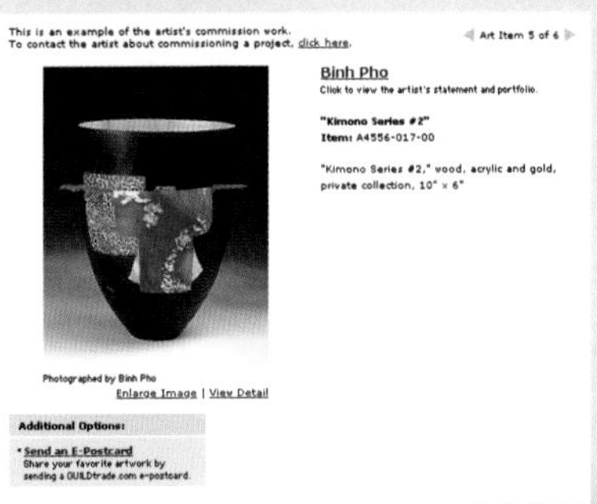

SEND AN E-POSTCARD

You can share your favorite artwork (and impress your clients) by sending e-postcards. Each postcard includes the image and title of the work you select, the artist's name, and a link to the GUILDtrade website. Look for the e-postcard link under the image on each item page. Just enter an e-mail address and a personal message (if you wish); your e-postcard will be delivered with a click of the Send button.

CLIENT PRESENTATIONS

You can also save pages and images from Sourcebook Online to your computer and incorporate them into client presentations. It's a quick and easy way to introduce your clients to artists available for commission projects.

TRADE SALES CONSULTANTS

Want to find out whether an artist is available for your project? Fill out the online Artist Contact form or contact one of our Trade Sales Consultants; they'll be happy to contact the artist on your behalf or show you additional examples of the artist's work.

Still can't find exactly what you're looking for? Fill out our online Post a Project form and we'll broadcast your project request via e-mail; GUILD artists will respond to you directly. If you prefer, GUILD's Trade Sales Consultants can assist with your search.

Finally, never hesitate to contact our Trade Sales Consultants. Their mission is to help you in any way they can as you select artists and make your vision a reality. Call 1-877-565-2002 (toll-free) or send us an e-mail: tradeinfo@guild.com.

Architectural Ceramics, Mosaics & Wall Reliefs

Columbus' Sky (upper deck), *da Gama's Sky* (mid deck), *Magellan's Sky* (lower deck), 2000, *Explorer of the Seas,* Royal Caribbean Cruise Line, glass and stone mosaic, approximately 39' x 6.5' each

Michel Verdure

Lynx (detail from *da Gama's Sky*) 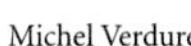 Michel Verdure

Camelopardalis (detail from *da Gama's Sky*) Michel Verdure

Station Clock, 1999, Glendale Transportation Center, Glendale, CA, glass mosaic, 4'Dia. Tom Bonner

Station Clock Tom Bonner

Paravento, 2001, ceramic relief, 12" x 13" x 1.75"

Gemelli, 2001, ceramic relief, 12" x 13" x 2"

Abbey, 2001, ceramic relief, 20" x 14" x 2"

Dome, 2001, ceramic relief, 22" x 18" x 2"

Photos: Bill Quinnell

Company of Women: Turquoise, 2001, ceramic tile, 12" x 12"

Toucans Mural, 2001, 6" x 6" ceramic tile totaling 18" x 12"

Photos: Erik S. Lieber

Mimi Moore

Mimi Moore is responsible for the art program at Denver International Airport. This means she administers and oversees the public art collections — including site-specific art commissions — as well as rotating exhibits. ■ The Denver Percent-for-Art ordinance specifies that one percent of the total costs of any new city construction be set aside for art at that site. Because the Denver International Airport was one of the largest public construction projects in recent years, the facility was awarded a substantial art budget. ■ One such commission includes *Mountain Mirage,* which greets travelers arriving at the center terminal. This breathtaking vision of the Rocky Mountains Front Range was created using 3,200 brass nozzles, which project streams of water into the air. ■ But Moore emphasizes that the art and the changing exhibits are not just for travelers. "We have a couple of thousand employees at the airport, so the rotating shows are for them too. We change these exhibitions four times a year. By the end of the third month, the employees always ask: 'What's next?'" ■ The most recent exhibition coincided with the National Stock Show. Moore worked with Paul Stewart, private collector and founder of the Black American West Museum, to create *Shadow Cowboy,* an installation on the history of African-American and Hispanic cowboys. ■ Because art at the airport is funded with public dollars, each proposal goes through a strict review process. Although this can make Moore's job stressful, she believes in the process. ■ "These public facilities are for everyone," she says, "so you have to be very conscientious. The review process is really a good thing."

Jamy Jones

Cellular Micrograph: Epithelial Tissue, Vanderbilt Univ. Medical Research Center, Nashville, TN, 2000, limestone panel, 3.5' x 5' x 3"

Cellular Micrograph: Nerve Tissue, 2000, limestone panel, 3.5' x 5' x 3"

Cellular Micrograph: Connective Tissue, 2000, limestone panel, 3.5' x 5' x 3"

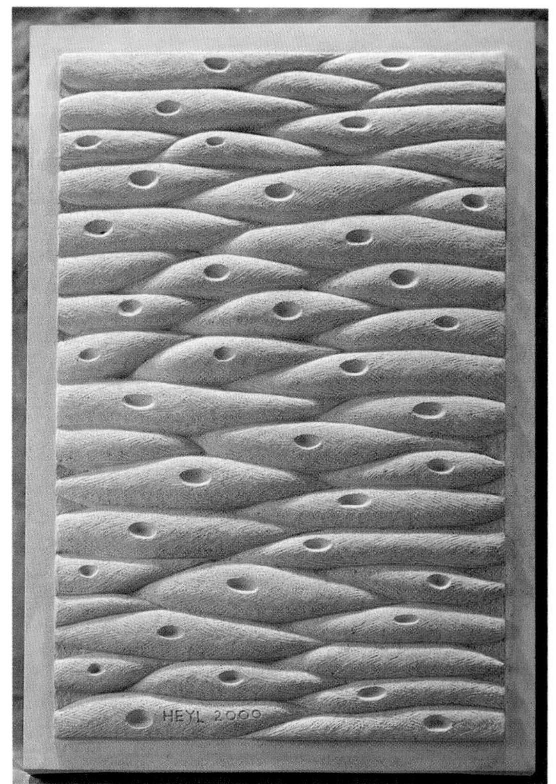

Cellular Micrograph: Muscle Tissue, 2000, limestone panel, 3.5' x 5' x 3"

Photos: Charles Behlow

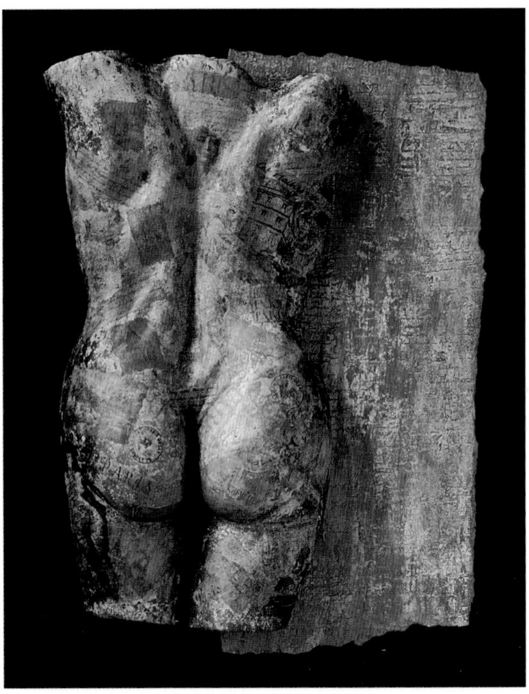

Paris (Travel Series), 2001, private residence, porcelain with Xerox transfers, 18" x 14" x 4"

Provence (Travel Series), 2001, private residence, porcelain with Polaroid emulsion and dry transfers, 18" x 16" x 4"

Geoff . . . 30 years, 2001, Nike, porcelain with Xerox and Polaroid emulsion transfers, 1' x 2' x 2.5"

Photos: Grace Weston

Peaceable Kingdom, installed March 2000, Mercy Hospital, Oshkosh, WI, 8'H x 18'W

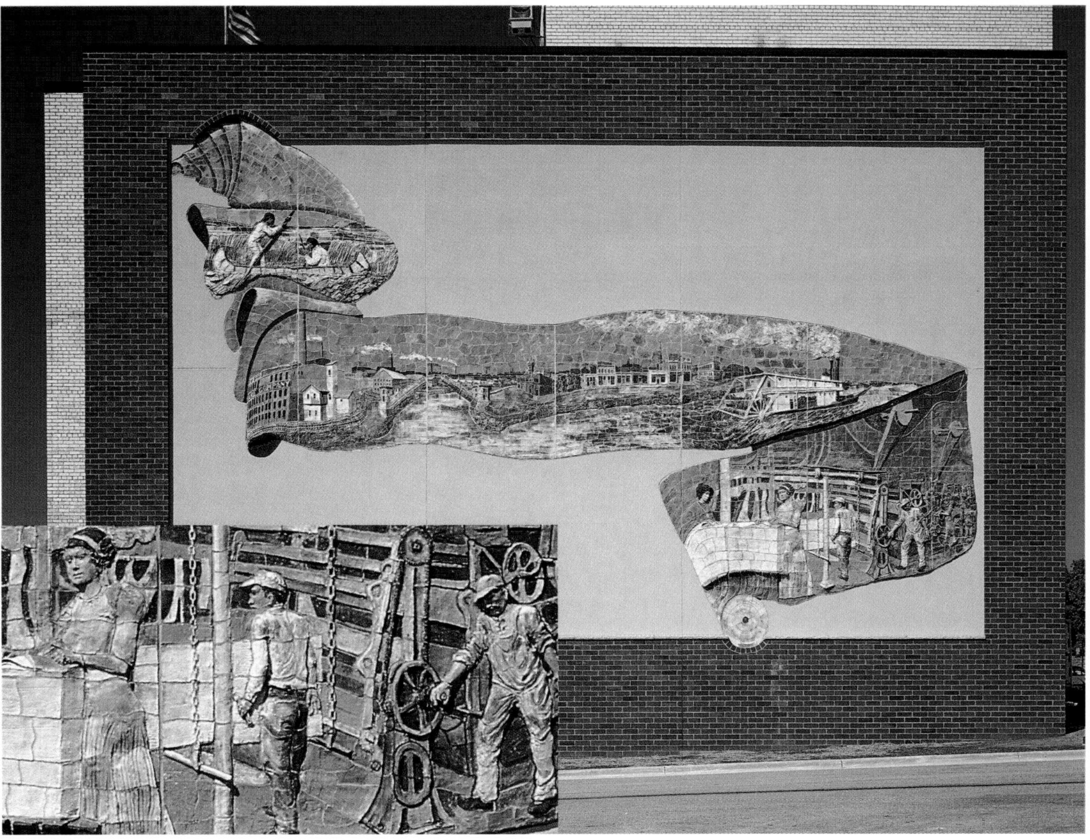

Ceramic relief, installed May 2000, City Hall, Menasha, WI, 53'W x 32'H

Photos: Munroe Studios

Carol Spiegel

Carol Spiegel is a seasoned professional. She has owned her own art consulting firm, The Art Group, for 22 years. The company works with architectural design firms and deals in all kinds of art, including original paintings and sculpture. Projects range from large public sculptures to corporate interiors. Spiegel also assembles collections of art for corporations. ■ Seven years ago, when an industry recession hit Los Angeles, Spiegel was prompted to open a second branch of her corporate consulting company in Las Vegas. She says her business has changed since the L.A. recession. ■ "I think people's priorities have changed. The artwork I buy for companies today isn't as expensive as it used to be. I'm buying as much as I used to, but spending less." ■ She now finds herself buying more work from emerging artists — artists whose work is just beginning to sell well. This change in business style fits right in with GUILD. ■ "GUILD has a number of artists who do well but aren't world famous," Spiegel says. "That's the market I deal in most, where a piece can sell from anywhere between $400 and $2,000. Instead of paying $60,000 for a sculpture, as we used to, we might now find an artist who will create a comparable piece for $30,000." ■ In her spare time, Spiegel sits on the board for a committee called NEON, whose mission is to preserve the classic neon signs from old Las Vegas hotels. Even when she's off duty, Spiegel is still committed to art.

Layered pigment over painted markings on clay relief, 2001, squares: 14" each; 7.5' x 6'

Randy Clark

Artemis, Acrobats, Divas and Dancers (detail), 1999-2000, MTA, 66th Street Lincoln Center Station, New York, NY, 2000-square-foot ceramic tile and glass mosaic, 42 panels, each panel: 4' x 12', original artwork by Nancy Spero

Artemis, Acrobats, Divas and Dancers (detail)

Photos: Stephanie Berger

Artemis, Acrobats, Divas and Dancers (detail)

Mission Creek Mural, collaboration with Lillian Sizemore, 1999, San Francisco, CA, ceramic tile and mirror mosaic, 15' x 8.5' Alon Picker

Velocity Circus mural (detail), 2001, San Francisco, CA, glass mosaic, 16' x 2' overall David Meiland

Pat's Bench, 2000, Kottinger Park, Pleasanton, CA, ceramic tile mosaic, 48" x 60" x 22" Laurel True

Architectural Metal

The Gregarious Swamp Village Collective, 2001, cast aluminum and fabricated steel railing, 65' x 6' x 22"

The Gregarious Swamp Village Collective (detail)

The Gregarious Swamp Village Collective (detail)

BRUCE PAUL FINK

Testing the Dawn (view from inside)

Testing the Dawn, 2001, Miami Blue Lagoon office entrance screen, cast aluminum and fabricated steel, 12' x 8.6' x 1.4"

Forged log rack with horse head, mild steel, 37"H

Entry/garden gate, forged mild steel and bronze, 65" x 37"

Forged split picket railing, mild steel, 150' (linear)

Classic-designed forged railing, mild steel, 111' (linear)

Forged and fabricated platter, mild steel, 37" x 20"

Tea Cup Gate, 2000, Perks Coffee Bar, Lampasas, TX, metal layers, 42" x 72" x 1.75"

Harold Harton

Custom-etched nickel mural, 2001, Hyatt Park Tower, Chicago, IL, 15' x 10'

Art Initiative, Inc.

Kimberley Campbell (right, below) and Kristen Rolando (left), who co-own Art Initiative, Inc. in Atlanta, Georgia, are a unique pair of art consultants. "Our complementary skills benefit our clients," says Campbell. Rolando agrees: "We work very well together." ■ The women describe their collaboration as a symbiotic merging of talents arising from their respective areas of expertise. Campbell, with her strong background in art history, aids not only in the initial presentation and planning of a project, but also with an explanation of how a piece of art fits within the historical context of location and theme. Rolando, who has studied at the Penland School of Crafts and worked in various mediums as an artist, is able to oversee standards of craftsmanship. ■ Together, the team accomplishes artistic feats such as placing a twenty-foot-high steel sculpture by Georgia artist Andrew Crawford in a two-story rotunda in Atlanta. Crawford fabricated the sculpture off-site in his studio and transported it to the site by truck. Once in place, the artist used an electrostatic technique to paint the piece a striking cobalt blue. ■ Campbell and Rolando feel a successful project such as this one allows the viewer to engage in a dialogue with the art. "The communication can be verbal or it can be internal," says Rolando, "It doesn't matter, so long as it's there." ■ Campbell agrees. "Whether it's a positive or negative reaction, that dialogue with the art is important."

Sarah Hobbs

Rock Art, dining room table, 1997, Cor-Ten steel

Bronze Age Dancers, floor lamp, 1999, Cor-Ten steel

Ode to Suzan (detail)

Ode to Suzan, sideboard table, 2001, Cor-Ten steel

Photos: Rob Melnychuk

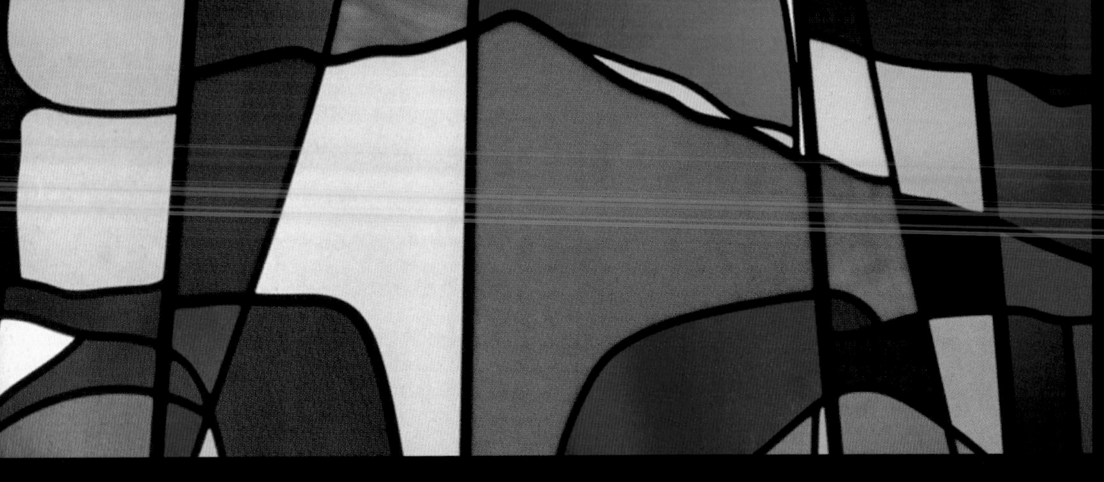

Architectural Glass

ARCHITECTURAL GLASS ART, INC.

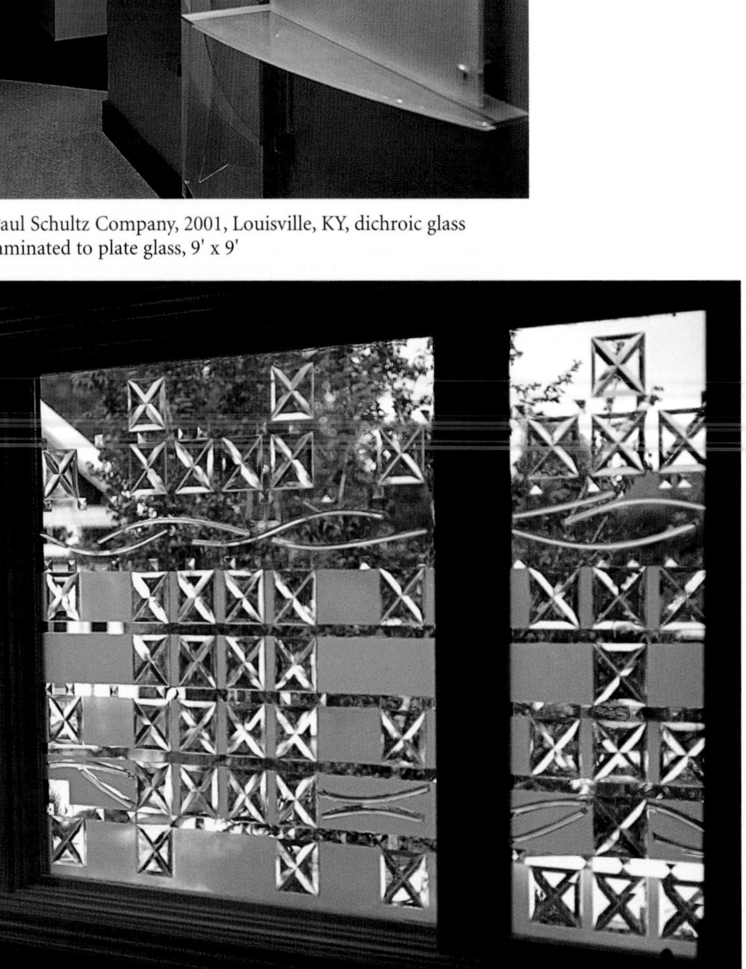

Paul Schultz Company, 2001, Louisville, KY, dichroic glass laminated to plate glass, 9' x 9'

Levinsky Residence, 2001, Louisville, KY, laminated beveled glass, 8' x 3'

Optically clear, etched and beveled glass installation, 5' x 5'

Photos: William A. Porter, San Francisco, CA

Cascades Entry, 2001, Stanley Hotel, Estes Park, CO

Jim Osterberg

The Magic Doors, 1999, Foothills Library, Glendale, AZ — Kathy Bradford

The Magic Doors (detail) — Kathy Bradford

Circus Bear (detail) — Photo provided by the Russian Tea Room

Bear Ballroom, 1999, the Russian Tea Room, New York, NY, sandcarved glass, ten arched panels, each 5' x 10' x .5" — Photo provided by the Russian Tea Room

Vestige, 1999, part one of *Chronos Trilogy,* Lincoln House office tower, Hong Kong, 26' x 15' x 5'

Inset: *Chronos Trilogy* (*Vestige,* center; *Sea of Time,* left; *Approach of Time,* right)

Photos: Gerry Kopelow

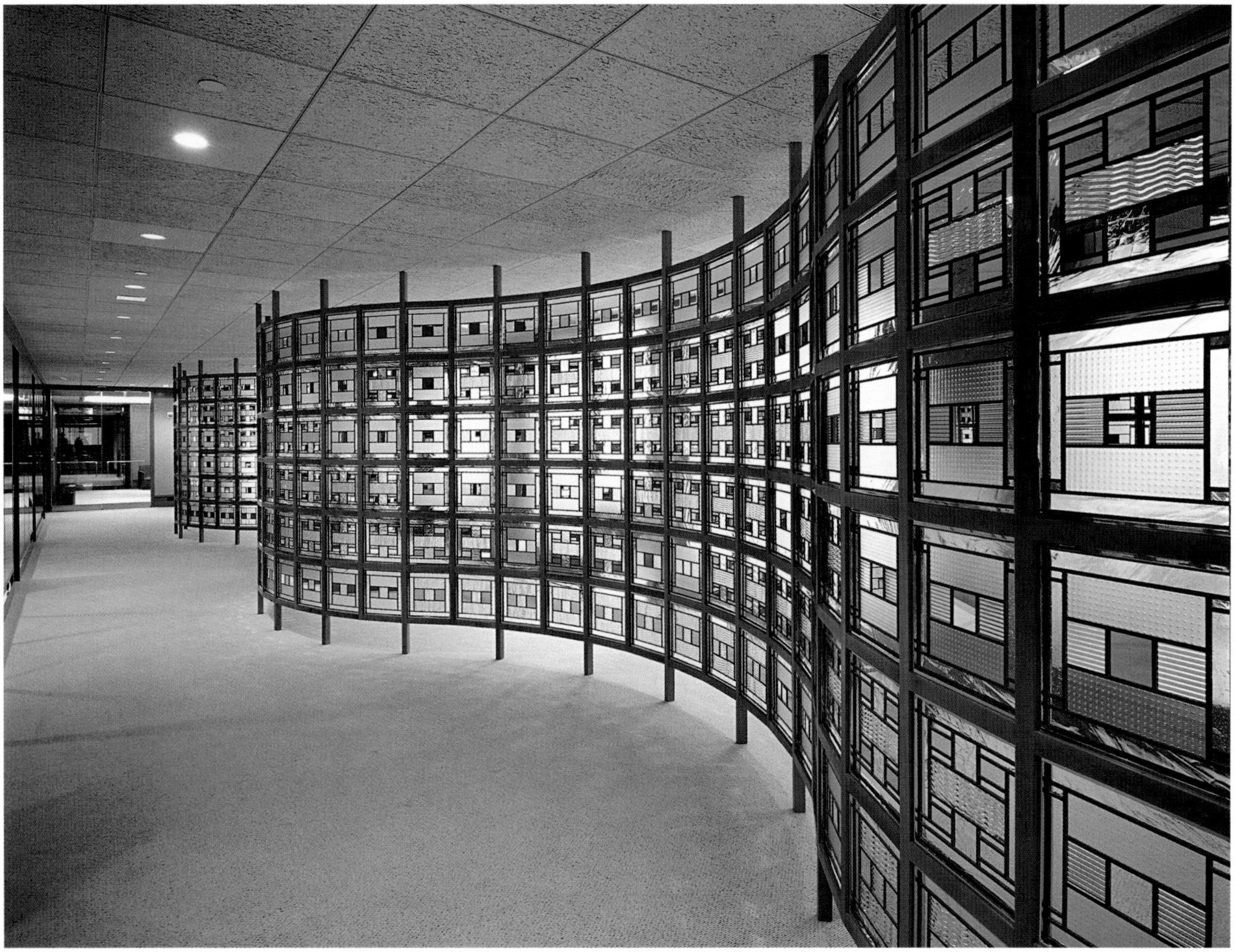

DAVID WILSON DESIGN

Wave Wall, 2000, Corning Incorporated, New York, NY, glass, 6' x 60'

Resurrection, Concordia Cemetery Mausoleum, Fort Wayne, IN

General Anthony Wayne, office window at City Glass Specialty, Fort Wayne, IN

Glass Landscape, 2000, South Carolina Aquarium, Charleston, leaded glass, silk screen and glass painting, 30' x 18' Timothy Hursley

Adath Jeshurun Synagogue Windows, 1995, Minnetonka, MN, leaded glass and glass painting, up to 12' Saari & Forrai

The Resurrection, 2001, Marian Woods Chapel, Hartsdale, NY, leaded glass and glass painting, center window 13' x 4.5'; side panels 10.5' x 3.5' Stephen Ostrow

Interior installation, 2001, private residence, stained and leaded glass Robert Holman

Entryway, 1999, private residence, stained and leaded glass

Lobby installation, 1999, Shared Systems Corporate Headquarters, stained and leaded glass, 12' x 8'

Ceiling installation, 2001, private residence, stained, leaded and sandblasted glass, 12' x 14' Robert Holman

Decorative Glass Skylight, 2001, Conference Center, 35'Dia.

Goddard & Gibbs Studios Ltd.

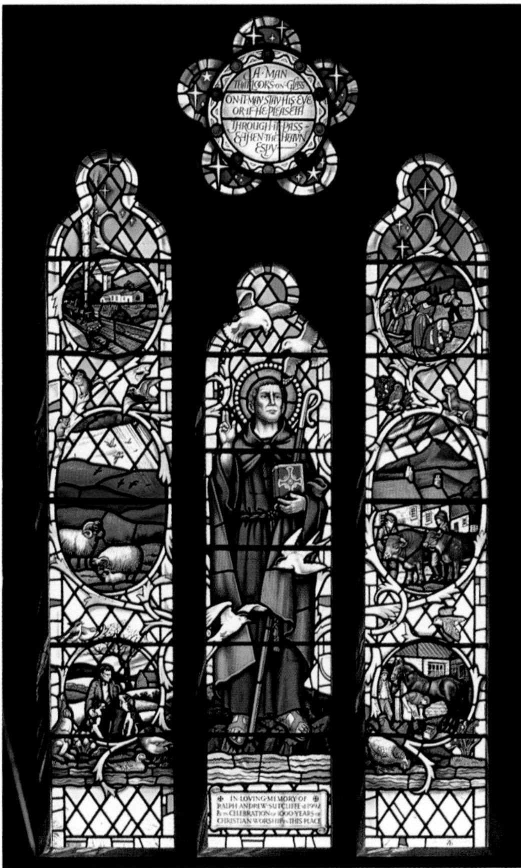

Memorial Window, 2000,
St. Cuthberts Church, Kildale, England

Goddard & Gibbs Studios Ltd.

Stained glass dome, 2001, UAE Chancery,
Washington, DC, 30'Dia.

Robert Creamer, Baltimore, MD

Laminated glass screen, 2002, Sisters of St. Joseph of Orange, Orange, CA, laminated stained glass on tempered, powder-coated steel, 55' x 9'

Laminated glass screen (detail)

Photos: Greg Epstein

Untitled glass wall, 2001, The Peninsula Chicago Hotel, fused/cast glass, 12' x 9' Jon Miller/Hedrich Blessing (large photo)

Hall residence, 2001, glass, 23" x 72" each

Quiet Room Triptych #1, 2001, glass, 22" x 48"

Medallion, UCSF Mt. Zion Quiet Room, 2001, glass and patinated steel, 56" diameter

Bratton Sculpture, 2001, glass and stainless steel, 4' x 8'

Photos: Michael Bruk

Two kiln-formed art glass entryways (detail), Worcester Public Library, MA, each: 80" x 12'

The Crystal Quilt (detail), Love Library, University of Nebraska-Lincoln, kiln-formed art glass wall, 77" x 52'

Two kiln-formed art glass entry doors (detail), Worcester Public Library, MA, each: 80" x 12'

Front Door, 1997, Tucson, AZ, cast glass and steel, 8' x 6'

Rotunda Wall #1 (detail), 2001, Westminster, CO, cast glass and steel, 5' x 5'

Larry George

Consilience, 2000, University of Colorado, Colorado Springs, cast glass and steel, 8' x 23'

Lee Milne

Altar, Our Lady of the Woods Chapel, Bellarmine University, Louisville, KY

Choir, Our Lady of the Woods Chapel, Bellarmine University, Louisville, KY

Overview, Our Lady of the Woods Chapel, Bellarmine University, Louisville, KY

Photos: Walt Roycraft

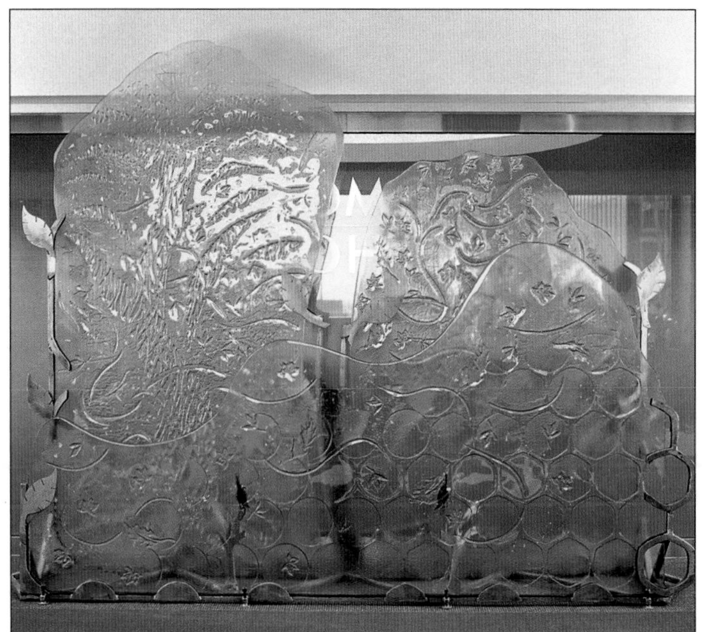

Tree of Life, 1999, Metropolitan Chicago Healthcare Council, Chicago, IL, cast glass and steel, 72" x 94"

J.B. Spector

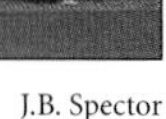

Serendipity, 2001, private collection, Nashville, TN, cast glass with dichroic, 72" x 60"

Shane Johnson

Joy of Creativity, 1999, Sheraton Hotel, Phoenix, AZ, cast glass, 120" x 60", opposite page: *Feeling Fall,* 1999, American Express Corporation, Phoenix, AZ, cast glass, 96" x 420", photo by Richard Abrams

Robin Stancliff

Consider Truth, one of four lobby-area windows totaling 460 square feet, Nesbett Federal Courthouse, Anchorage, AK, stained glass

Chris Arend

Front entry and middle conference room windows, Property and Facilities Management Center, Durham, NC, cast glass

Greg Plachta

Gates, Mississippi Museum of Art, 1998, etched glass with steel frame, 230.5" x 95.5"

Study doors, 2000, private residence, leaded, beveled and stained glass, 60" x 95"

Pompeii, 2001, antique flashed glass, sandblasted and etched, with kiln-fired glass paint, 30" x 40"

Perry residence, 2001, Medina, WA, bas-relief cast glass doors

Dick Springgate

Gordon Moore Memorial Window (detail of *Arch of Reconciliation*)

Gordon Moore Memorial Window (detail of two gothic arches)

Gordon Moore Memorial Window, Trinity Episcopal Church, Houston, TX, 11.5' x 27.5'

Photos: Ronald E. Chambers

Fountain of Faith, three-part glass panel, White Bear Lake Nursing Home, MN, flat glass with sandblasting, each panel: 18" x 60"

Photos: Ted Wentink

Holmes Regional Medical Center, Melbourne, FL

Spring (detail)

Winter (detail)

Photos: Randall Smith

Janet Perry

It's difficult to catch up with Janet Perry, interior designer for J. Banks Design Group in Hilton Head, South Carolina, but when you do, she describes the appeal of her company's work with genuine enthusiasm. ■ "It's our look," Perry states. "We're not afraid of color and we like to mix the old with the new; it's a very comfortable and lived-in feel. We go to London and France at least twice a year to buy antiques. Very low-country, easy-maintenance. You can walk into a space we've created and say, 'J. Banks did this.'" ■ That look makes J. Banks one of the most sought-after design firms in the area. It has landed them on the cover of *Southern Living* and *Carolina Architecture* magazines. Their houses have been featured on TV's "Dream Drive." According to Perry, the J. Banks style is incredible — and it's Southern. ■ "If you want to know the South, the plantation, the wide planks in the wood floors and the dark brown (not shiny red) mahogany, you should get to know our work. It's like the South: different." ■ The J. Banks look also stresses the incorporation of a client's treasures and artwork. "Art is almost always the most important thing I deal with. I create homes around the artwork." ■ Though half of J. Banks' assignments are commercial, it doesn't change the emphasis of the work. "We give commercial projects a residential feel," Perry says. "Everybody wants that safe and comfortable feeling — even when they're at work. We give commercial settings that at-home kind of feeling, just on a larger scale." ■ Work or play, office or home, J. Banks makes living feel good.

JEFF G. SMITH

Trinity, St. Matthew Catholic Church, Windham, NH, 14.3' x 13.6'

Trinity (detail)

Transfiguration (one of twelve Nave windows), St. Matthew Catholic Church, Windham, NH, 4' x 7.3'

Transfiguration (detail)

A Celebration of Faith, A Celebration of Worship, 2001, St. Luke Lutheran Church, Ann Arbor, MI, leaded handblown and plate glass with beveled glass prisms, 40' x 18'

Arthur Stern

Center Cross (detail), 2001, St. Luke Lutheran Church, Ann Arbor, MI, leaded handblown and plate glass with beveled glass prisms, 18' x 17'

Arthur Stern

Fireplace, 32" x 63" x .38" Art & Clarity

Garden Panel, 2001, metal fused in glass, 49" x 30" x .25" Phil Cohen

Spa Room, San Francisco, CA, 7' x 20' Art & Clarity

Untitled entry, 2001, private residence, Chicago, IL

Richard Bruck

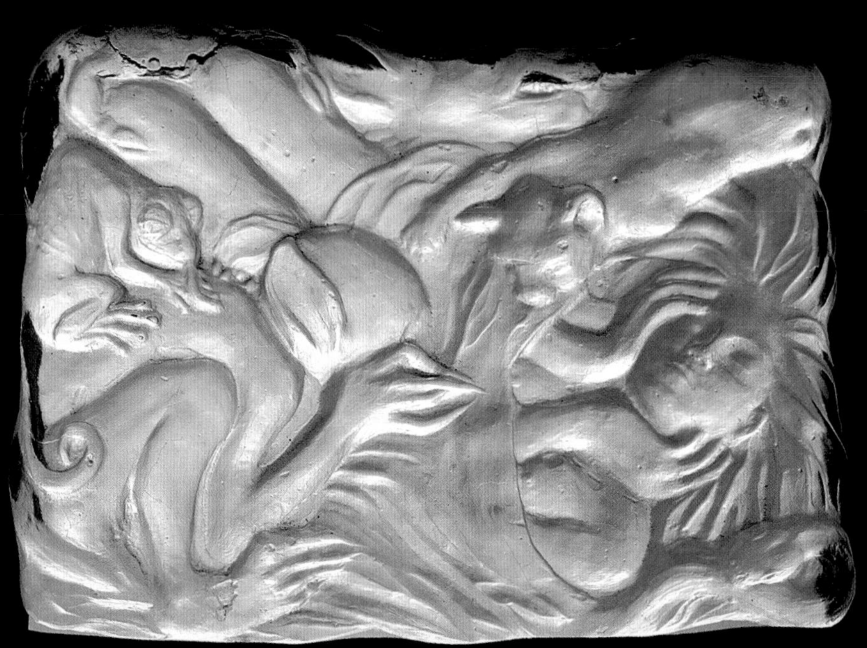

Architectural Elements

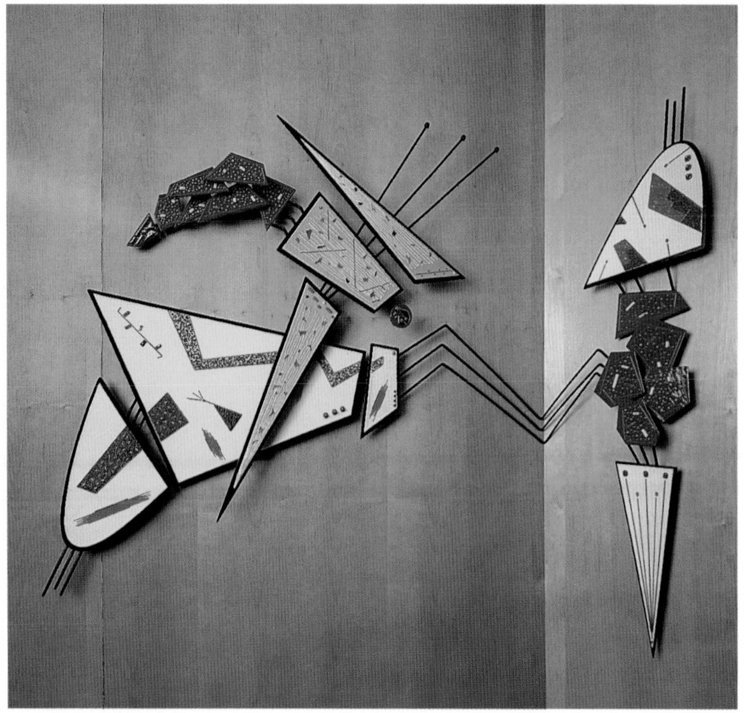

Dynamic Forces, 2001, AVAYA Communications, glass and steel, 4' x 8'

Retro Techno, 2001, Lucent Technologies, glass and steel, 5' x 6'

Dynamic Forces (detail)

Photos: Scott Service

Meditation on Flow – A Koan, 1998, San Francisco, CA, cast black concrete bowl, pink neon, recycling water flow, 8'Dia Katherine McDonald

Climbing Sculpture on Mosaic Rubber Plane, 2001, San Francisco, CA, concrete, steel and rubber, 9' x 6' Ian Reeves

The Presence of Absence, 2001, Marriott Corporation, Emeryville, CA, stone tile mosaics, 10' x 10' Topher Delaney

Turning on a World of Words, 2001, Marriott Corporation, San Francisco, CA, silicone bronze and gear mechanisms, 7'Dia Ian Reeves

Ladies Fireplace, carved white oak, 11' x 7'H — Don Tuttle

Renaissance Fireplace, carved beaumaniere French limestone, 10' x 6.6'H — Jean Michel Addor

Ritual Dancer, 2002, sand-cast glass, ground and polished, enamels, metal leaf and steel, 79" x 11" x 6" x 16"Dia. steel base

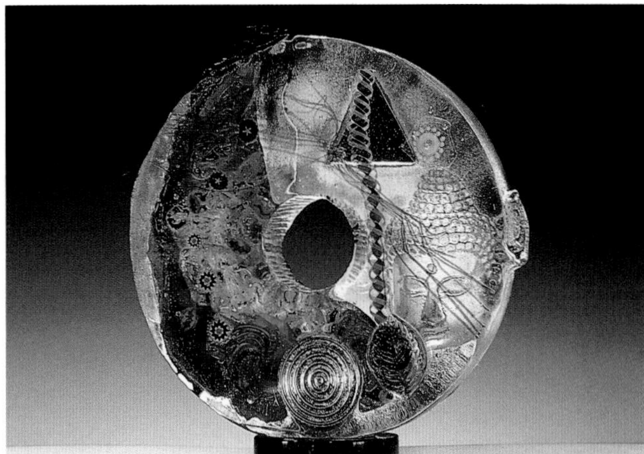

Green Buddha, 2002, sand-cast glass, ground and polished, copper, enamels and marble, 14" x 13" x 4"

Jerry Mesmer

Port Tampa Benches, 1999, Hillsborough County, FL, kiln-cast glass tiles with enamels and metal leaf, set in steel, 18" x 60" x 17"

Pegasus, 2002, University of Central Florida, Orlando, cast glass, silicone, 23K gold leaf, 5'Dia. x 4"

Libation, cast glass in frame, 13" x 7"

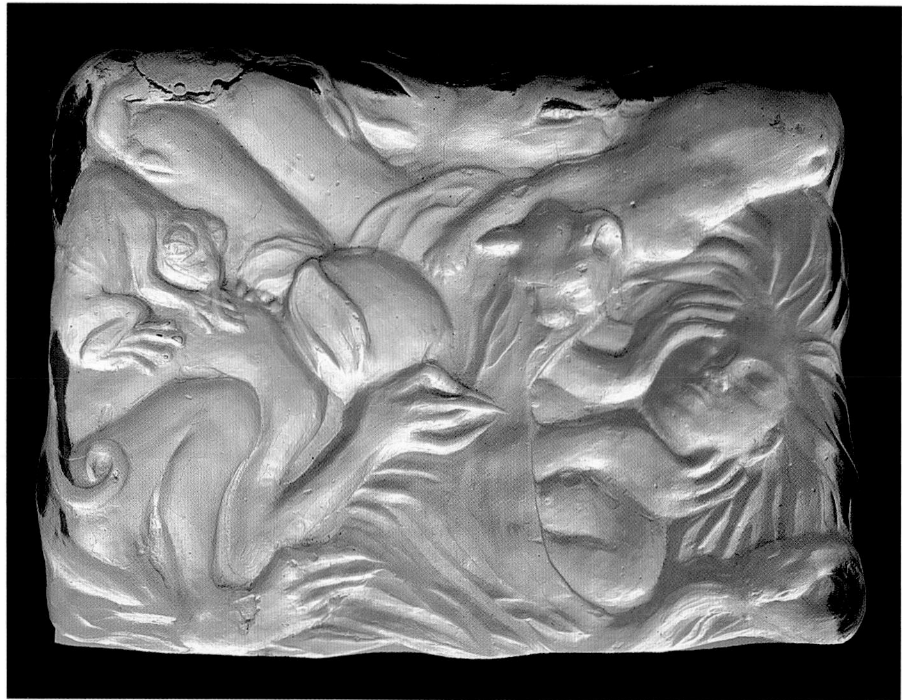

Pandora's Imprudence, clear cast glass bas-relief photographed against colored background, 10" x 13"

Primate, clear cast glass bas-relief photographed against colored background, 10" x 10"

Born Again, cast glass, 5" x 6" x 2"

Photos: Marlin R. Wagner

Swanky Fish Weathervane, 2001, copper with 23K gold leaf, 40"H

Mark Lennihan

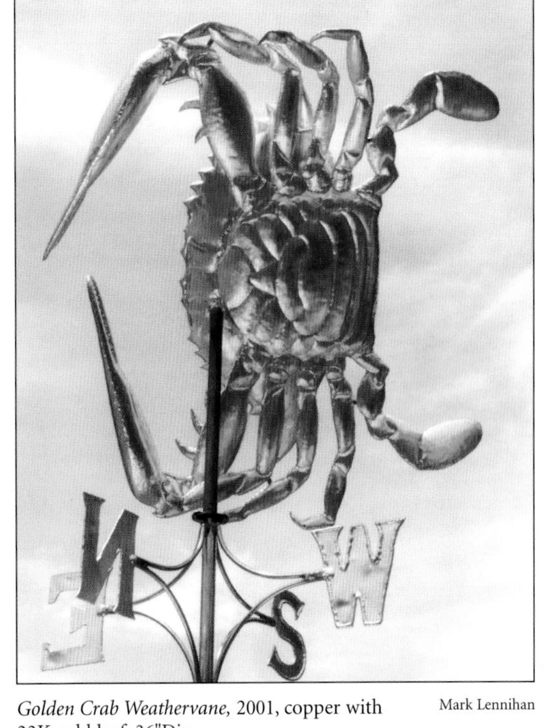

Golden Crab Weathervane, 2001, copper with 23K gold leaf, 36"Dia.

Mark Lennihan

Nittany Lion Weathervane, 2001, Beaver Stadium, Penn State University, 10.25' x 5', weight: 2,000 lbs.

Greg Greico

Geo Square-style fused and thermal-sealed door panels, 2001, 72" x 85"

Geo Square-style fused glass ceiling lamp, 2001, 24"Dia

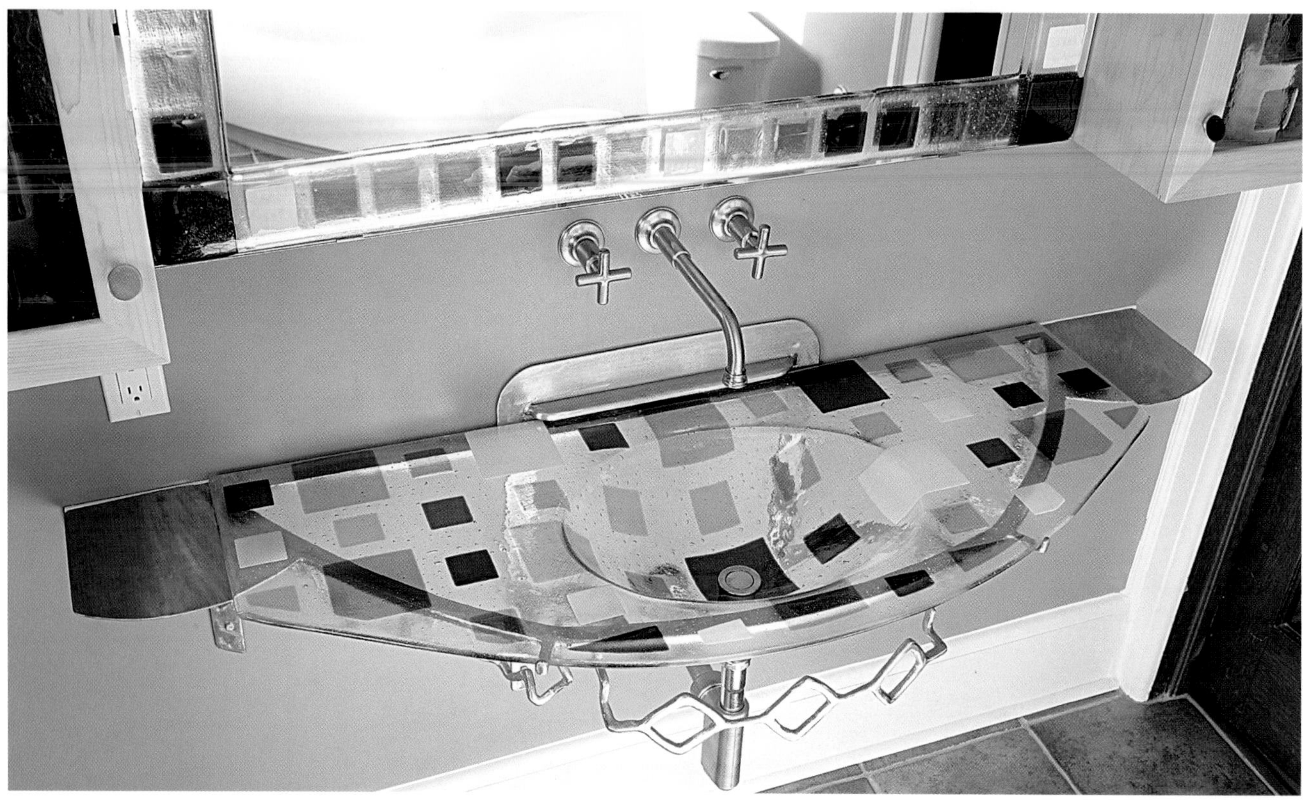

Geo Square-style fused glass sink, 2001, 47" x 21"

Photos: JPB Photography

Nagoya Marriott Associa Hotel, 52nd floor Sky Lounge ceiling art, 2000, JR Towers, Nagoya, Japan, mixed-media thermoset plastic painting on 31 sandwiched aluminum panels, 19' x 47'

Atrium Sculpture

Jeremy Elliott

Trent Foltz

One part of a three-part installation for Northwest Plaza, St. Louis, MO, layered Plexiglas, painted aluminum, 1' x 10.5' and 2' x 18', total width: 8'; inset: *Sunrise/Sunset,* entry sculpture, City of Montclair, CA, painted aluminum, Plexiglas, 20'H x 13'W

Canticle to a Blue Planet, 2000, painted aluminum and pear veneer, Royal Caribbean International's *Explorer of the Seas,* 42' x 10'

Jeff Baird

Summer Days, 2001, University of Arkansas, Little Rock, nylon, 160'L x 16'W x 60'H

Rainbow Waves, 2000, Centre Club, Fitness and Wellness Center for Condell Medical Center, Libertyville, IL, nylon, 56 banners, each: 50" x 44"

Central Illinois Regional Airport, 2001, Bloomington, IL, nylon, kites: 9', swags: 42" x up to 80'

Rich Sistos

Tango, 1999, Towers Perrin, San Francisco, CA, expanded aluminum, 8' x 12' x 2'

Wings, 1993, Synoptics, Santa Clara, CA, expanded aluminum, 12' x 12' x 12'

Ascension, 2001, private collection, glass and steel, 100" x 30" x 30"

Jeffrey White

Jeffrey White, owner of the architectural firm Direct Design Enterprises, first decided to be an architect when he was six years old. ■ "It's quite something to carry that kind of career goal with you from such a young age. I'm originally from the Chicago area, so I was greatly influenced by the Prairie School architects: Wright, Sullivan and, of course, Richardson. I grew up in the presence of great American architecture." ■ Although Direct Design Enterprises is located in New York, it takes on projects from all over the country. White runs a broad-based practice that includes everything from kitchen additions to multimillion-dollar train stations. ■ "My philosophy of design in architecture is based on using materials, forms and elements that are local to an area," White says, "as opposed to those that must be imported." ■ White has worked with many GUILD artists — so many, in fact, that he often can't remember which artists he initially found through GUILD. He does remember one GUILD artist in particular, however. Cabinetmaker Tony Clarke was responsible for constructing much of the cabinetry and woodwork in one of White's projects, a Connecticut estate. ■ White calls architecture the "world's greatest profession and the world's worst business." ■ "We're completely computerized these days," he says. "It used to be pretty simple: a board, a parallel rule and $20 worth of instruments. It's not like that anymore. Technology has to be respected for what it is, but it's certainly not a substitute for talent. The mind and the hand are faster than the best computer out there."

Seth Rogers

Stories from Light (detail)

Stories from Light (detail)

Stories from Light, Women and Babies Hospital, Lancaster, PA, dichroic glass, stainless steel and cables, 26' x 26' x 5.5'

Lyrick Studios, Allen, TX — 24 oval sculptures: anodized aluminum frames with stretched fabric

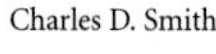

Charles D. Smith

Mishima Hospital, Shizuoka Prefecture, Japan — Brass and copper mesh leaves on enameled tube vines and tree trunk

Toshinori Hattori

PNC Firstside Center, Pittsburgh, PA — 480', anodized aluminum tubing, stainless steel cable and polycarbonate strips

Edward Massery

Mishima Hospital, Shizuoka Prefecture, Japan — Presentation drawing

GEORGE PETERS & MELANIE WALKER / AIRWORKS, INC.

Tree Talk, fiberglass, aluminum and prismatic film, 40' x 16' x 16'

Pieces of the Puzzle, fiberglass rod, fiberglass sunscreen and acrylic color, 20' x 7' x 60'

Flight Patterns, fiberglass rod, fiberglass sunscreen and acrylic color, 20' x 10' x 20'

Blue Blossoms, 1999, polychromed aluminum and stainless steel, Pharmacia Upjohn, Peapack, NJ, 16' x 15' x 9'

Blue Blossoms

Spectral Microcosm, anodized niobium and stainless steel, 14' x 8' x 8'

A Mist of Fragrant Time, 2000, private residence, acrylic, 10' x 12'

Sky Ballet, Metro Plaza, San Jose, CA, acrylic, 4' x 6' x 17'

Spectral Arc, 1998, Lucent Technologies, FL, acrylic wall hanging, 4' x 5' x 11'

Dawn of Spring's Bouquet, 2000, City Hall, Hayward, CA, acrylic, 15' x 15' x 18'

Photos: Paul Sable

Representational Sculpture

General Joshua L. Chamberlain, 2000, private collection, fiberglass, 24"H x 20" x 10.5"

Mermaids, 1995, private collection, fiberglass, 44"H x 42" x 30"

Chief Massasoit, 2001, private collection, bronze, 24"H x 5.5" x 5"

Photos: Virtual Productions

DIESEL Jeans, © 2002, limestone and oil stains, 29" x 12" x 6" Edward Peterson

Milano Cookies, © 2002, bag: marble and acrylic, cookies: resin and acrylic, 3.5" x 15" x 8" Edward Peterson

Milk and Cookies, © 2001, glass: alabaster and acrylic, plate: limestone and oil stains, cookies: resin and acrylic, 6.5" x 12" x 12"

Boot in Motion, © 2000, limestone and oil stains, 12" x 8" x 4"

Dragonfly, 2002, Vancouver, WA, etched copper on stainless steel supporting structure, 7' x 5' x 3'

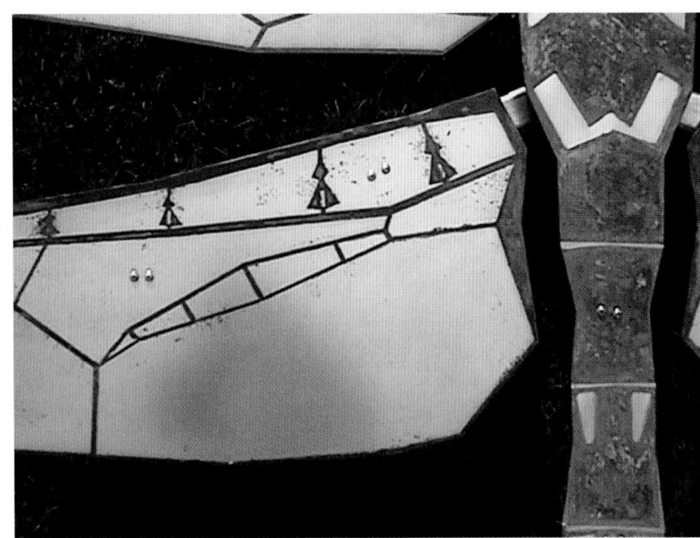

Dragonfly (detail)

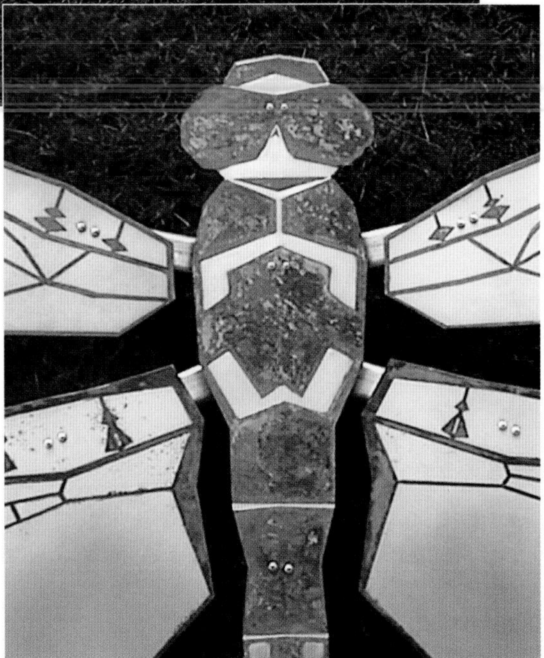

Dragonfly (detail)

Celebration, 2001, New Mexico, clay with crater glaze, 4' x 4' x 7'

Wood Nymph, 2001, Illinois, clay with crater glaze, 9.5' x 1' x 1.5'

Reflection, 2001, Michigan, clay with crater glaze, 12' x 4'

Three Levels, 2001, Georgia, clay with crater glaze, 12'

Cor Ad Cor Loquitor, Sacred Heart Hospital, SD, sculptor: James Michael Maher

Hush, private collection, sculptor: Edward E. Hlavka

South Dakota's World War II Warriors, state capitol grounds, Pierre, SD, sculptor: Lee Leuning, assisted by Sherri Treeby

Bill Groethe

The City of Presidents: John Adams, Rapid City, SD, sculptor: John Lopez

Paul Tierney on Coffee Jeff, Pro Rodeo Hall of Fame, Colorado Springs, CO, sculptor: John Lopez

Red Shell, 1998, tiger eye alabaster on marble base, 18"H x 8"W x 7"D

Orange Delight, 1999, translucent alabaster on marble base, 18"H x 11"W x 9"D

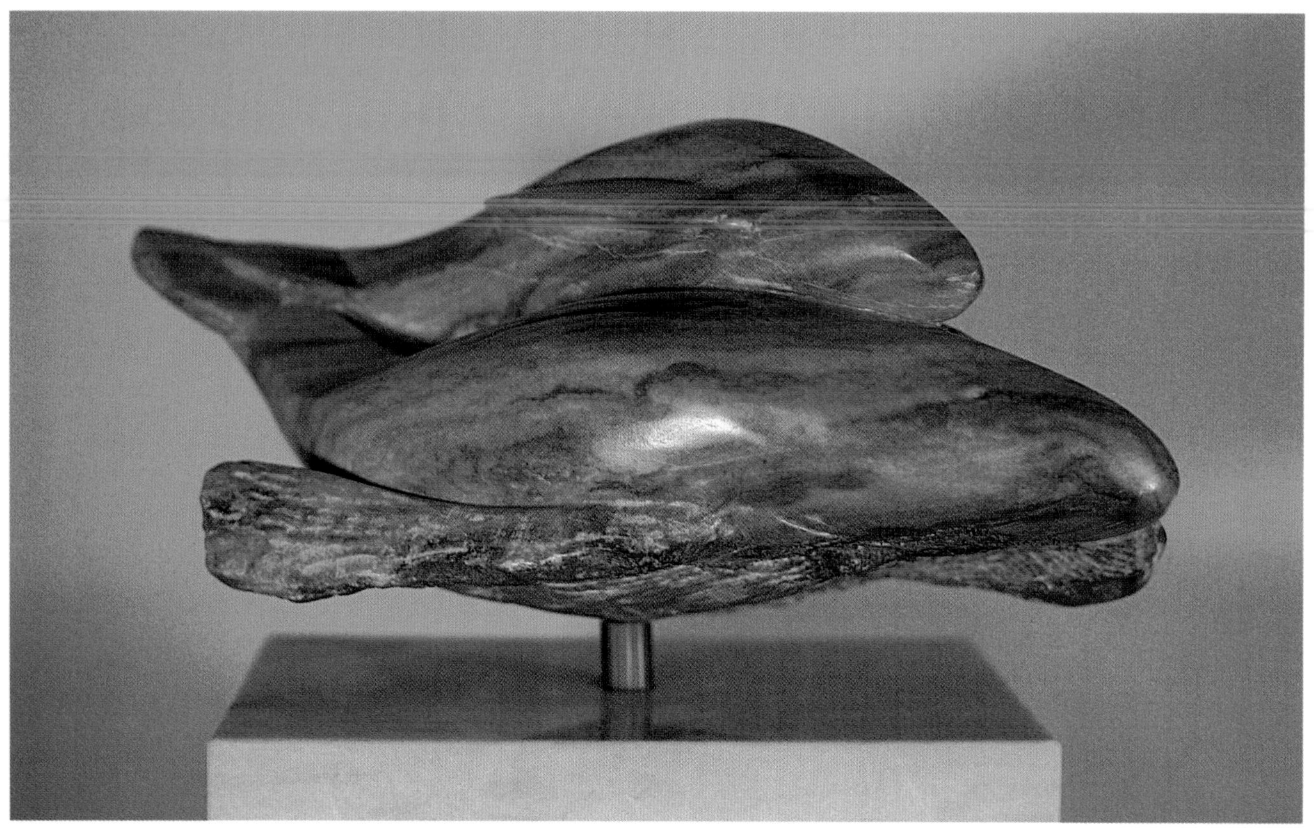

Whales, 1999, cockscomb alabaster on marble base, 10.5"H x 17.5"W x 10.5"D

Pearl Diver, 1998, bronze, 22" x 18" x 14", edition of 90

Paleontologist: The Perfect Find, 1997, terracotta, life size, edition of 40

Mannature Balanced, 1999, bronze

Andre Dubus III, FGR gypsum, life size

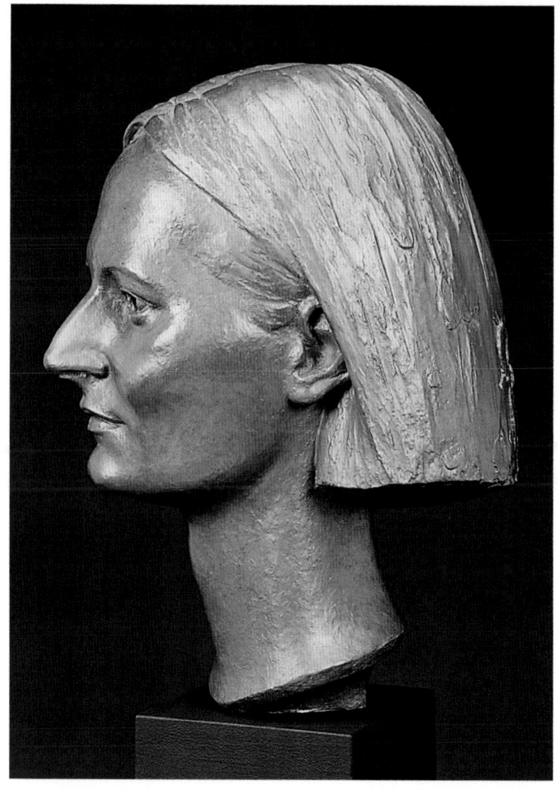
Gail Feretti, bronze, life size

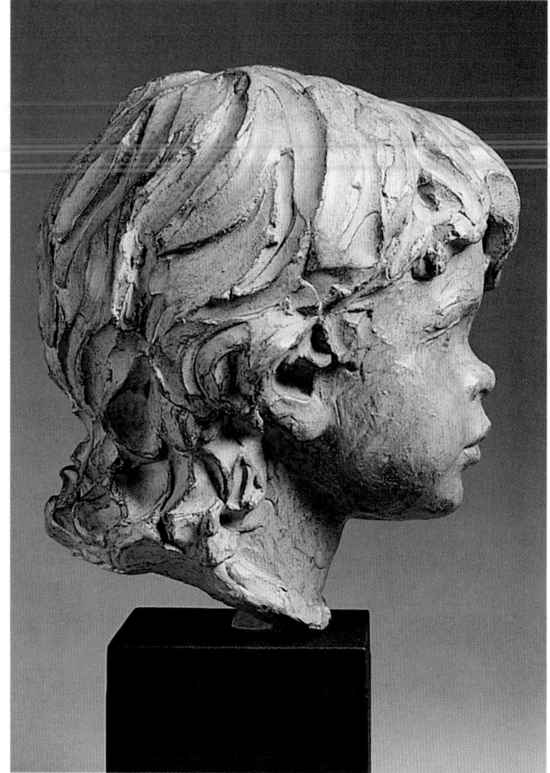
Portrait of a Child, plaster, life size

Ben Kamihira, FGR gypsum, life size

Photos: Sheldan Collins

Three Stags, (detail)

Three Stags, Boldt Castle's entry arch, Hart Island, Thousand Islands region, NY, bronze

Sisters in Learning, St. Scholastica Plaza, Benedictine College campus, Atchison, KS, (clay in progress)

Sisters in Learning (detail)

Dance of Creation, from the *Circle of Life* sculptures, 2001, Bronson Hospital, Kalamazoo, MI, life-size figure on 5' sculptured bronze column, edition of seven

Educators, 2000, Mishawaka, IN, 9' bronze figures creating a 16' archway, edition of seven

The Circle of Life, 2001, Bronson Hospital, Kalamazoo, MI, life-size figures on 5' sculptured bronze columns, edition of seven

Herman B Wells, 2001, Indiana University, Bloomington

Solitude Monument, 2001, bronze, 11'H

Bear Bryant Monument, bronze, Alabama Sports Hall of Fame

Mud Buddies, 2000, bronze

Canadian Honker, 1998, fabricated steel and alabaster, 60" wingspan

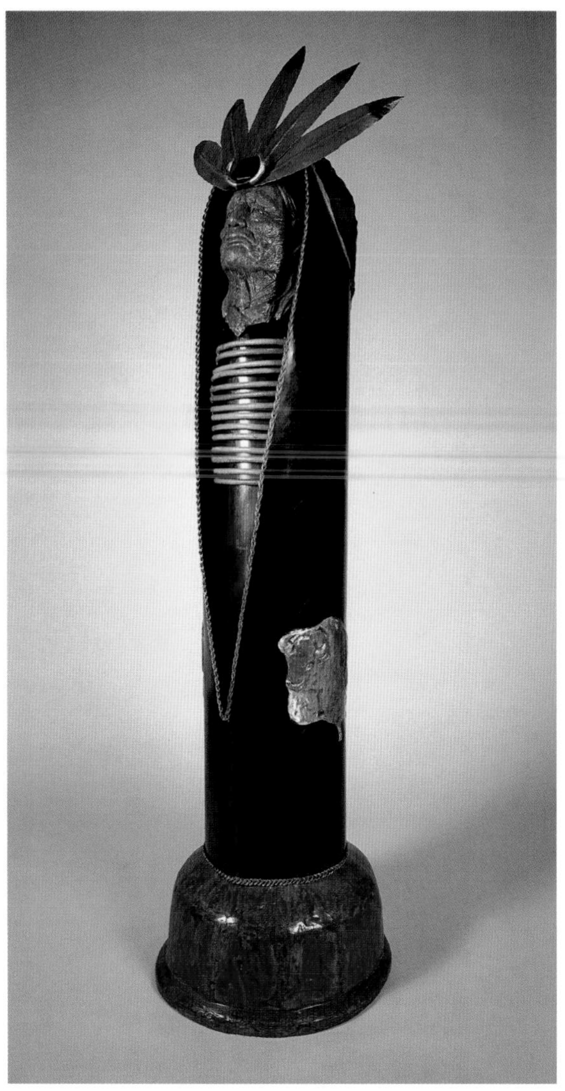

Buffalo Keeper II, 2002, fabricated steel and poly cement, 80"H

One More Season, 2002, fabricated steel and poly cement, 123"H

Photos: Robert Fike

Edward and Clay, bronze, 40" x 28" and 36" x 30", editions of 10

Tea Party, bronze, 36" x 28", limited edition

Avalon's Legacy, 2001, City of Brea "Artisan Walk," bronze, 6.5' x 6.5' x 3'

Cradle, 1990, painted resin triptych, each: 26"Dia. x 12", edition of nine

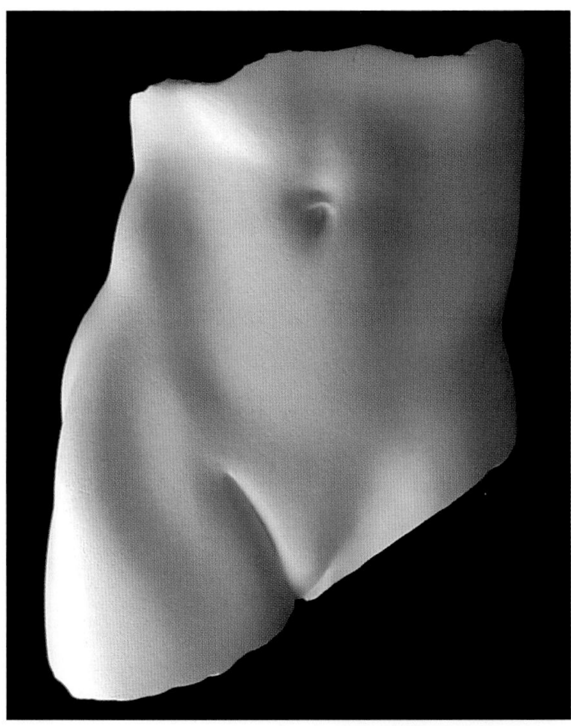

Curve, 2000, ceramic and wood, 17" x 14" x 5", edition of 9

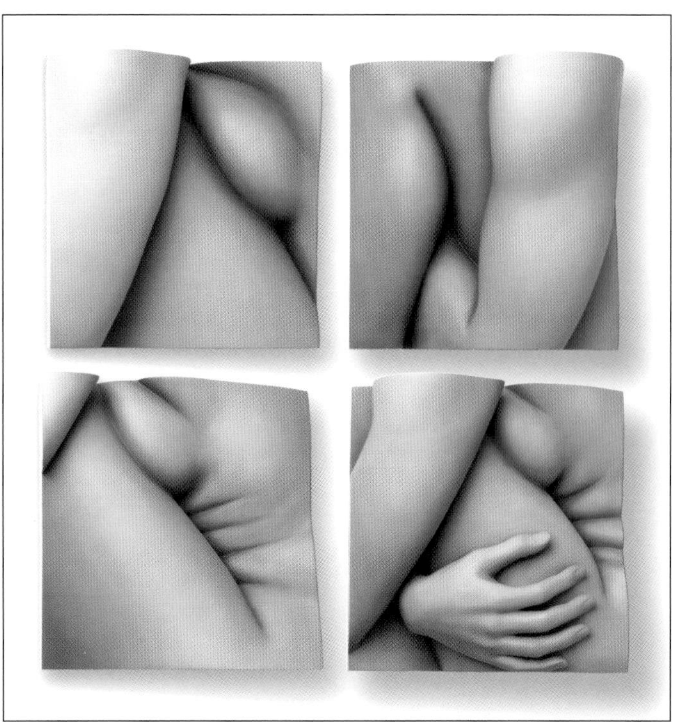

Progression of Four, 1997, painted resin, 22" x 22" x 7", edition of 9

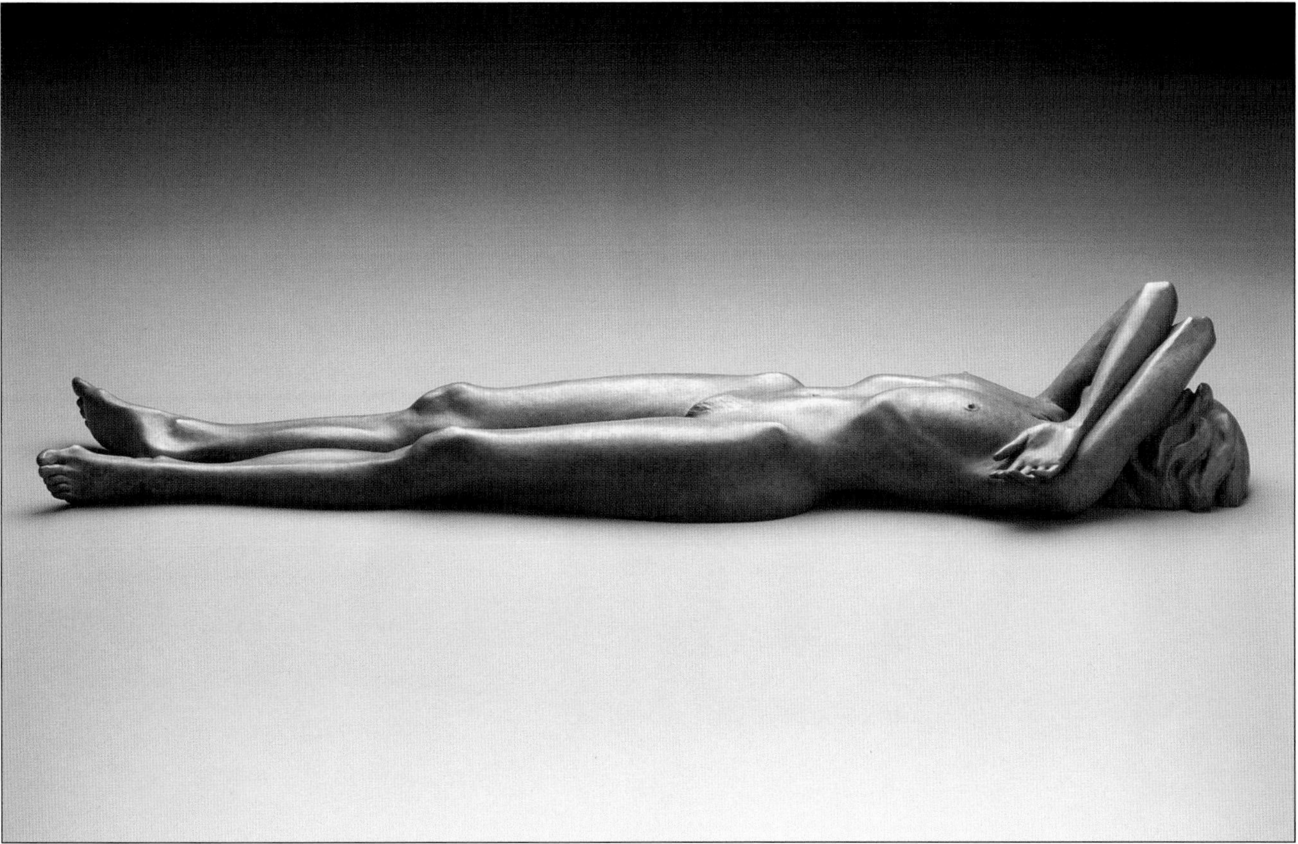

Intimacy, 1998, bronze, 32" x 6" x 6", edition of 9

Wind Spirit, Town of Mountain Village (Heritage Plaza), Telluride, CO, bronze, 13' x 9', limited edition of five

Al Loft

Sack Race, 2002, bronze, lifesize

Les Jeunes Femmes, 2000, bronze, 18" x 12" x 12"

My Book, 2001, bronze, 18" x 22" x 23"

Mining Monument, 2001, Bell Park, Sudbury, ON, Canada, cast bronze, 15'H x 9' x 4'

Mining Monument (detail)

Mining Monument (detail)

Mining Monument (detail)

Late for School, 2002, bronze, 11.5' x 5' x 4.5'

A Wing and a Prayer (back), 2000, bronze, 63"H

A Wing and a Prayer (front)

Photos: Marcia Ward/The Imagemaker

GLENN TERRY

Saint Paul, 2000, bronze on marble pedestal, heroic size

Sweet Surrender, 1996, bronze, 17"H

The Bountiful Well, 1997, bronze, 64"H

Photos: Gary Berman

Melody, bronze, 24"x 10" x 9", edition of 29

Marsha Ward

Lefty the Bluesman, bronze, 16" x 11" x 17", edition of 21

Richard Stum

After Midnight, bronze, 24" x 14" x 9", edition of 21

Richard Stum

Job, bronze, under life size

Family, bronze, life size

On Watch, bronze, life size

Tirza (detail), bronze with taupe patina, 35"

Ruth, bronze with light patina, 38"

Jamuna, clay (to be bronzed) with bismuth patina, 32"

Eve, bronze with ivory patina, 24"

Tirza, bronze with taupe patina, 35"

Non-Representational Sculpture

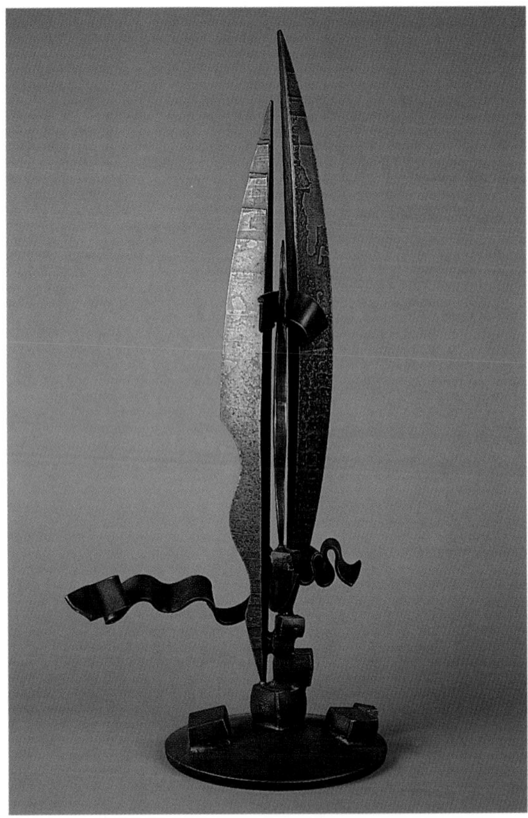

Interlude, forged steel maquette, 22" x 7" x 11"

Wing Ding Doodle, Baseline Corporate Center, Tempe, AZ, Cor-Ten steel, 24' x 8' x 6'

Tribal Figment, shown at Navy Pier, Chicago, IL, Cor-Ten steel, 19' x 6' x 7'

Millennium Bowl, 2001, Bishop Ranch, San Ramon, CA, stainless steel and water, 14' x 8'

Millennium Bowl (side view)

Exchange, 2000, Alza Corporation, Mountain View, CA, bronze, stainless steel and water, 10' x 10' x 23'

Unity, 2001, Howard Hughes Corporation, Las Vegas, NV, 4' x 7' x 15'

River of Life (series one), 2001, Eli Lilly & Co., Indianapolis, IN, steel, stainless steel and glass, 12' x 3' x 4'

River of Life (series two), 2001, Eli Lilly & Co., limestone, stainless steel and glass, 8' x 2' x 2'

River of Life (series three)

Photos: WM Photographic

River of Life (series three), 2001, Eli Lilly & Co., limestone, steel, stainless steel and glass, 12' x 3' x 4'

Through the Clouds, 2001, bronze and stainless steel, 13' x 9' x 9'

Through the Clouds #3, 2001, bronze and stainless steel, 32" x 24" x 20"

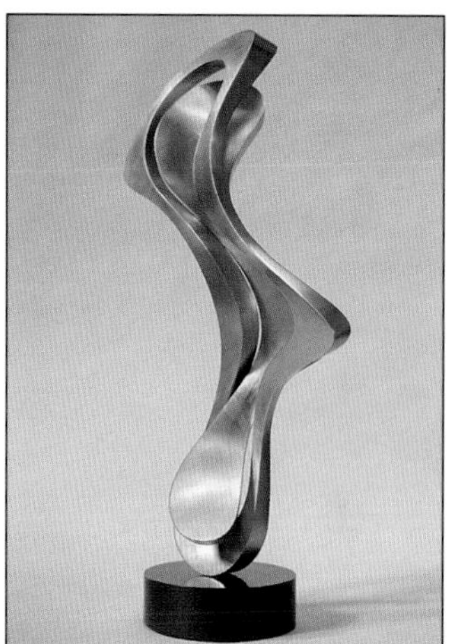

Spirit form "Emerging," 2001, bronze, 32" x 17" x 8"

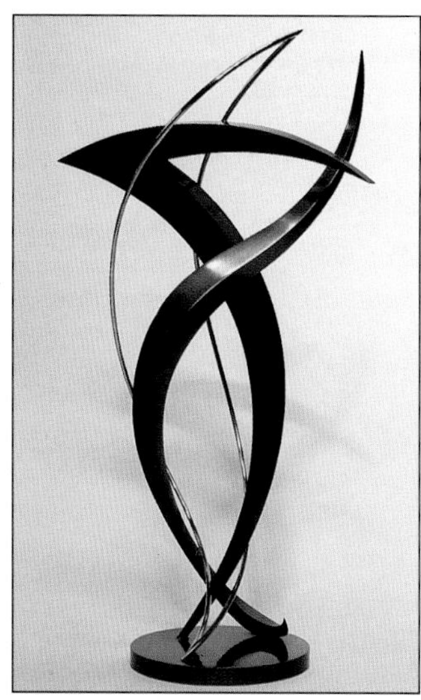

Synergetic #3, 2001, bronze, 42" x 16" x 12"

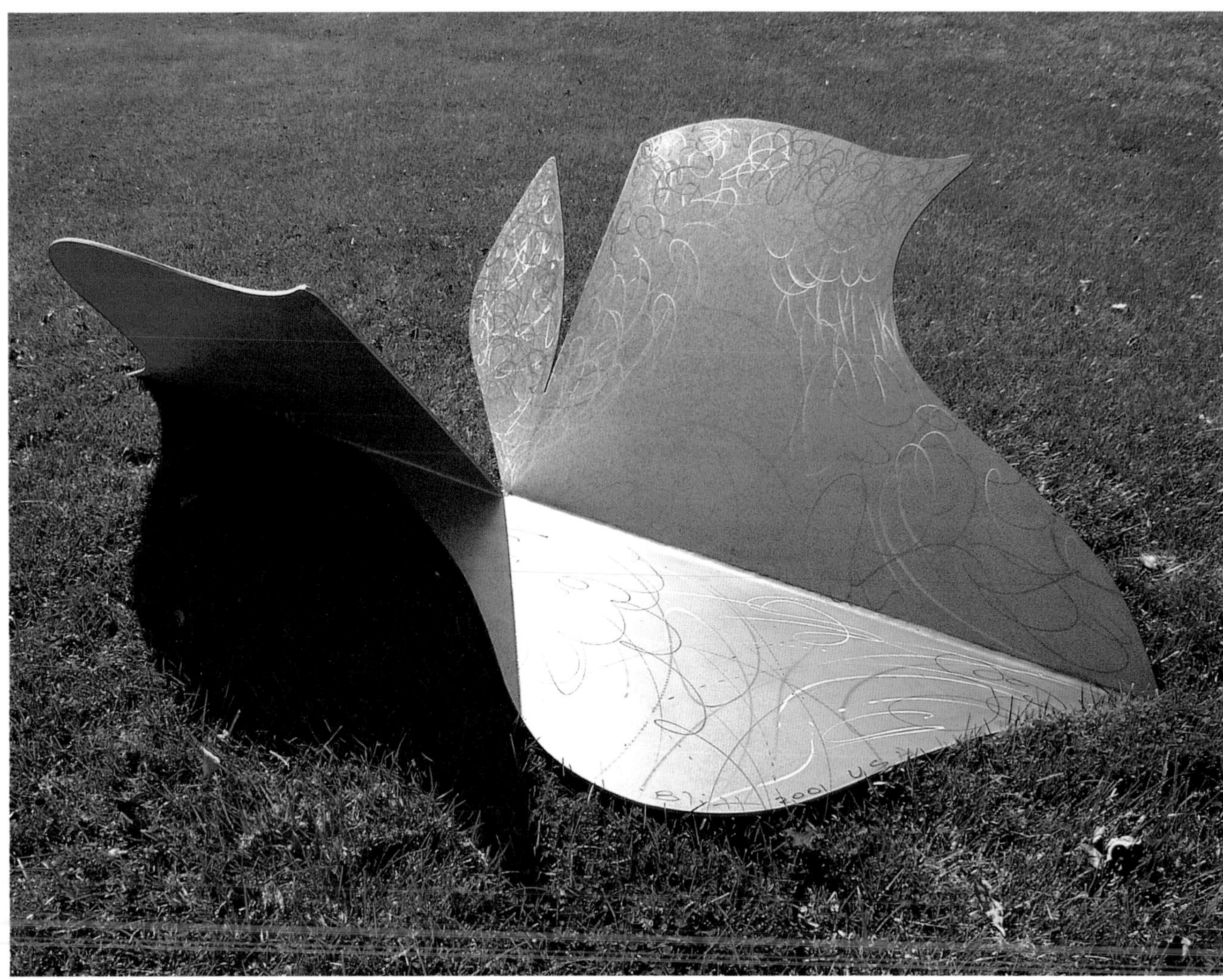

Liberation, Gold Coast Regional Art Center, Surfers Paradise, Australia, stainless steel, 4' x 5' x 10' James Maidhof

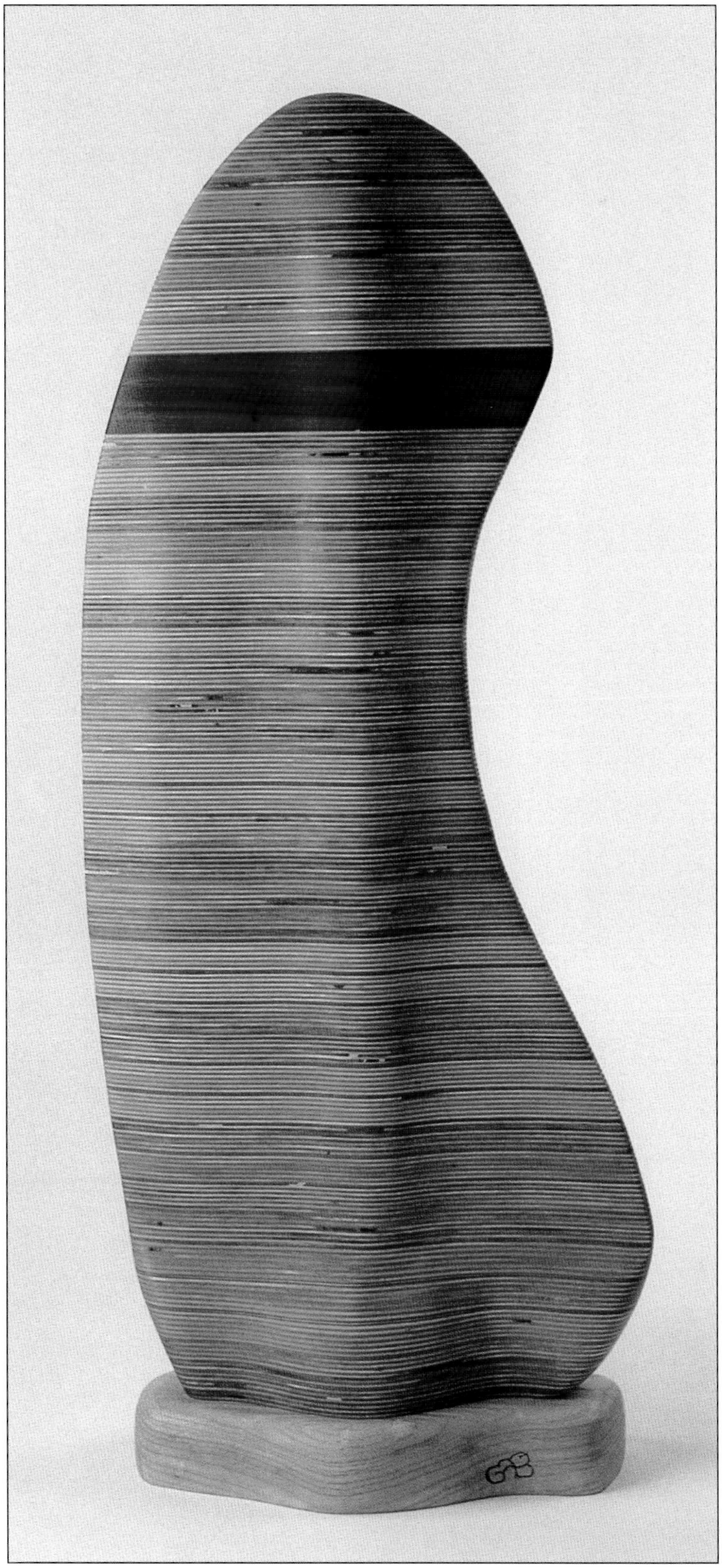

Illusion, 2001, Baltic birch, padauk and ash, 30" x 12.5" x 5"

Photos: Wilson Graham

Tropic Depression, 2001, Baltic birch, Aramath and granite, 25" x 23" x 10.5"

Soft Landing, 2001, aluminum, tropical walnut, padauk and marble, 19" x 18" x 5"

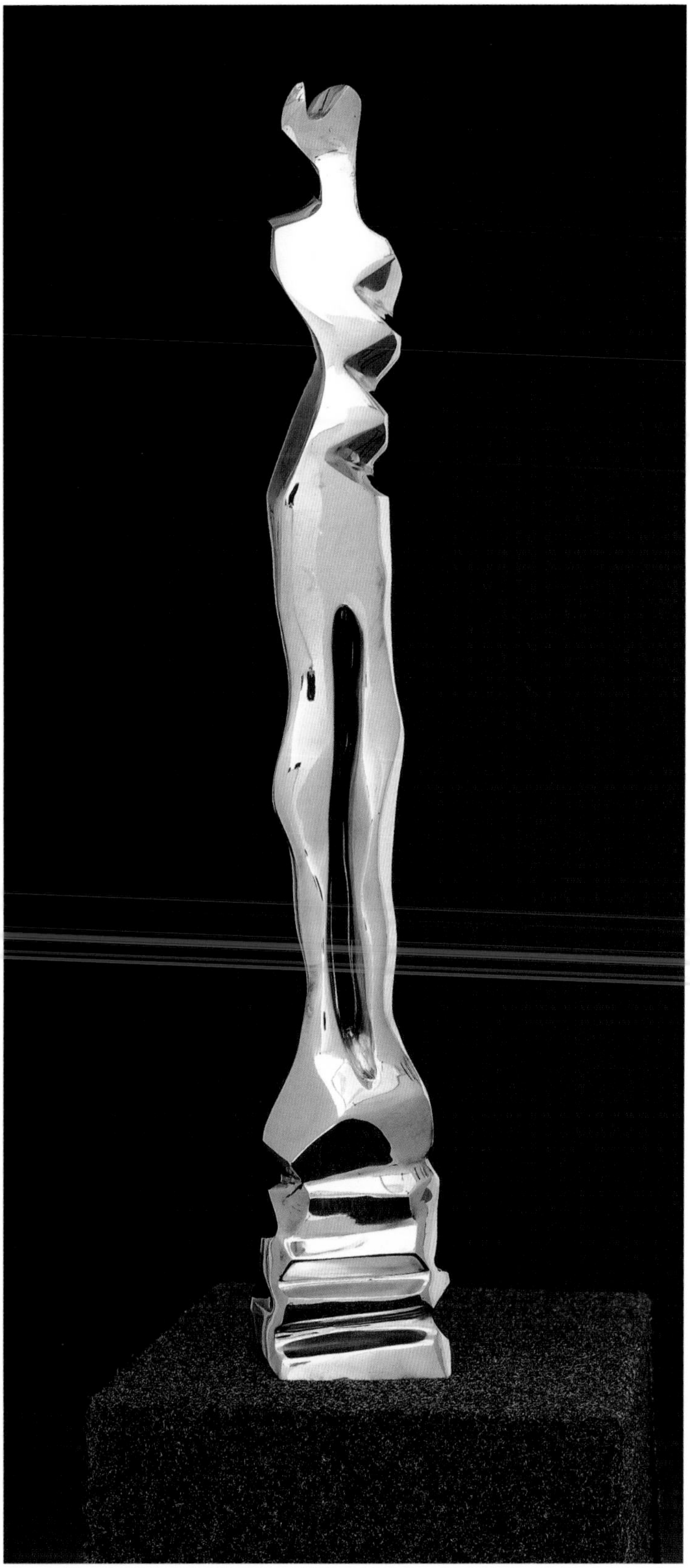

Colomba, bronze, 29"H x 4" x 3"

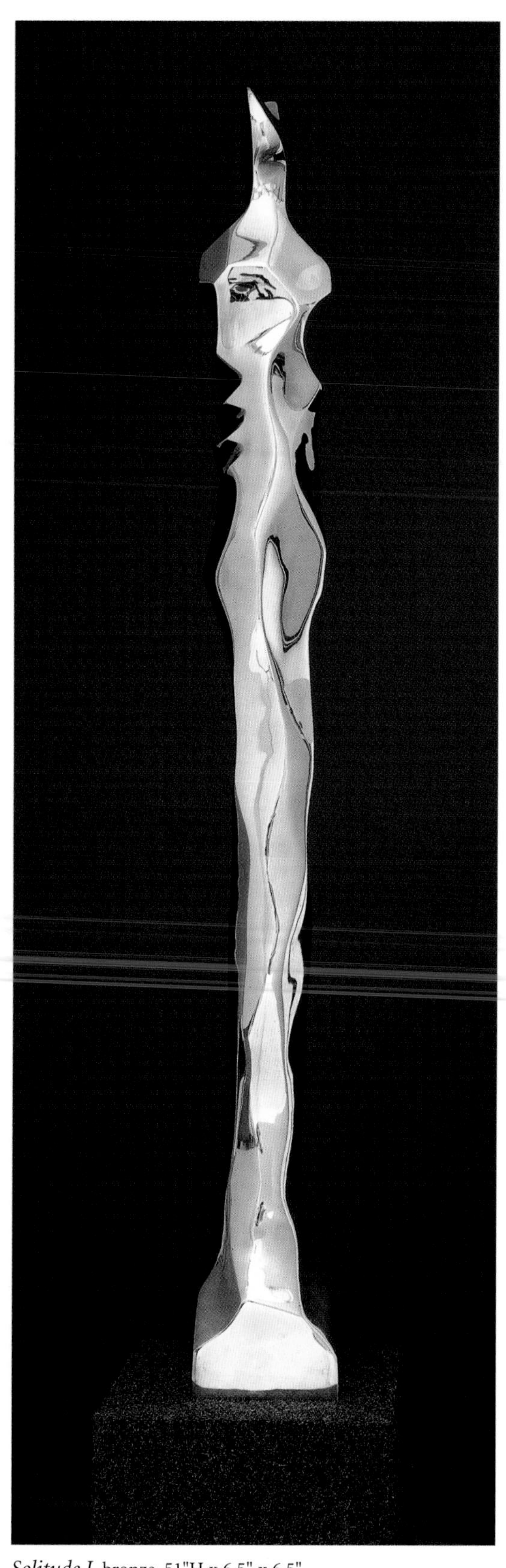

Solitude I, bronze, 51"H x 6.5" x 6.5"

Curvilinear Lady, 48" x 7" x 7" Stan Neimcicky

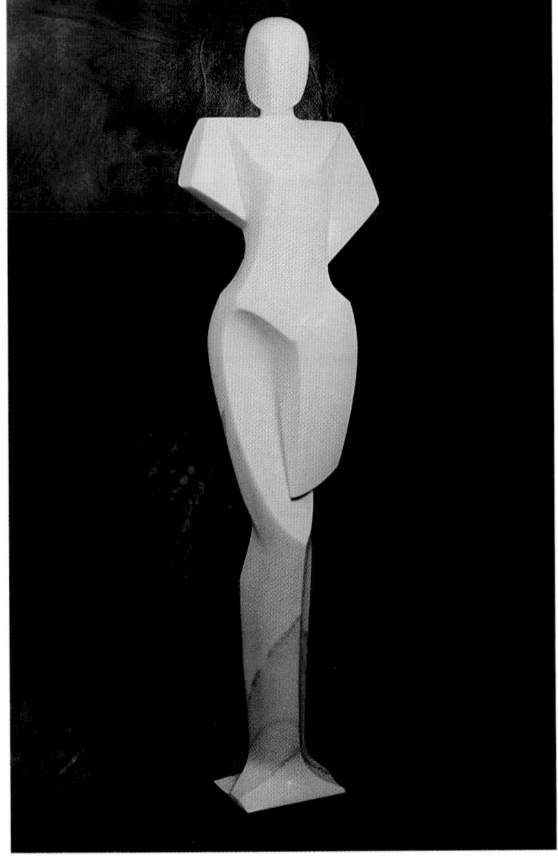

Elegant Lady, 72" x 24" x 12" Stan Neimcicky

Tenderness, 64" x 15" x 15" Jim Stayton

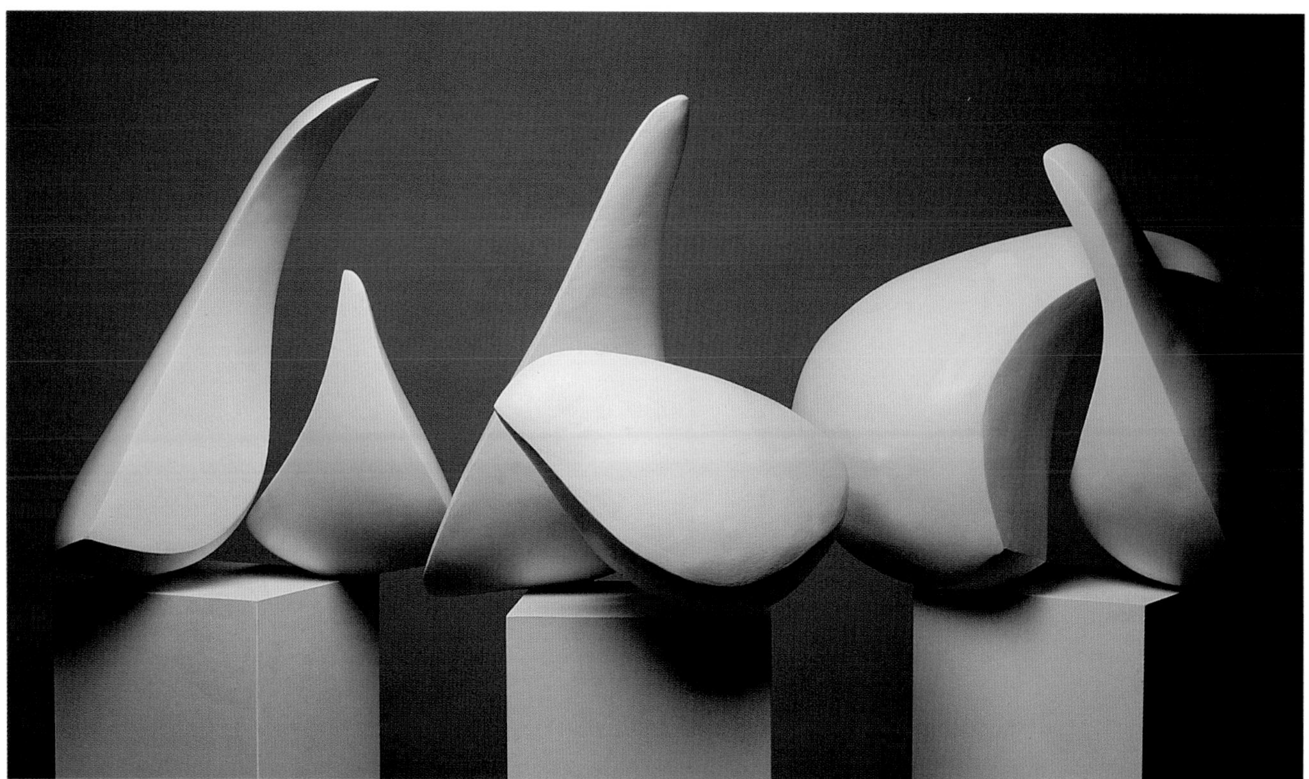

Relationship VI, VII, VIII, plaster (also available in bronze) Andrew Kent

Relationship Series IV, plaster, 19.5" x 20.5" x 21.75" (also available in bronze) Andrew Kent

Reverse Curve IV, bronze, 20.5" x 13.3" x 11.75" Mark Stehle

Birds of Paradise, blown glass, 60.5" x 11"; 61" x 11.25"

Photos: Latchezar Boyadjiev

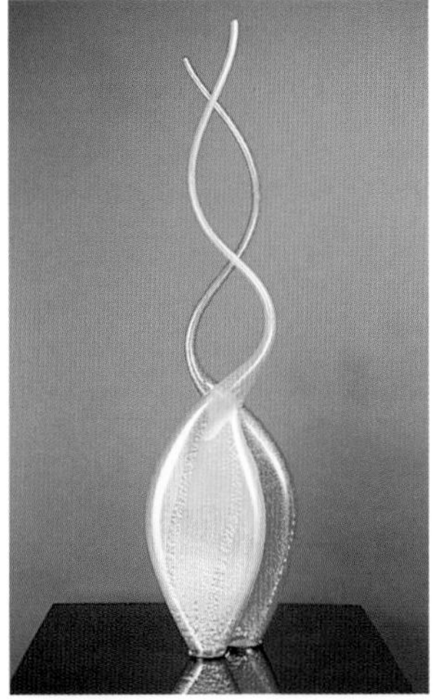

Birds of Paradise, blown glass, 61" x 12"; 57.5" x 12"

Birds of Paradise, blown glass, 51.5" x 11.5"; 59" x 13"

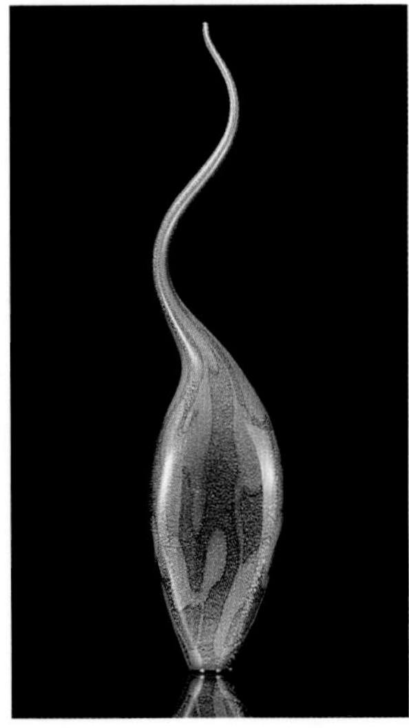

Birds of Paradise, blown glass, 55.5" x 12"

NICK EDMONDS

The Sharon Hill, 1991, carved wood and acrylic paint, 7' x 4' x 4'

Adam and Eve, 1997, wood and acrylic paint, 7' x 4' x 4'

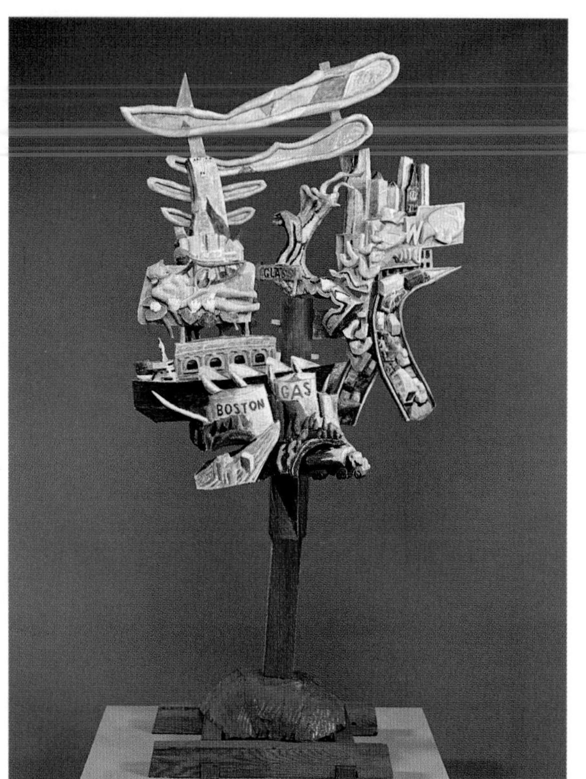

The Port of Cinderella, carved wood and acrylic paint, 7' x 3' x 2'

The Pilots, 2001, carved wood, 8' x 8' x 7'

Warren Patterson

Checkerboard of Pentagons, 2001, Emeryville, CA, granite, 10'Dia.

Eightfold Way, 1993, Berkeley, CA, white marble, black serpentine, hyperbolic heptagon tiling, 6' x 6' x 6', 3 tons

Hyperbolic pentagon tiling setting, 2001, Emeryville, CA, granite, 10'Dia.

Fibonacci Fountain, 2001, Bowie, MD, granite, 18' x 20' x 6', 45 tons

Photos: Jonathan Ferguson

Three ceramic columns, up to 9'H

Kalamazoo, 2002, Radisson Plaza Hotel, Kalamazoo, MI, etched and painted glass, granite and water jets with fiber-optic lights, 153"H x 132" x 132"

Michael Morin

Bat in Sunshine (at night), 1999, installed in front of ShaTian real estate building, Shanghai, China — Xu Yong Min

Bat in Sunshine (daytime) — Xu Yong Min

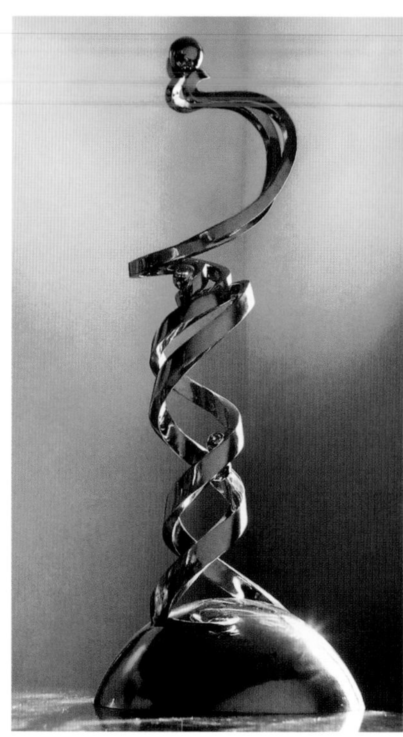

DNA Spiraling into the Universe, 1/10 scale, Art and Science Center, WV

Eshe, 1999, marble, 34" x 42" x 23" Patrick Vingo

Maya, 2001, marble and brushed stainless steel, 40" x 60" x 41" Erin Kiernan

Offering, 2002, silicon bronze and concrete, 87" x 60" x 32"

Romance, 2000, stainless steel and bronze, 49" x 45" x 3"

Protection While We Dance, 2001, silicon bronze, 70" x 20" x 33"

Lady of Justice, 2001, silicon bronze and stainless steel, 94" x 30" x 24"

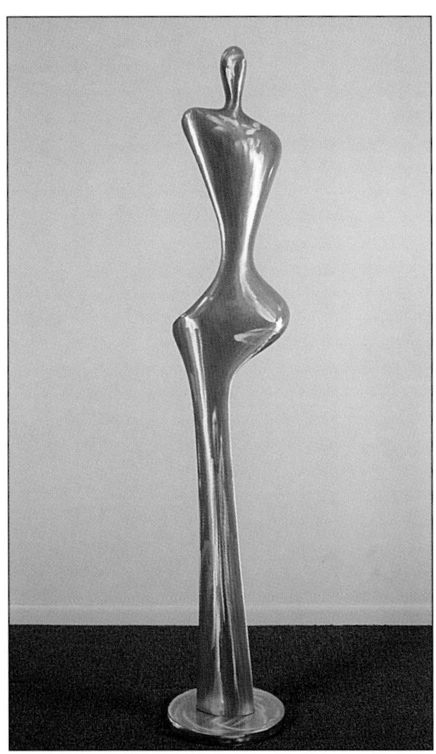

Single Form, 2000, aluminum, 82" x 18" x 15"

Southwest Forms, 2001, aluminum, 52" x 18" x 15"

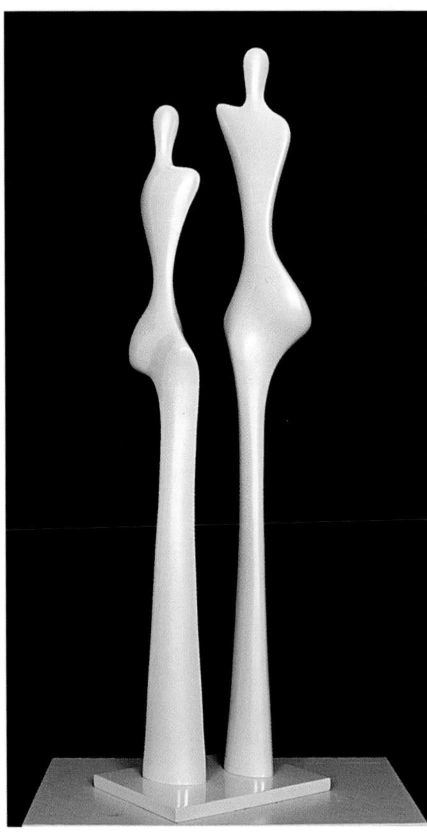

Two Forms, 2001, painted aluminum, 60" x 16" x 12"

Spring Forms, 2001, painted aluminum, 35" x 13" x 9"

Photos: Robert Ruschak

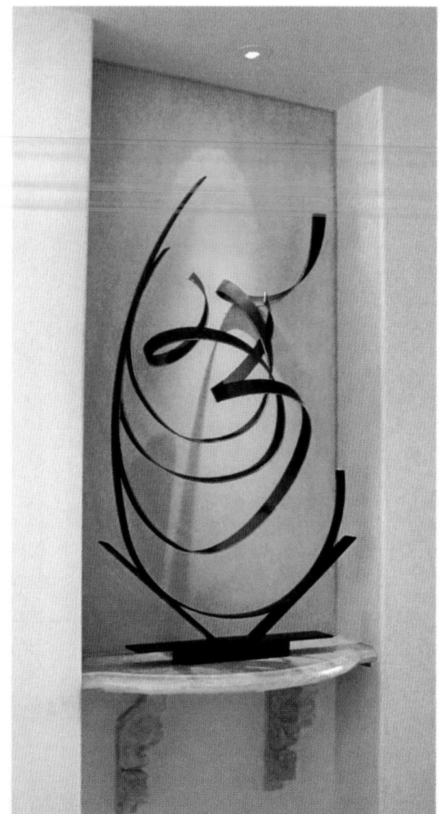

Chambered Nautilus, 2002, private residence, Palm Desert, CA, painted steel and anodized aluminum

Photos courtesy of Andrea Schwartz Gallery, San Francisco, CA

Lanterna, Jackson National Life Headquarters, Lansing, MI, stainless steel and painted metal on granite base, 9' x 15' x 11.5' Doug Elbinger

Lanterna Doug Elbinger

Protos Richard Frasier

Protos, Booz Allen Hamilton Headquarters, Tyson's Corner, VA, stainless steel and aluminum on granite base, 12' x 15' x 16' Richard Frasier

Books for Father, Vol. II, fabricated bronze, 14" x 26" x 18" on 8" base

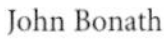

John Bonath

Astilla, cast bronze, 86" x 42" x 12" Kevin Robb

Think Outside the Box, stainless steel, 82" x 30" x 26" Kevin Robb

Cybele Rowe with a selection of her vessels, 2001

Brandy Burton

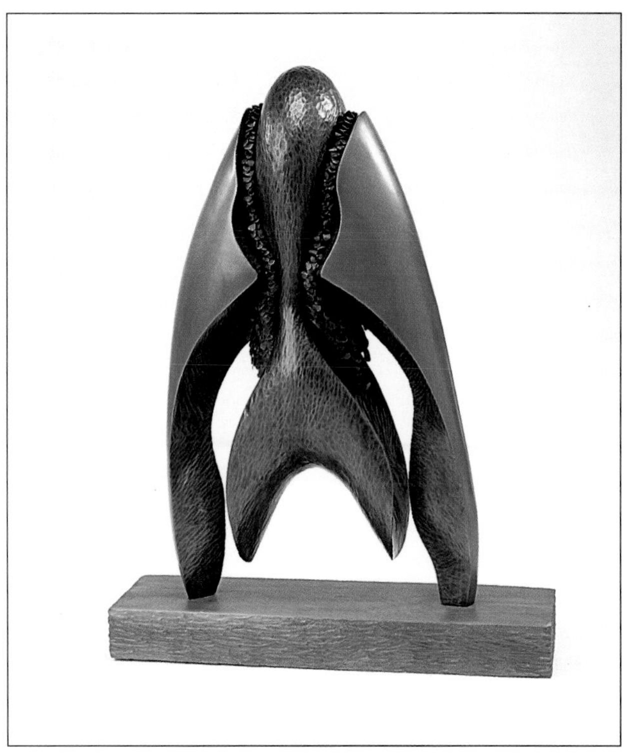

Totem, bronze, 36" x 24" x 12"

Centaur with Nymph, bronze, 54" x 12" x 7"

Mitosis, bronze, 29" x 15" x 10"

Guarded Form, bronze, 36" x 20" x 12"

Photos: Richard Schmidt

Red Bone 2, 2001, cast glass and forged steel, 76.75" x 33" x 16.5"

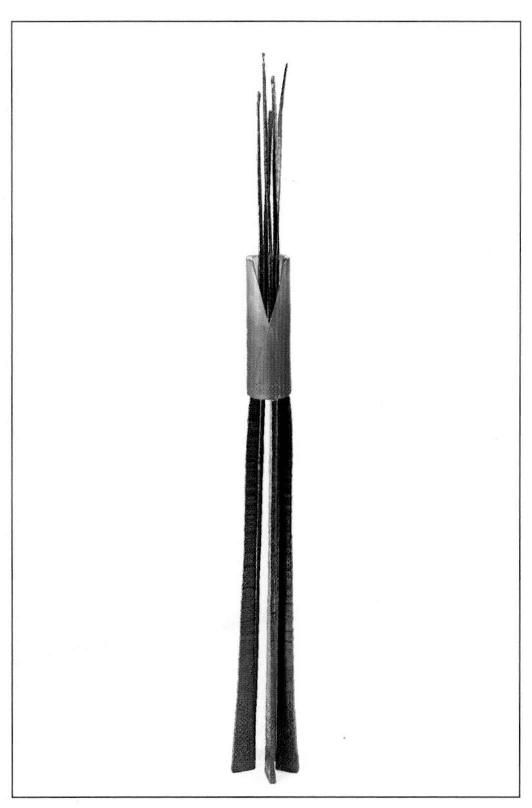

Internalization, 2001, cast glass and forged steel, 93" x 10.5" x 10"

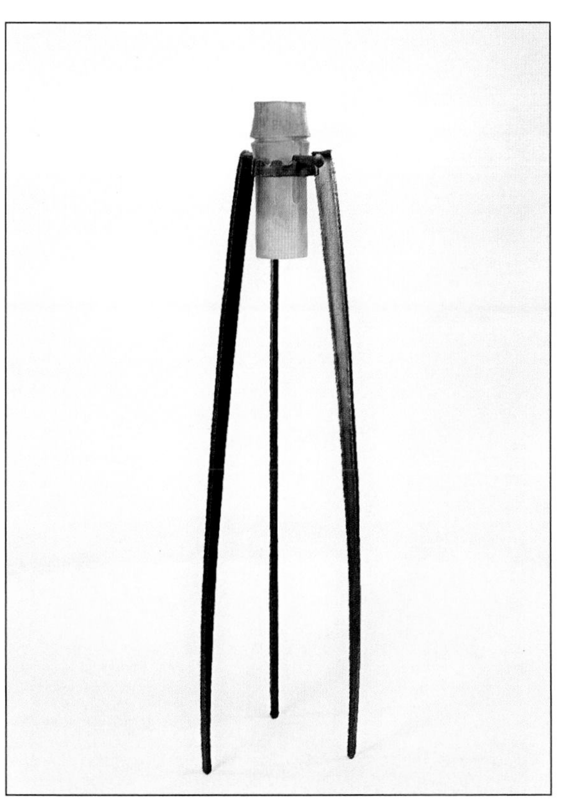

Beacon, 2001, cast glass and forged steel, 73.5" x 16" x 16"

Divergence, 2001, cast glass and forged steel, 74" x 12" x 13"

Photos: S.S.P.

Soaring Star, 2001, Chico Municipal Airport, Chico, CA, polished stainless steel, 9.5' x 10.5'

Springtime, 2001, Sunset Development Co., San Ramon, CA, polished stainless steel, 6' on 2' pedestal

Soaring Hope, 2001, Wausau Hospital, Wausau, WI, polished stainless steel, 6' on 4' pedestal

Red Planet, 1992, private collection, kinetic mixed media, 24" x 18"Dia. John Bonath

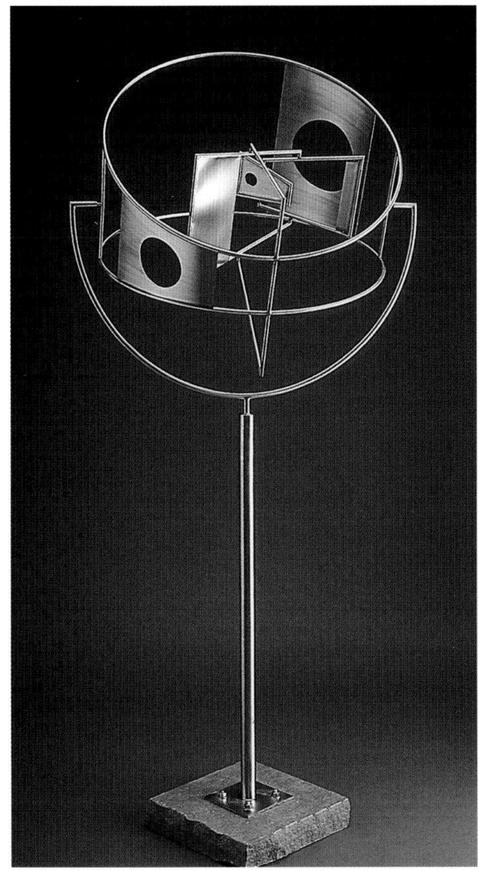

3-Point Perspective, 1995, private collection, kinetic stainless steel, 5' x 36"Dia. John Bonath

Wings of Knowledge, 2001, Lamar Community College, Lamar, CO, kinetic stainless steel, 40' x 22'Dia. C. Sturrock

Holly Jones

In 1991, Holly Jones was hired to create paintings for the SAS Institute, the largest privately owned software company in the world. Eleven years later, Jones is still at SAS, as the company's art consultant and artist-in-residence. ■ Jones first met company owner Dr. Jim Goodnight and his wife, Ann — both longtime art lovers — in the 1980s, when the Goodnights visited her studio and purchased her work. Soon thereafter, Jones received a life-changing phone call. It was Dr. Goodnight's secretary who told her, "We've got a wild offer for you. Dr. Goodnight wants you to come and work for SAS as the artist-in-residence." ■ Jones' reaction? "I said, 'This is just the biggest bluebird that ever flew in my window.'" ■ Jones now finds and buys art for the SAS headquarters in Cary, North Carolina, as well as its numerous offices across the United States. The company hosts a collection of 2,700 pieces of art. ■ Why do companies like SAS invest so much in art? "Dr. Goodnight wants the absolute best workplace for his employees, a place where people will want to spend time," Jones says. It seems to work. SAS has been named one of the top companies to work for in the United States by *Working Mother* magazine. ■ SAS is not alone in promoting and buying art. According to Jones, there's a resurgence in corporate art acquisition programs across the country. ■ "These companies share in the feeling that fine art motivates and inspires personnel," says Jones. "Art stimulates our minds so we can think beyond the frame."

Juliana Novozhilova

Los Acróbatas, 2002, aluminum, 10' x 12' x 6" Miquel Rocafort

Volumen Amarillo, 1998, aluminum, 12' x 4' x 3' José Jimenez

Public Art

Humpback Whale Tail traveling educational exhibit, fiberglass, 8.3'H x 15'W   William D. Bosworth

Baby West Indian Manatee, figured tiger maple, 7.5'L   Paul Keyserling

Topiary Lucere (The Shining Garden), illuminated sculptural environment with eight-color cycle, cast glass and acrylic embedded in concrete, with stainless steel and fiber optics, 30'W x 60' D x 14'H

Bill Lempke

Entry pylon, Lawrence-Dumont Stadium, Wichita, KS, three-dimensional bronze and brushed aluminum with internal illumination, 25'H x 11' x 3'

Wall of Balls, Lawrence-Dumont Stadium, triangular porcelain cabinet with cast aluminum baseballs and raised letters, 25'H x 6' x 6' x 6'

Satchel Paige, Lawrence-Dumont Stadium, porcelain with cast aluminum baseball and three-dimensional elements, 10' x 17' x 1'

Photos: Steve Rasmussen

Spiral of Life Totem (detail)

Spiral of Life Totem (detail)

Spiral of Life Totem, 2000, Rehmann Hall Justice Center, Tacoma, WA, carved, enameled and cast glass, powder-coated steel and stone, 32'H

Photos: Roger Screiber

New plaza sculpture suite, 1991, Federal Reserve Bank of San Francisco, Seattle, WA, stainless steel, 86"H x 864" x 64"

Fountain, 1975, Seattle Water Control Center, stainless steel, 144"H x 312" x 120"

Torque, 1982, Continental Plaza, Seattle, WA, stainless steel, 108"H x 72" x 48"

Fountain, 1998, SAP Labs, Inc., Palo Alto, CA, stainless steel, 156"H x 96" x 48"

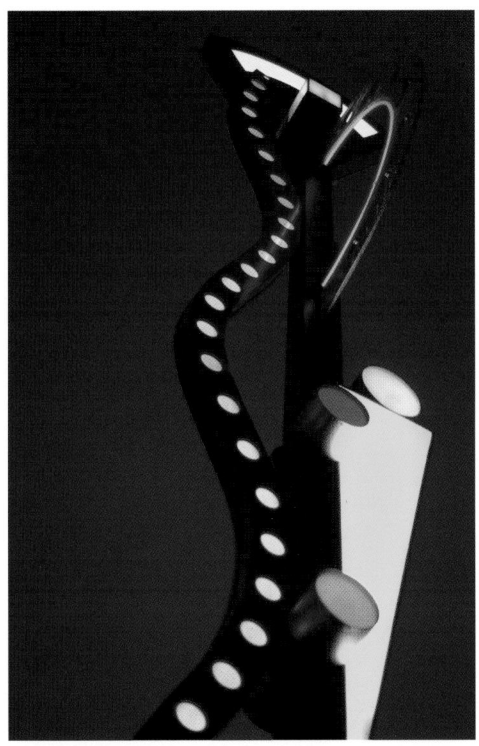

Zephyr, 2000, Los Angeles, CA, aluminum, neon and plastics, 24' x 4' x 3'

Dream with the Fishes, 1998, Milwaukee, WI, aluminum, neon and plastics, 250' x 90' x 1'

Singapore Rain, 1999, Singapore, aluminum, neon and plastics, 450' x 60' x 20'

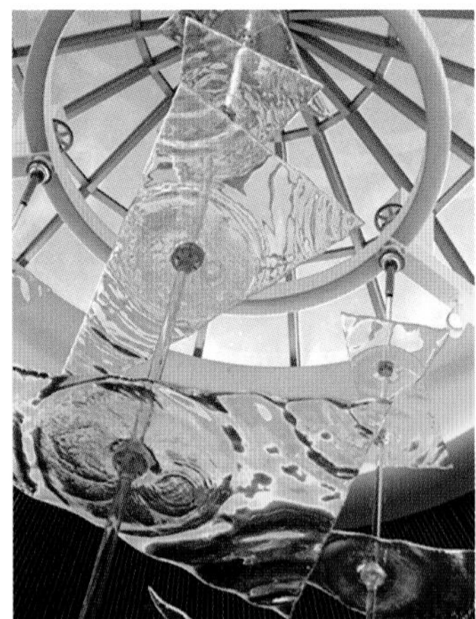

Serenity (detail)

Untitled, 2002, Gerard Center, Lima, OH, sculpted hardwoods, 11' x 24"

Serenity, 2001, St. Ritas Regional Cancer Center, Lima, OH, rotating acrylic forms with pooled and cascading water, granite and natural stone, 30' x 25'

Photos: Michael J. Ayers

Kenosha, 2001, Kenosha, WI, painted aluminum and stainless steel, top forms are wind-turned, 35' x 40' x 60'

Untitled, 2000, The Ohio State Univ./Lima Technical College, painted aluminum and acrylic, 50' x 50' x 20'

Origins: Part One – The Story (detail), 1996, Notre Dame University, South Bend, IN, sculpted hardwoods, 9' x 22.5'

Photos: Michael J. Ayers

Smysor Fountain, 1999, Murphysboro, IL, forged and fabricated bronze, 10' x 6' x 6'

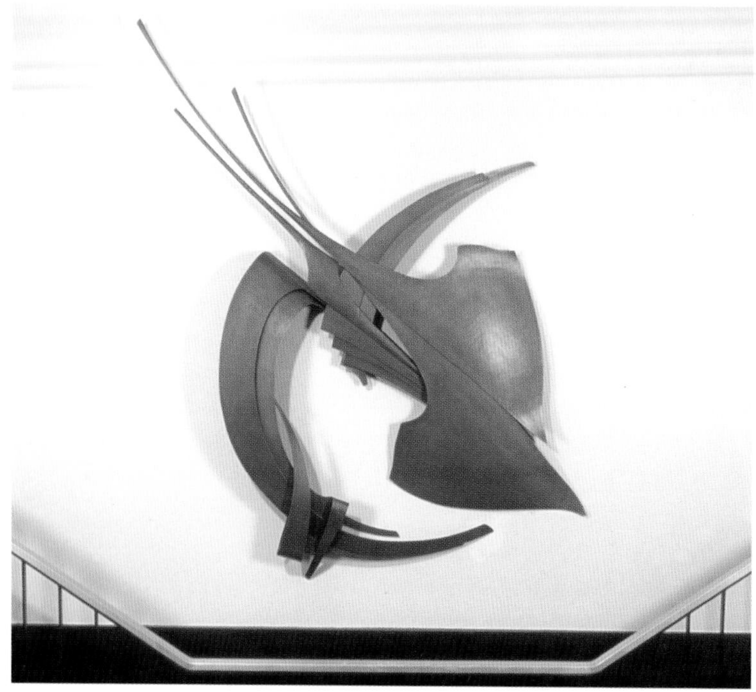

Cosmic Combustion, 2000, Southern Illinois University at Carbondale, Communications Building, forged and fabricated steel, 8' x 7' x 8"

Untitled sculpture, 1998, collection of the Minneapolis Institute of Art, forged steel, 26" x 19" x 30"

Whirl, 2001, Vance Park, Memphis, TN, forged and fabricated steel and aluminum, 18' x 21' x 8'

Photos: Jeff Bruce

Gold Panner, sculptor: Dee Clements, Blackhawk, CO, bronze, lifesize, edition of 15

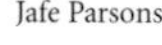

Jafe Parsons

I Am You, sculptor: Denny Haskew, Cerritos, CA, bronze with gold leaf, 156"H, edition of seven

Jafe Parsons

Steel Obelisk, sculptor: Bruce Gueswel, steel, 216"H x 25" x 25"

Bruce Gueswel

On the Alert, sculptor: Rosetta, Lakewood, CO, bronze, 64"H x 53" x 40", edition of eight

Mel Schockner

Descending Eagle, sculptor: Sandy Scott, Glen Eagle Development, Overland Park, KS, bronze, 120"H x 228", edition of 25

Solar Sails, sculptor: Mark Leichliter, Paramount, CA, powder-coated steel, 215"H

Alex Fong

Flame, 2001, Wausau Hospital, stainless steel, 15' x 4' x 4'

Interim Series, 2000, Niemi Sculpture Gallery, stainless steel, 5.8' x 27" x 27"

Celestial Trio, 2001, Niemi Sculpture Gallery, stainless steel, 15.5' x 7' x 5.5'

Light Rapids (detail)

Light Rapids, 2001, Miami University, Middletown, OH, dichroic glass, limestone and stainless steel, 10' x 35' x 35'

Eve's Apple, 1998, Windsor Sculpture Garden, Windsor, ON, Canada, painted steel, 12.3'H

Kevin Kavanaugh

Character Through Competition, 2001, Hillsborough County, FL, concrete and steel, 15' x 15' x 6'

This Forest Primeval, 1999, concrete and steel, 14' x 10' x 6'

Steps in the Sand, Laguna Beach, CA, 63" x 174" x 12"

Infinity Art Photography

Mandril de Rosa, Brea, CA, 78" x 48" x 12"

Portals, Brea, CA, 90" x 60" x 40"

Dance of the Prairie Dawn II, 2001, copper and stainless steel, 56" x 40" x 22"

Icarus Descended (detail), Chang-Won, Korea, Korean granite, 13.8' x 6.6' x 3.3', inset: *Icarus Descended*

Kaftan for Kabbaj, Seaside Park, Tangiers, Morocco, African travertine, 7.5' x 4.6' x 4.3'

Kaftan for Kabbaj (side view)

Hope for Life, Stowers Institute for Medical Research, Kansas City, MO, stainless steel, 31' x 11' x 11' Larry Young

Pegasus and Bellerophon, Grounds for Sculpture, Hamilton, NJ, bronze, 9' x 9' x 6' Larry Young

Nexus, Boone Hospital Medical Park, Columbia, MO, bronze, 17' x 16' x 8' Carole Patterson

Tango, Pier Walk '98, Chicago, IL, bronze, 11' x 4' x 2' David Wagenaar

Liturgical Art

Mary at the Wedding in Cana, 2001, Mother of Divine Providence Chapel, Pittsburgh, PA, bronze, figure 8.5' x 3' x 3' John Madia

The Crucifixion on the Tree of Life, St. Vincent DePaul Church, Fort Wayne, IN, bronze, 14'H

Ann Sherman

Mary and Infant Jesus, Prince of Peace Church, Plano, TX, bronze, 7'H

St. Francis, artist's studio, Albuquerque, NM, bronze, 6'H

David Nufer

The Immaculate Conception, Gate of Heaven Mausoleum, bronze, 7'H

St. Joseph and Family, 2001

St. Joseph and Jesus, 1998

St Peter, created for Pope John Paul II for the shore on the Sea of Galilee, bronze, 11'H

Crucifix, 1985, Resurrection Catholic Church, Destin FL, cast bronze, 5'H

Crucifix, 1988, Pastor's office, Destin, FL, cast bronze, 24"H

Mary and Child, 2001, Meridian, ID, oil-colored linden wood, 6'H

Martin Luther, 1992, Wisconsin Lutheran Seminary, cast bronze, 7'H

Tina Foulker

Interior designer Tina Foulker works for the architectural firm of Flad & Associates in Madison, Wisconsin. Established by the Flad family seven decades ago, the firm — like the Flad name — still stands for the Midwestern values of commitment, integrity, honesty and a passion for excellence. ■ Interestingly, Flad & Associates is better known around the country than it is in Madison. In the firm's early years, it designed many of the buildings downtown and on the University of Wisconsin campus. More recently, however, it has undertaken a greater number of out-of-state projects. ■ Foulker, who started with Flad & Associates two years ago, describes the company's collegial approach. "We work in teams of interior designers, landscape architects and structural engineers," she says. "I love that environment. You gain a lot from the experience of the people on your team. It's amazing what I've learned — especially as a younger member of the staff." ■ Flad & Associates offers clients a full range of architectural and engineering services, everything from preliminary designs to finishes, furniture and artwork. Flad clients work in fields as diverse as healthcare, research and development, academia and industry, as well as the corporate market. "We offer the gamut," Foulker says. ■ Flad recently completed construction on a neonatal intensive care unit they designed for a hospital in Iowa. "The client was looking for art that was both multicultural and child-oriented," Foulker says. "We were having a hard time finding that piece. Through GUILD, we commissioned two original paintings from Wendy Mattson." ■ True to the longstanding Flad tradition, excellence was achieved once more.

Portraits Express, Madison

Corpus, 2001, St. Patrick Catholic Church, Fremont, NE, laminated basswood, 7.5'H

Richard Rader, Fremont, NE

Open Your Heart, 2001, St. Paul the Apostle RCC, New Middleton, OH, clay original, 8'

A Quiet Moment, Bethlehem, Israel, clay original of the monument to the holy family

Joy of the Family, various locations, U.S. and Canada, bronze, life-size

Standing Holy Family, clay original, opposite page: *One Body,* 2002, Vatican Gardens, Rome, Italy, 10' clay original (prior to casting)

Communion Window (detail), 2001, St. Luke Lutheran Church, Ann Arbor, MI, leaded glass with beveled glass prisms, total: 6.5' x 10'

Arthur Stern

Holy Spirit Window (detail), 2001, St. Luke Lutheran Church, Ann Arbor, MI, leaded glass with beveled glass prisms, total: 6.5' x 10'

Arthur Stern

Furniture & Objects

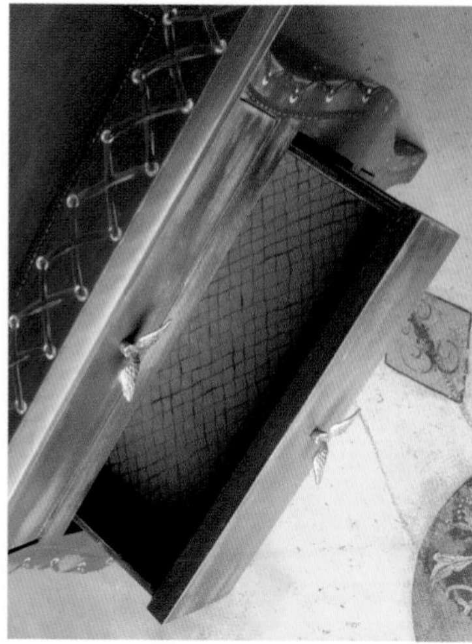

Angel Baby, three-drawer dresser

Beauty, accent table, 25" x 19" x 30.25"

Nightbird, two-drawer bombé, 36.5" x 17" x 31.75"

Avalon, wardrobe armoire, 46" x 25" x 81"

Photos: Andrew Matusik

FLUX

Wall unit, mahogany, steel, stained glass, 120" x 60" x 12"; inset: detail

Tier table, pear, satinwood, figured cherry, walnut and steel, 22" x 52" x 43"

Hall table, teak, white oak, steel and stained glass, 32" x 48" x 12"

Photos: Rick Maloof

Plea, 2002, cast glass and steel, Kaelin Gallery, Boston, MA, 6' x 12' x 1", inset: full view

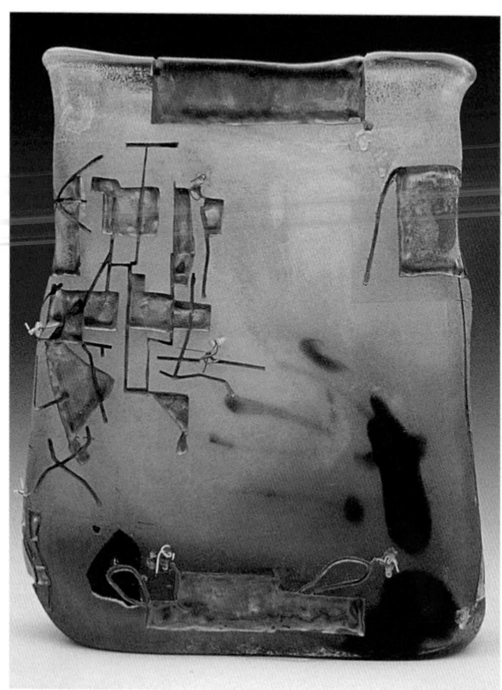

Dusk, 2001, blown and carved glass with electroformed copper, 1' x 14" x 4"

Circumnavigation, 2001, blown and carved glass with electroformed copper, 1' x 1' x 10"

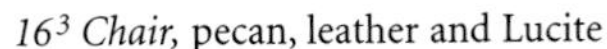

16^3 *Chair,* pecan, leather and Lucite

Flutter Weight Coffee Table, wenge and wrought steel

Keyedeco Chair, maple, wenge and leather

Anti-Kitchen Island, stainless steel, longleaf pine and maple

Photos: John Langford

Desk, mahogany veneer top, ebonized legs and mechanical drawer guides, 29" x 42" x 22" Richard Walker

Nile Cabinet, stained cherry and zebra veneer, 71" x 25" x 16" Sylvie Ball

Cherry Bijou, cherry veneer and gold leaf, 30" x 32" x 18" Richard Walker

Padauk and ebony contemporary trestle table, 42" x 72" x 30"

Dana Kershner

Figured cherry and bubinga curved buffet, 22" x 60" x 36"

David Scherrer

Brave New World, 2000, Shamel ash, palo verde, exotic woods, stainless steel rod, lacquer finish, 26.5"H x 36"Dia.

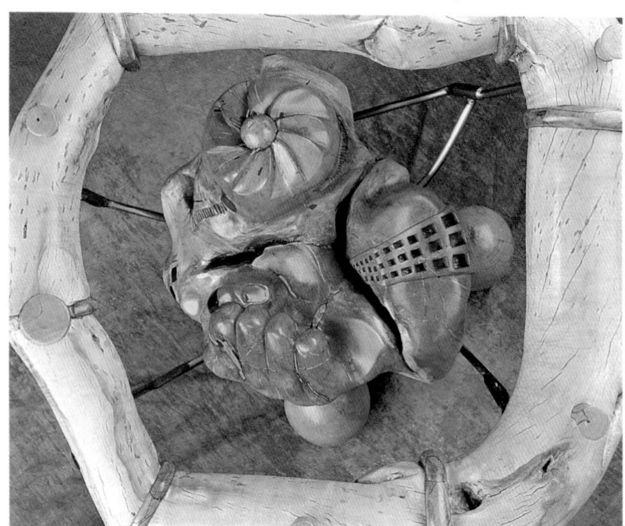

Brave New World (detail)

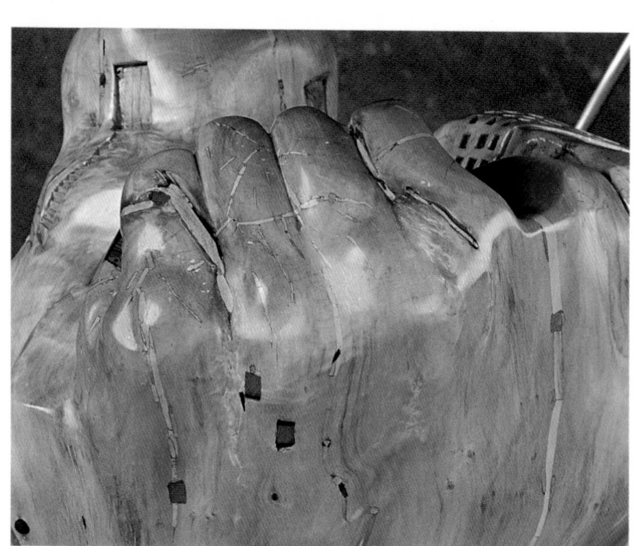

Brave New World (detail)

Photos: Randy Brink

Illuminates Bath Screen, wood and Oguru paper, two panels, each: 62" x 20"

Lee Thomas

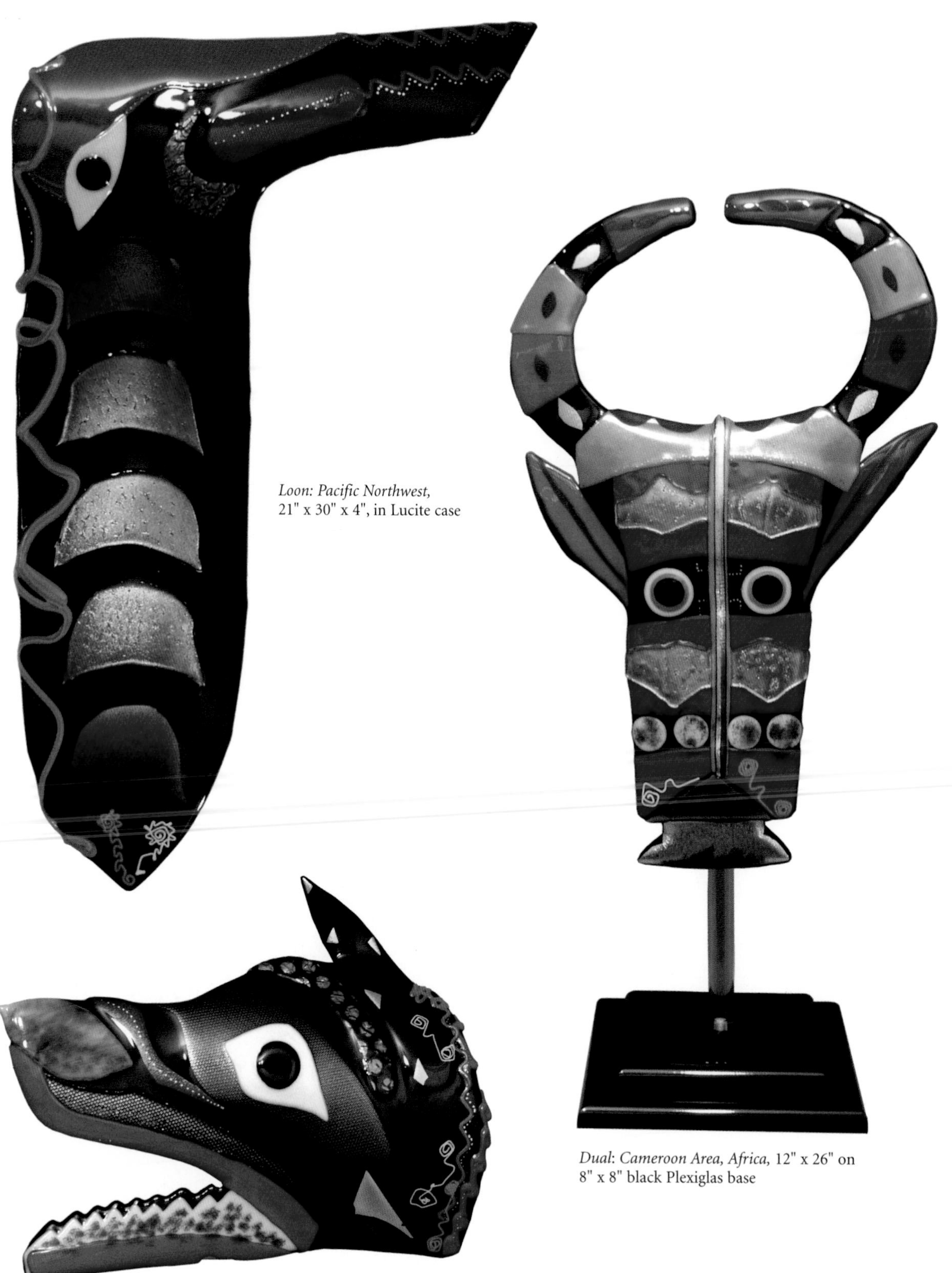

Loon: Pacific Northwest,
21" x 30" x 4", in Lucite case

Dual: Cameroon Area, Africa, 12" x 26" on 8" x 8" black Plexiglas base

Wolf: Pacific Northwest, 24" x 20" x 4", in Lucite case

Haida: Pacific Northwest, 11" x 22" on 8" x 8" black Lucite base

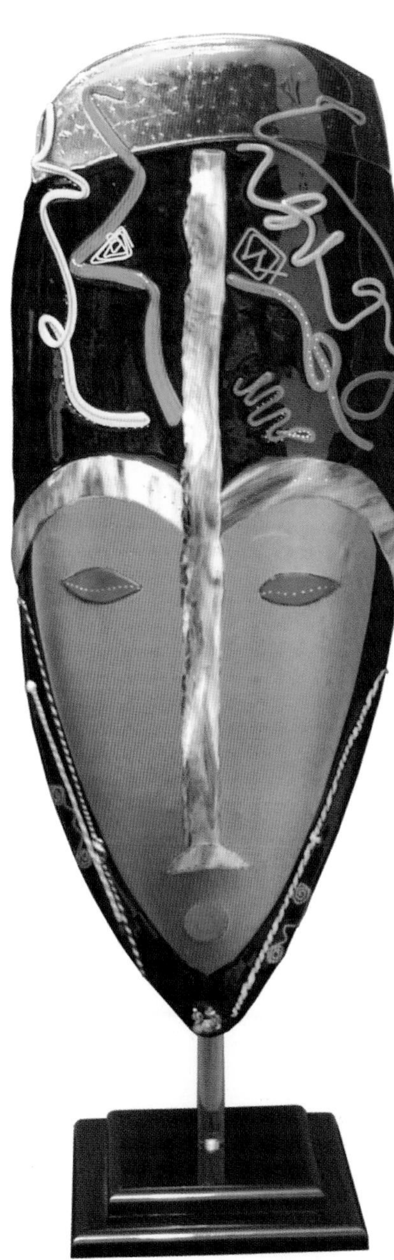

Large Fang: Africa, 12" x 34" on 10" x 10" black Lucite base

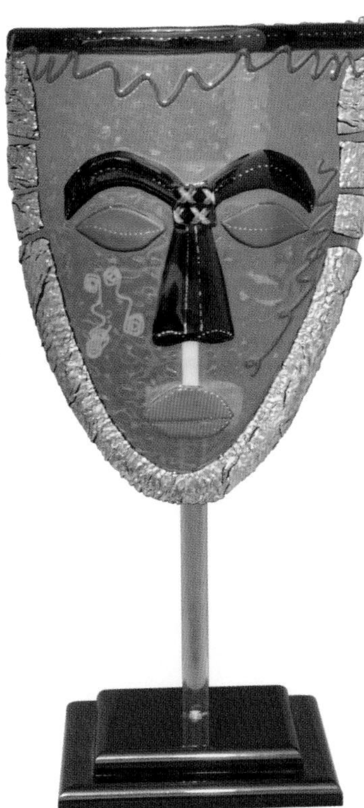

Kuba: Africa, 11" x 22" on 8" x 8" black Lucite base

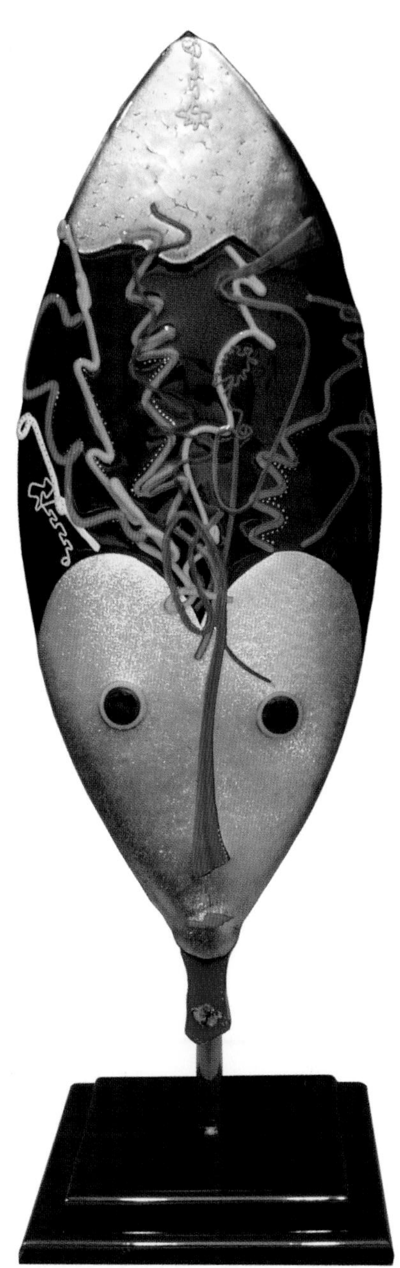

Flute: New Guinea, 12" x 34" on 10" x 10" black Lucite base

Dynasty, 2001, sycamore, dye and acrylic, 14" x 10"Dia

Warrior I, 2001, quilted oak, dye and acrylic, 11" x 6"Dia

Dynasty (detail)

Photos: Binh Pho

Nature's Windows vase, manzanita and ebony, 13" x 7"

Natural edge vase, white oak and ebony, 12" x 6.5"

Rimmed hollow-formed bowl, oak and ebony, 7" x 13"

Photos: McNabb Studio

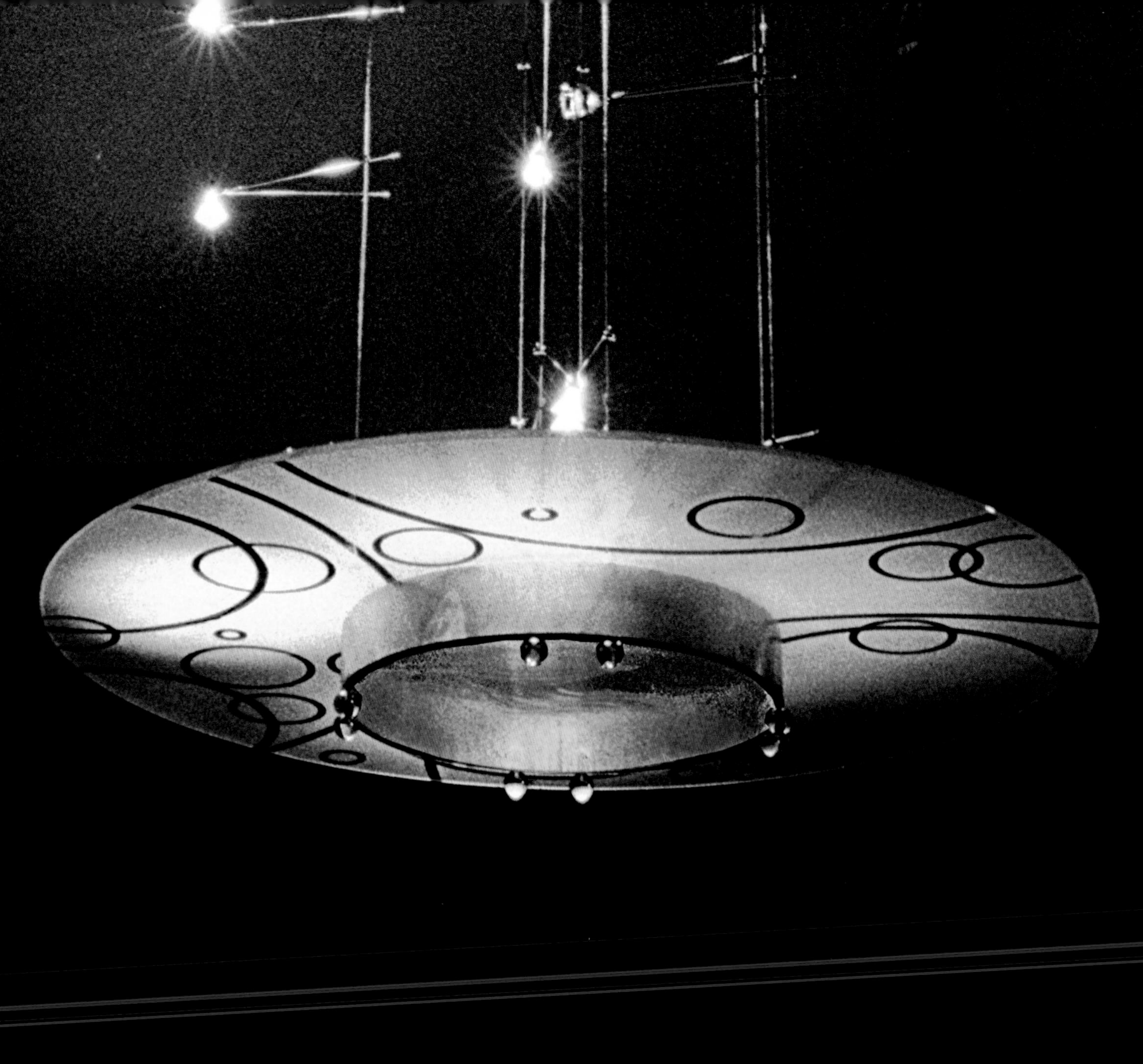

Lighting

Carly Smith

Carly Smith is busy. An art consultant for the Annex Gallery and the Warren-Garrett Fine Art Advisory in San Diego, California, Smith always has multiple jobs going on at the same time. ■ "We're all over the country, all over the world," she says. "We're doing a project in Saudi Arabia right now. We're constantly traveling." ■ Although her firm consults for hospitals and corporations, many of Smith's projects are in the hospitality industry.

Elizabeth Clinkenbeard

As part of that focus, she collects fine art for upscale hotels. ■ "The best hotels seem to be geared towards installing art collections, rather than just decorative pieces," she says. "It's amazing to see the hotel without all of the artwork, then again once the artwork is in place. It's just an amazing transformation." ■ One of the firm's projects, a collection of artwork for the Ritz-Carleton in New York City's Battery Park, was installed after a delay of several months. The opening had originally been scheduled for October 2001; however, the attacks on September 11th changed that. Smith had been in the process of picking up pieces from the artists' studios when everything was put on hold. Because of the hotel's location in lower Manhattan, she and her colleagues at the firm were concerned that the project might be abandoned. They were delighted when word came that it would go forward early in 2002. ■ "It's an incredible collection," Smith says. "I can't wait to see it installed. Many established artists — as well as up-and-coming artists — are involved, and it features all kinds of work: paintings, photography, glass and sculpture."

San Jose Repertory Theatre lobby, 2001

Wave Pendant, kiln-formed glass, 32" x 32"

Oliver, hand-blown art glass, cherry, mica shade with Japanese maple leaves, 15" x 19.5"Dia., glass by Joseph Morell — Linda Svendsen

Silent Times, Honduras mahogany and amber mica with Japanese maple leaves, 20.5" x 24"H — Carl Nelson

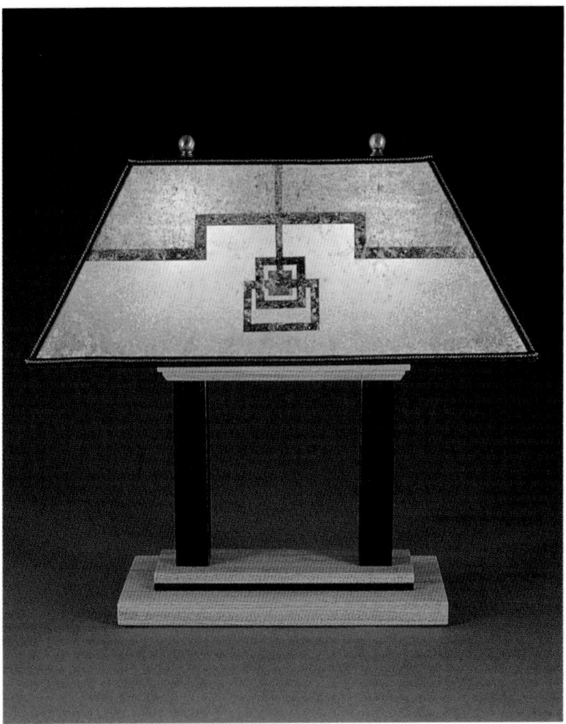

Library Interlocking Square, Honduras mahogany and alkyd mica with handcut motif, 20" x 18.5"H — Carl Nelson

Deanne Andolina

Among Deanne Andolina's clients are some of the most technologically savvy people in the world. Andolina, of Deanne's Decor in San Jose, California — at the heart of Silicon Valley — designs and decorates cutting-edge homes and offices for entrepreneurs in the technology industry. ■ When the technology changes, Andolina is right there, adapting to the constant flux in needs and design. "Flat-screen televisions, flat-screen computer monitors: the technology is amazing," she states. "And changed technology means changed design. We don't need huge desks for these new screens; the desk can be contoured: wider where you need drawers and narrower where the monitor sits." ■ But the driving force behind Andolina's style isn't function — it's art. "From the time humans first painted pictures on their cave walls," she says, "art has been used to make our mark on our living spaces." ■ For Andolina's clients, the choice in art often reflects their personal style. In one recent project, she mounted a beautiful backdrop of exotic wood behind a hanging television. Her client, who didn't want the constant opening and closing of entertainment center doors, chose this artful way to display his flat-screen TV. ■ Andolina often turns to GUILD in her search for signature pieces; through GUILD, she's found skilled artists to make, for example, kidney-shaped desks and dressers with round drawers. ■ She quotes Aldo Leopold: "Acts of creation are ordinarily reserved for gods and poets, but humbler folks may circumvent this restriction if they know how." ■ "For that," Andolina adds, "we've got GUILD."

Nicholas Robert

Chandelier and wall sconce, 1997, Japengo Restaurant, cast and blown glass, iron, chandelier: 48", sconce: 24"

Chandelier, 1999, Biggs residence, blown glass, iron, 48" x 40"

Chandelier, 1998, Jasper's Restaurant, blown glass, salvaged fixtures, 45"

Blown glass pendant lights, 1999, Waugh residence

Photos: Tim Pott

Summer

Murals & Trompe L'Oeil

Crestview Summer, Children's Wing, Northwestern Hospitals, Chicago, IL

Hudson Valley Panorama (2 panels), American Renaissance Center, Scottsdale, AZ

Work In Progress, Northwestern Hospitals, Chicago, IL

Photos: Carriage House Art Studios

JOHN J. DeVLIEGER

Versailles (detail), 200 square feet

Bill & Connie's Vista, 10' x 30'

Kristi & Kelly's Vista, 20' x 40'

Photos: Todd Murray Photography

Shirley Myers

With more than 20 years of experience in the art consulting field and as a resource for other art consultants, Shirley Myers feels she can help interior designers understand the services that art consultants provide and how their expertise can support a designer's work. ■ "Art consultants do a great deal of research for sources for art. If we're not working on a specific job, we're visiting galleries and artists' studios or gathering printed materials.

David G. MacKay

When a designer calls us and says, 'I have a corporation that has gone with craftsman-style furniture or a 1930s look in these colors,' we can say, 'I know just what you're looking for; let me show you some pieces.' That can save an interior designer weeks of work and everyone wins — especially the client." ■ Myers says the best scenario is when art consultants and designers form informal partnerships. ■ "I once worked with a designer who was very bold and talented," Myers recalls. "He was designing a one-bedroom apartment in the Watergate. One wall was all glass, but there were no other windows, and the entire apartment was designed in black. I suggested a single huge, colorful painting and told him to leave it to me. I found a large, bright abstract and we placed it near the window. Along another wall, he installed a long glass shelf with beautiful blown glass in hot pink, turquoise, yellow and white. The place honestly looked like sunshine and light. He had used all of the reflective surfaces against the black, and the apartment literally sparkled. The client adored it. The designer's talent and my discovery of the perfect piece of art made all the difference."

Knowledge, 2001, lobby of Glencoe/McGraw-Hill Publishing, Columbus, OH, transparent overlapping images painted in acrylic on 18 canvas panels, total size 77" x 173" x 2"

Knowledge (detail)

Photos: Tommy McNabb

Bedroom mural, 10' x 22'

Wall mural

Ceiling fresco, private residence, CA

Mural over fireplace mantle, 18' x 10'

A Little Monkey Business (detail)

Eric Michael Hilton

A Little Monkey Business (detail)

Eric Michael Hilton

A Little Monkey Business, 2000, silicate paints on masonry, Sarasota, FL, 62' x 90'

Greg Wilson

Paul Adelson

Paul Adelson is an art consultant and gallery owner who lives his work. Literally. His home in Dallas, Texas, is a private art gallery that inventories 700 pieces of art. Everything is for sale, he'll inform you if asked, except for his wife and the two dogs. He daily leads heads of corporations and CEOs of Fortune 500 companies through his home; a list of his clients includes Disney, Dr. Pepper, General Electric, Honeywell, Intel, Nokia and Volvo. ■ But Adelson is interested only in placing art, no matter for whom. "Art is my love and passion in my life," he states. "I was put on earth for a mission — to share art with the world." ■ It all began 16 years ago when, after leaving a business career of 15 years, he purchased two original etchings over the phone: a Salvador Dali and a Joan Miró. ■ "I got those pieces framed and up on my wall and they just altered my life. I got so lit up, so turned on to what art could provide for people. I just dropped what I was doing and I went out and started knocking on doors, meeting artists." ■ That was the beginning of a long, passionate and successful career devoted to helping people find art. That pursuit involved GUILD when Adelson was working with a law firm in Lubbock, Texas. The firm's new building had a very specific niche — 48 inches tall by just 12 inches wide — that they wanted to fill with art. Adelson found the perfect solution in a GUILD sourcebook; when he showed his clients Jeremy Cline's *Birds of Paradise* glass sculptures, everyone knew immediately that the niche had been filled.

Lori Lawrence

Metro Center mural (left side), Washington, DC, subway, acrylic 15' x 15'

Metro Center mural (right side), Washington, DC, subway, acrylic, 15' x 15'

Mt. Vernon Mural (young Geroge Washington), entrance, visitor center, Mt. Vernon, VA, 7' x 20'

Mt. Vernon Mural (elder George Washington), partial view

Chamber of Commerce mural, Washington, DC, acrylic, 8' x 15'

Photos: Greg Staley

Light Walk (left half of mural), Palo Alto Medical Foundation, CA, 6' x 26'

Light Walk (trompe l'oeil detail)

Gates of Opa Locka II (partial view), state building, Miami, FL, 10' x 18'

Path Around Son, mural in main lobby, El Camino Hospital, Mountain View, CA, 10' x 32'

Photos: Brian Brumley

Cycles of Nature, Cycles of Life (detail of left segment of wall mural), Children's Hospital at Montefiore, Bronx, NY, 33' x 6.4'

Grape Harvest (detail), digital print, 16" x 13", limited edition

Wall mural and collateral identity (detail), Opus One Restaurant, Naples, FL, 5' x 7'

Fantasy Voyage (detail of wall border art in teenage patient rooms), Children's Hospital at Montefiore, Bronx, NY, 15' x 2' (repeated around rooms)

Paintings, Prints & Drawings

The Chase, oil on canvas, 60" x 60"

The Race, oil on canvas, 60" x 60"

Cottonwood in Fall, 36" x 48"

Bison Range, 36" x 48"

Sky & Ice, 2002, oil on canvas, 22" x 66"

Rivers & Tides, 2001, encaustic on wood, 40" x 30"

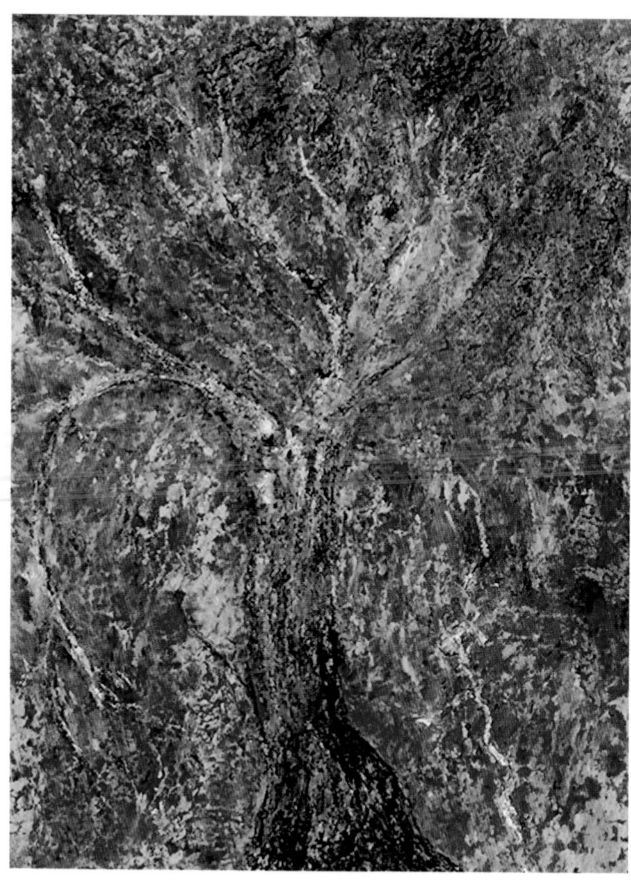

Archetype, 2001, encaustic on wood, 40" x 30"

Una Dolce Vita, 1996, oil on canvas, 20" x 16"

Portofino, 1996, "Dawn Princess," Princess Cruise Line, oil on canvas, 3' x 5'

Fishing Shack-Simi, 1996, watercolor, 14" x 20"

Riflessi di Santa Margherita, 1999, "Ocean Princess," Princess Cruise Line, oil on canvas, 4' x 8'

Elisabeth LaSalle Wilkinson

Elisabeth LaSalle Wilkinson's career was launched with a first job, fresh out of college, at New York's illustrious Parish-Hadley Associates. ■ "It was a God-given opportunity," she says of the experience. "I really lucked into it. I was set to go to the Lord & Taylor executive training program, but I really wanted to go into interior design instead. One day I stopped into a little shop on 5th Avenue, and the owner said, 'I know where you belong.' He arranged an interview with Sister Parish, the best interior designer in the country for 60 years and renowned for her clientele." ■ From Parish-Hadley, Wilkinson began building an impressive list of clients, including Mr. and Mrs. Donald Trump, Senator and Mrs. Ed Brooke, and Governor and Mrs. John "Jay" Rockefeller. (Of Rockefeller, she notes, "He used my bathroom once and seemed very impressed!") ■ Today, Wilkinson works out of Chateau de La Salle, her interior design firm in North Carolina, where she uses the same design principles that have served her well over the years. One of these principles is the use of art to add style or humor to a space. ■ Wilkinson prefers to use original artwork whenever she can and uses GUILD sourcebooks to help her clients find work they like. ■ "Original artwork is always my preference," she says, "but I'm not the type to come in and say, 'Clear off the walls, we're going to do it my way.' I try to work with my clients' tastes and guide them toward a great outcome. If I see something that's too small in scale, for example, I'll tell them they should go bolder and larger. That's where GUILD sourcebooks come in."

Akeem #1, pastel on paper, 26" x 30"

Akeem #2, pastel on paper, 26" x 30"

Pipe Dreams, pastel and sand, 24" x 18"

Fish Girl, pastel on paper, 28" x 24"

Feeling of Water Skiing, acrylic on wood

Tomiko Gumbleton

Fireplace, 2000, giclee print on paper, 17" x 26"

Cypress Roots I, 2001, giclee print on paper, 19" x 26"

Photos: Everett & Soule

When Shadows Fall, 2000, mixed-media oil on canvas, 6" x 8"

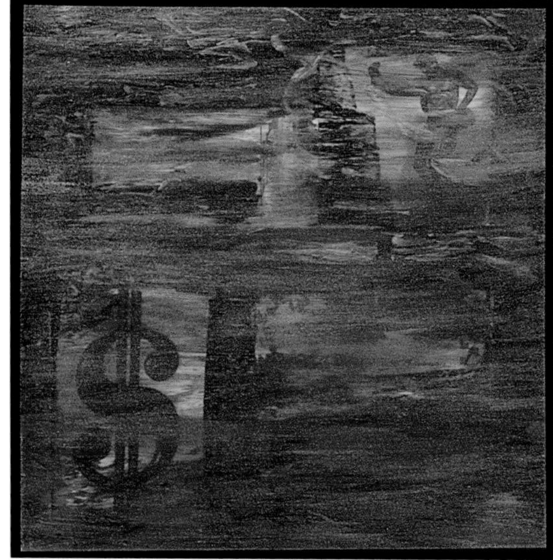

Rome, 2000, mixed-media oil on canvas, 12" x 12"

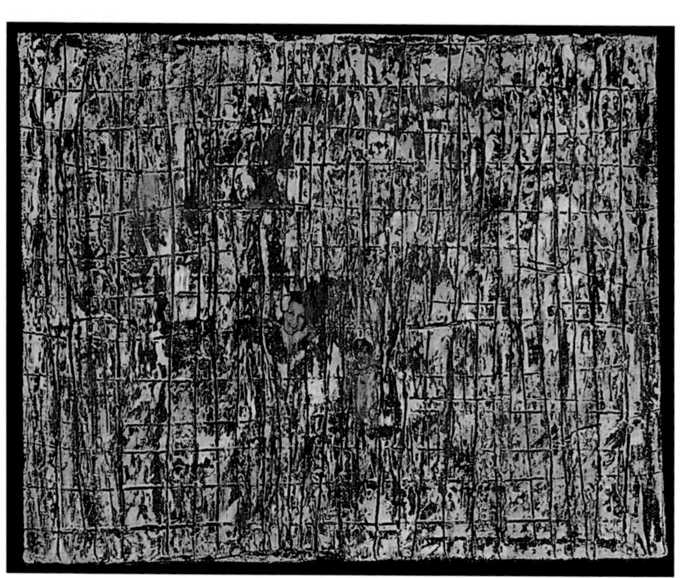

Our Times, 2001, mixed-media oil on canvas, 20" x 16"

Water Colors, oil on canvas, 52" x 50" Charles Mayer Photography

Beached in a Rainbow, oil on canvas, 36" x 38" Color Services Inc.

Full Moon With Wild Grass, 2000, gold, silver leaf and oil paint, 42" x 64"

New Moon, 2000, silver leaf and oil paint, 42" x 64"

Photos: Ira D. Schrank

STEVE HEIMANN

Bird of Knowledge, 2001, oil on canvas, 12" x 16"

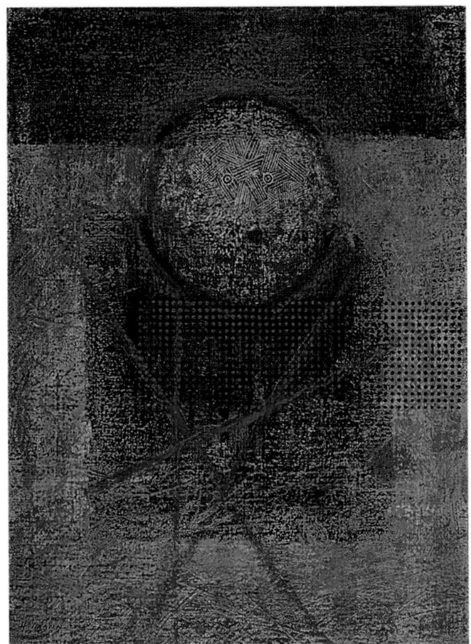

Drama Queen, 2001, oil on canvas, 16" x 12"

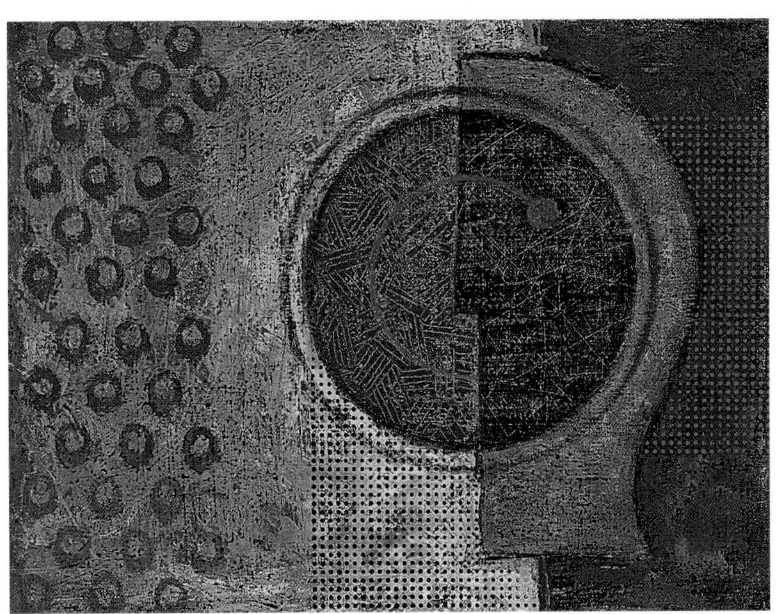

Tech Support, 2001, oil on canvas, 12" x 16"

Lindy Hop Ballroom, 1998, mixed-media linoleum block print on paper, image size: 24" x 36"

Ken Wagner

Vessels 4, 2001, mixed-media linoleum block print on paper, image size: 15" x 15"

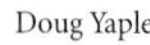

Doug Yaple

Vessels 2, 2001, mixed-media linoleum block print on paper, image size: 15" x 15"

Doug Yaple

Tundra Girl, 2002, private collection, acrylic on canvas, 36" x 36"

Blue Ridge Lullaby, 1999, acrylic on canvas, 36" x 36"

Moon-Vivaldi-Spring, private collection, acrylic on canvas, 32" x 32"

Photos: Silja Lahtinen

River-Fall, © 2001, acrylic on canvas, 24" x 24"

Western Strata, acrylic on paper, 40" x 40"

Riverview-Fall, © 2002, acrylic on paper, 22" x 30"

A Walk in the Park, 2001, oil on canvas, 38" x 58"

New Hampshire Avenue and S Street NW, 2001, oil on canvas, 36" x 54"

Photos: Greg Staley

Rosalyn Cama

Rosalyn Cama, of Cama, Inc., in New Haven, Connecticut, is one busy designer. Her firm's list of awards and publications is lengthy and prestigious, and clients range from hospitals to concert halls to that famous New Haven institution: Yale. ■ "They've been a client of ours forever," explains Cama. "Not only the University, but the Medical School and Hospital as well." ■ Part of Cama's success in managing such a varied and busy roster lies in her attitude. "We're only as good as our clients let us be," she says firmly. "A client has to be clear on their strategic direction in order for us to deliver an appropriate solution. If their budget doesn't match that direction, then we need to be creative with financial solutions as well." ■ Case in point: the Yale-New Haven Children's Hospital. Because the hospital was facing a curtailed art budget, Cama worked with a woman from a children's museum in Brooklyn, New York. The woman, who had a United Nations connection, solicited art depicting brave acts, both great and small, from children around the world. Titled *Tales of Courage,* the project — a phenomenal body of children's artwork from all over the world — opened in 1992 to international acclaim. ■ Cama often finds her art through GUILD, working with artists to create exactly what she feels is needed in a given space. A good example is the pediatric outpatient facility at Riley Hospital in Indianapolis, Indiana. Cama wanted artwork that children would interact with, something that would make them smile. Through GUILD, she found a glass artist to create a railing — incorporating dichroic glass — that appears to change color as children walk by. It's a functional, and magical, solution.

Frank Poole

Crossing, 2000, acrylic on canvas, 48" x 36"

Boat, 2002, acrylic on canvas, 24" x 20"

Fisherman, 2001, acrylic on canvas, 42" x 56"

Photos: Daniel Portnoy

JAMES C. NAGLE

Mislaid Artifacts, 2001, acrylic on canvas, 24" x 30"

Spirit House, 2001, acrylic on canvas, 30" x 24"

Breached Mischiefs, 2001, acrylic on canvas, 48" x 48"

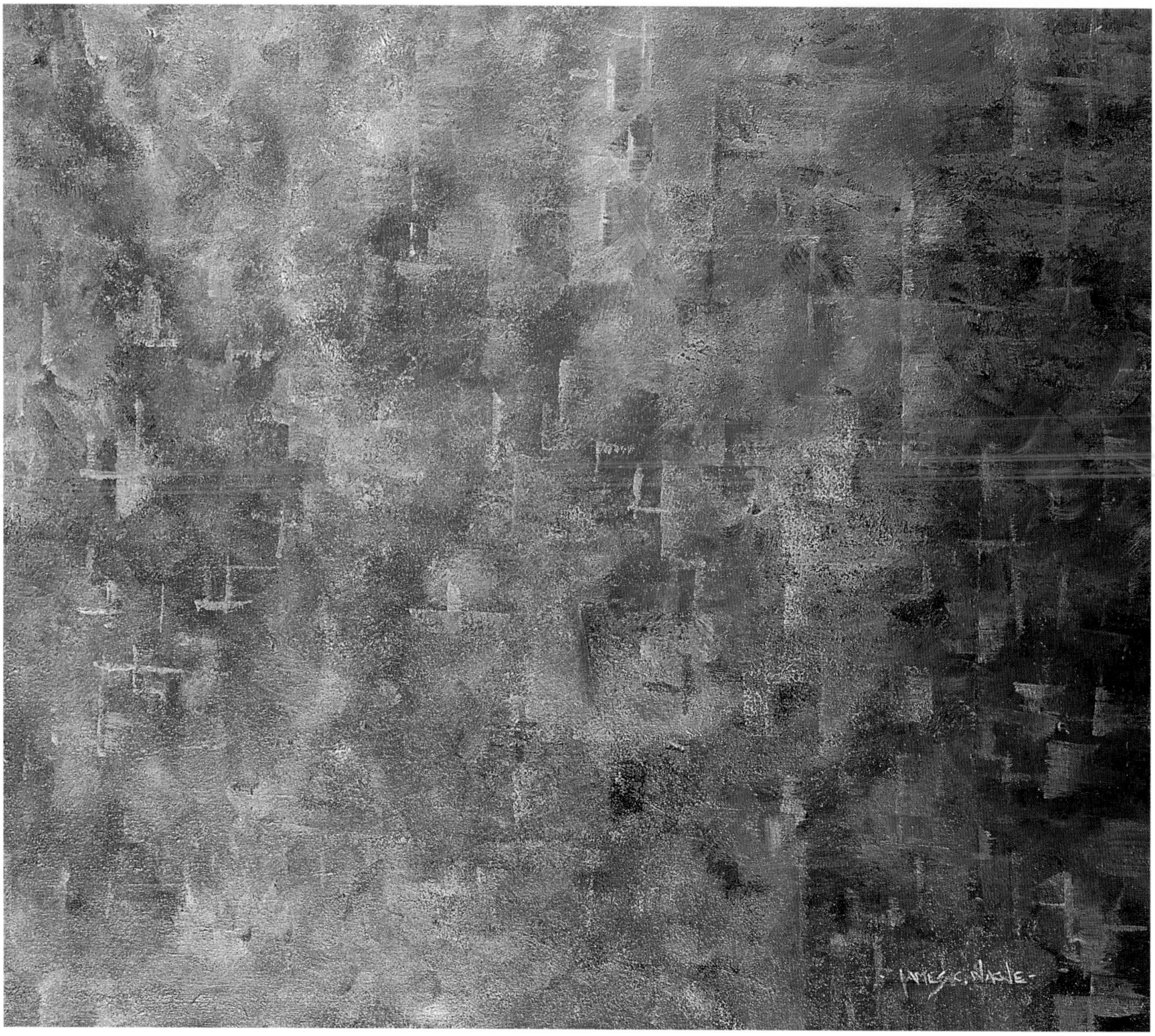

The Last Trace (detail), 2001, acrylic on canvas, 36" x 60"

Photos: Craig Smith

Cayman Palms, image size: 22" x 30"

Jennifer France

Jennifer France started Big Sky Design, Inc., in 1997, leaving the architectural firm where she worked as an interior designer to strike out on her own. She chose the company's name carefully, as a way to express its goals and mission to her clients. "We encourage our clients to think big," she says, "beyond the norm." ■ A recent project illustrates the Big Sky philosophy. An old supermarket in Wilmington, North Carolina, was to be turned into a new library branch featuring a state-of-the-art computer station. France, collaborating with the architect assigned to the project, came up with the theme of exploration, symbolized by the construction of a giant boat plowing the waves. ■ "The library now has an ocean liner penetrating the front wall of the building as you enter," she explains. ■ The use of recycled materials became an outgrowth of France's "big" concept. "We used recycled rubber flooring made out of tires," she says, "It's soft on the feet and has great acoustic value. From a design standpoint, it worked great because the curve of the tires mimicked the wake of the water." ■ The library design also incorporates panels made of post-consumer plastics — specifically, old detergent bottles — that display bits of shredded text. "The library donated some of its old books, which we shredded and then sent to a company that presses recycled plastic. They mixed the paper into their vat of plastic and pressed the panels." ■ It was an extremely successful project. The director of the library was recognized as "Director of the Year" by a regional library association and attributes the award, in part, to the design of the new facility.

See (from *Six Stages of Wine Tasting*), print, 12.5" x 15"

Smell (from *Six Stages of Wine Tasting*), print, 12.5" x 15"

Evening to Remember, watercolor, 41" x 51"

Sunrise, silkscreen print, 30" x 30"

Midday, silkscreen print, 30" x 30"

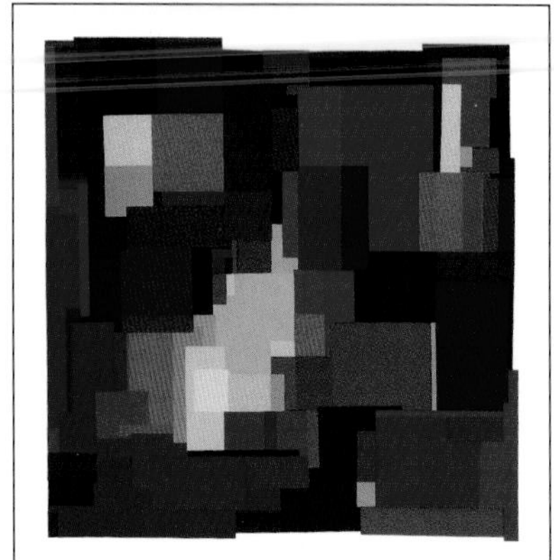

Sunset, silkscreen print, 30" x 30"

A San Francisco Night, silkscreen print, 60" x 40", edition of 250

BZ-R104, custom wool area rug, available in 7' x 9', 9.6' x 12' and larger custom sizes

Chess, 2001, iris print, image: 35" x 28"

Cactus 5, #5, 2001, collage, 13.5" x 11"

Twins Flying, 2001, iris print, image: 29" x 29"

Cactus 5, #4, 2001, collage, 13.5" x 11"

Photos: John Ferrentino

Fine Art Photography

Tears from Heaven #82, 2000, black and white sepia toned, 14" x 11"

MARIAN JONES

Beginnings, gicleé print, 11" x 16", limited edition

See Change (three parts), gicleé prints, 8" x 10" each, limited edition

TOM FERDERBAR

Abandoned Route 66 Near Stroud, OK, 1980, archival giclee print available in a variety of sizes

Yellow Truck, Route 66, Cuervo, NM, 1999, archival giclee print available in a variety of sizes

Garage Doors, Route 66, Bernalillo, NM, 1999, archival giclee print available in a variety of sizes

View Through an Arch, limited-edition photograph or Iris print

Shapes, limited-edition photograph or Iris print

African Red Sunset, limited-edition photograph or Iris print

Curtained Window, Riga, Latvia, © 2001

Geometry in Stone, Riga, Latvia, © 2001

Ornamentalism – Garage, Riga, Latvia, © 2001

Three Trees, © 2001

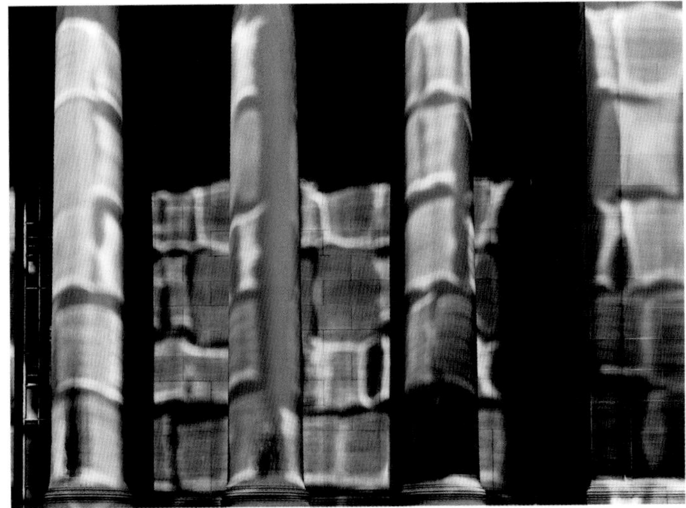

Bathed in Reflection, Carnegie Mellon Institute

San Felipe de Neri, Albuquerque, NM

R & R Hall, Cleveland, OH

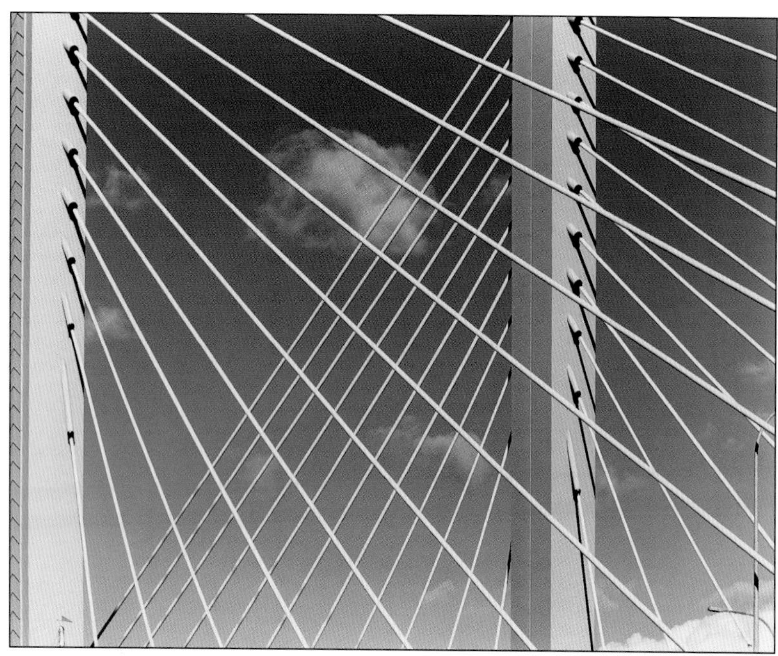

Cable Stay Bridge, Thea Foss Waterway, Tacoma, 2000, silver gelatin print, 8" x 10"

White Shadows, Sheraton Hotel, Tacoma, 2000, silver gelatin print, 8" x 10"

Plastic Bag, Wind and Shadow, Seattle, 1979, silver gelatin print, 8" x 10"

Green Point from Garage at 62 Island Blvd., Fox Island, 1994, silver gelatin, 8" x 10"

Cedar & Periwinkle, Fox Island, 1991, silver gelatin, 8" x 10"

Fan Light over Green Point, Fox Island, 2000, silver gelatin, 8" x 10"

Purple Tulips, © 1999, cibachrome or color print, any size

Yellow Orchids, © 1999, cibachrome or color print, any size

Three Rocks at Lake McDonald, limited-edition photographs and giclee prints up to 40"

Yellowstone River in Fall, limited-edition photographs and giclee prints up to 40"

Fern Canyon, limited-edition photographs and giclee prints up to 40"

Art for the Wall | Mixed Media

Cowboy, GSD&M Advertising Agency, Styrofoam, neon and paint, 10' x 60'

Shark, GSD&M Advertising Agency, Styrofoam, 7' x 2'

Galveston Dock, Bob Bullock Texas State History Museum, glass fiber reinforced concrete, 11' x 17'

Scott van Osdol

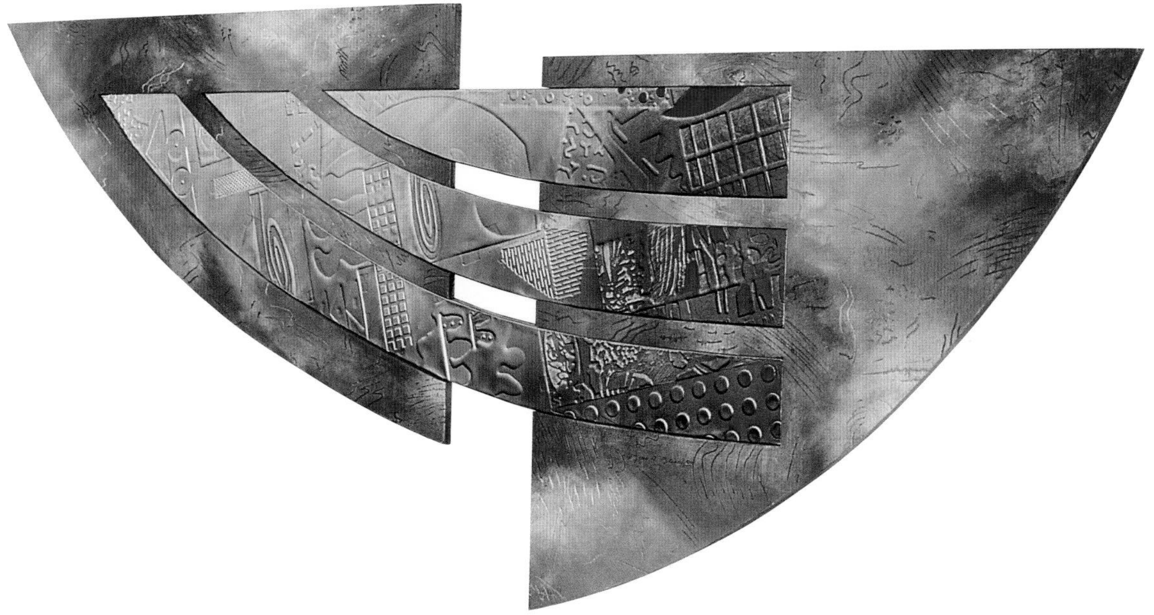

Untitled wall sculpture 02, painting on aluminum and wood, 4' x 7', installation: Booz, Allen & Hamilton Inc., VA

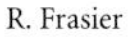

R. Frasier

Evening Embers I, monoprint collage, 24" x 36" Rod MacDonald

Evening Embers II, monoprint collage, 24" x 36" Rod MacDonald

Plan for Nuevo Bosque, 2000, carved wood, willow and paper, 30" x 29" x 7.5"

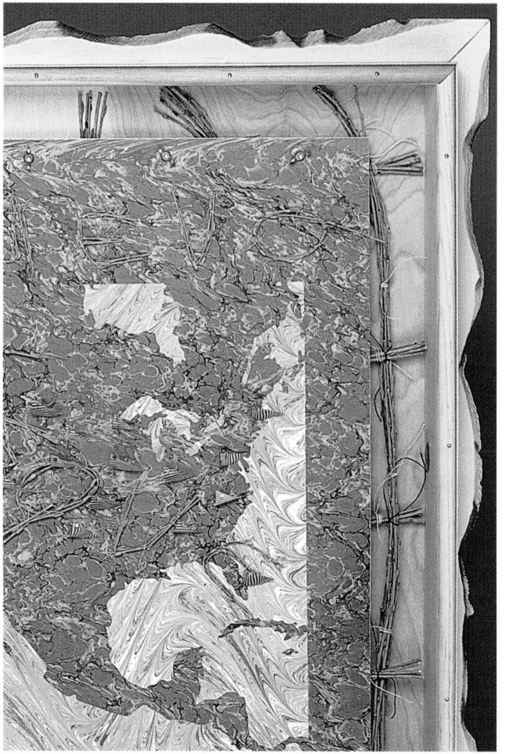

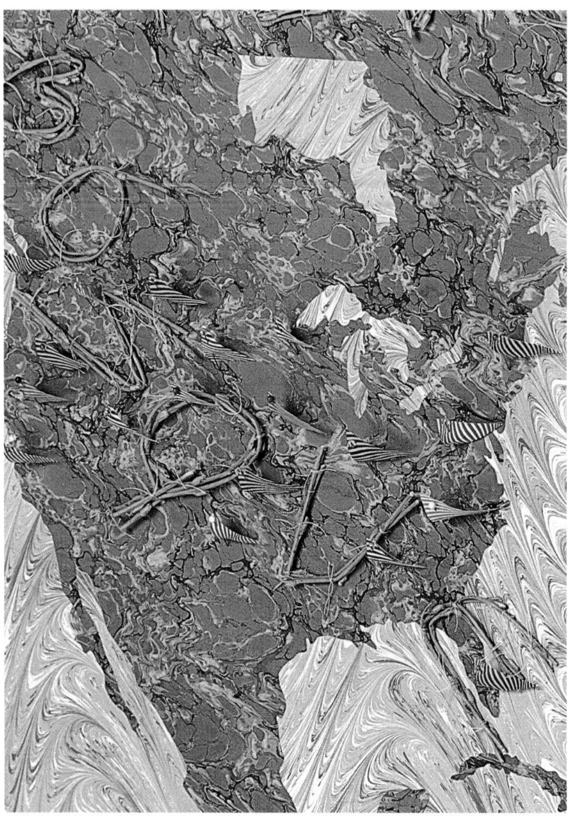

Photos: Eugene Sladek, College of DuPage

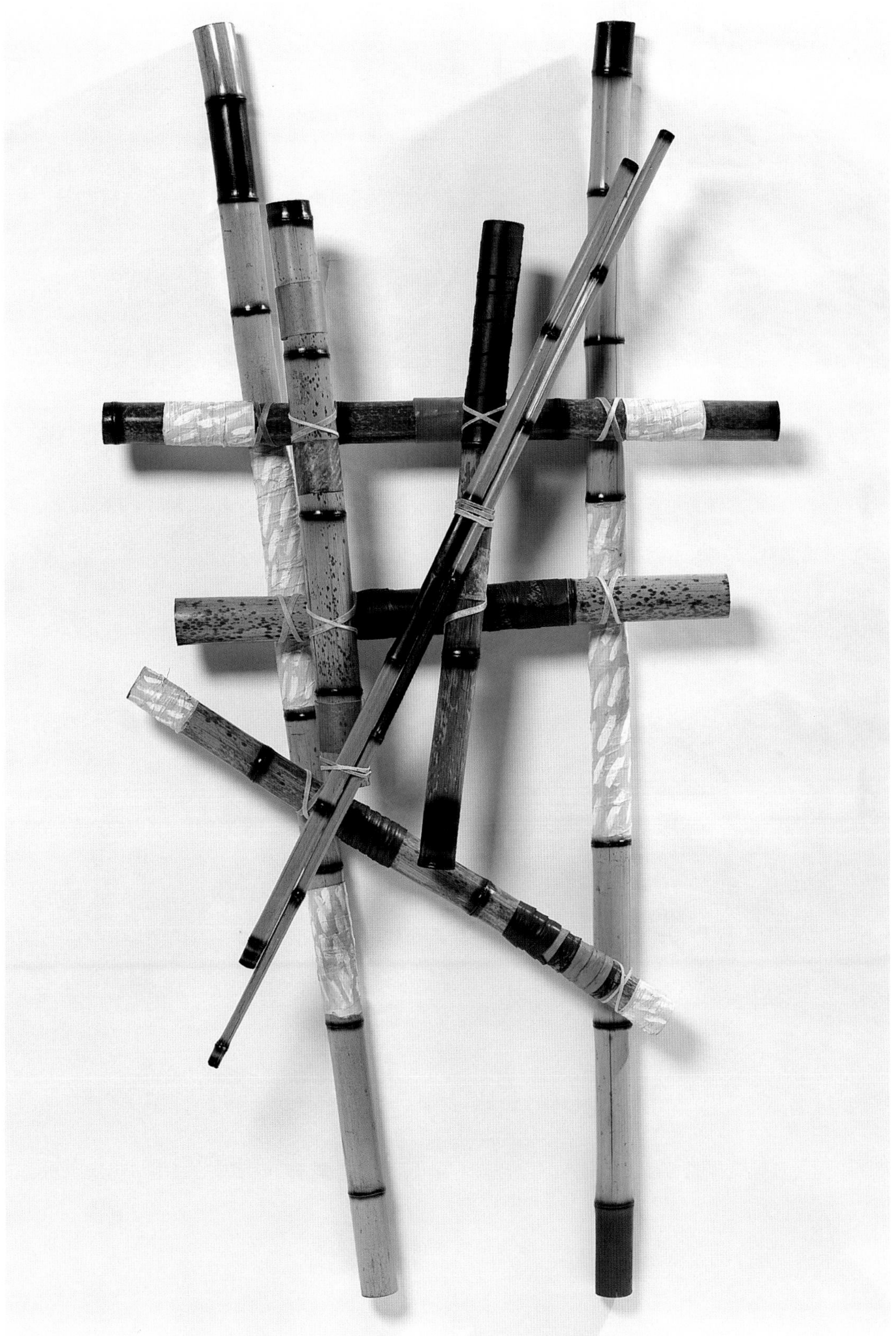

Fisherman's Friend, 2001, bamboo construction with mixed media and acrylic, 72" x 34" x 6"

David Nester

STEPHANIE GASSMAN

Tego Bay Bar and Grill, 2001, oil on canvas, 4'H x 6'W x .75"D, Troy, OH

OMS Photography

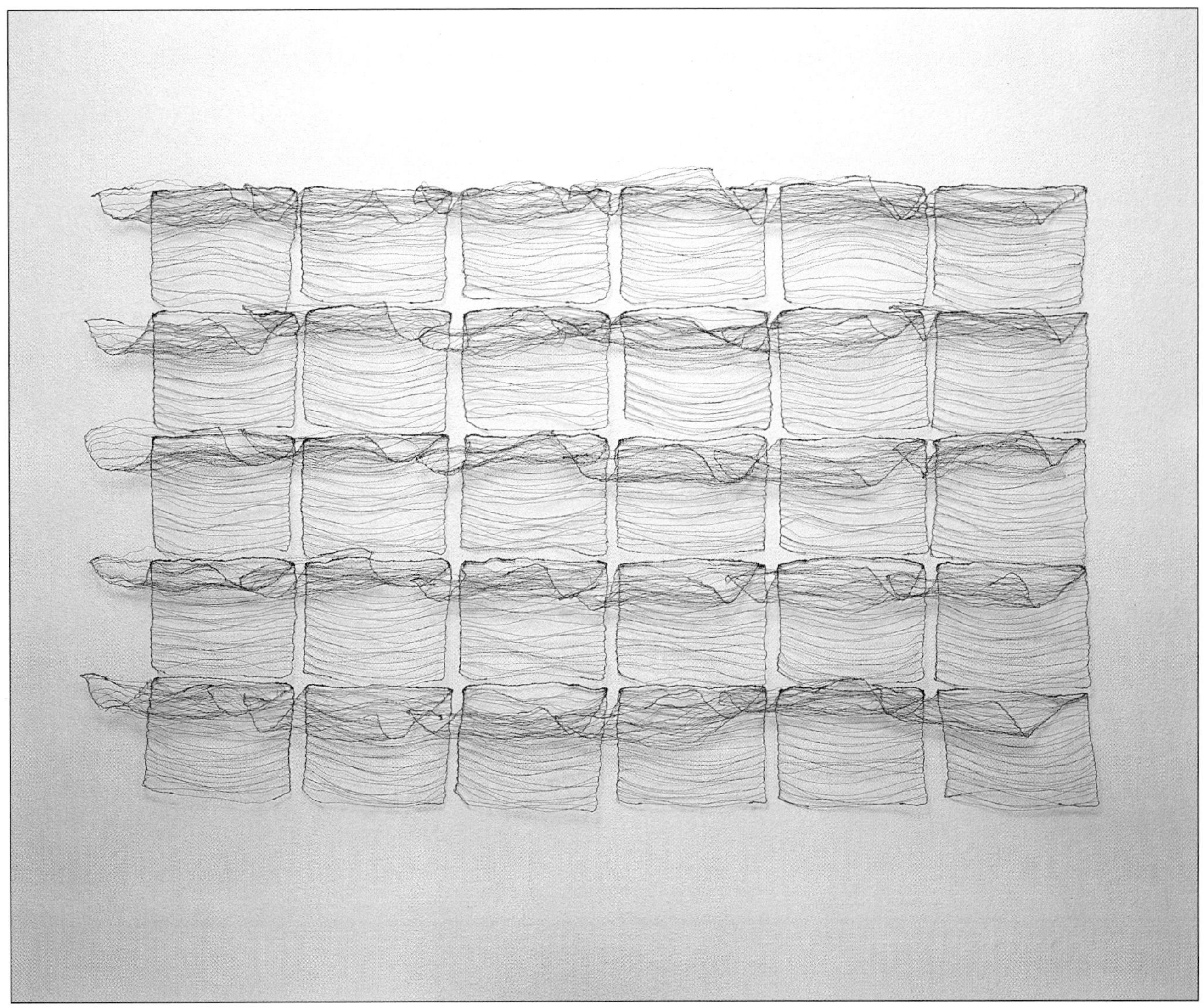

Lifting the Veil, steel wire, 3' x 5' x 4"

Gerry Ratto

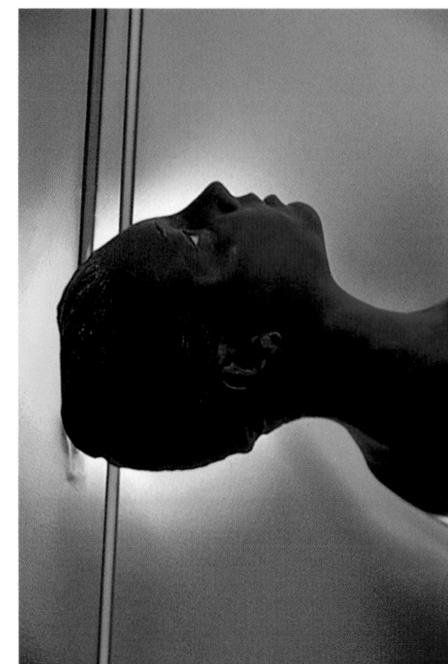

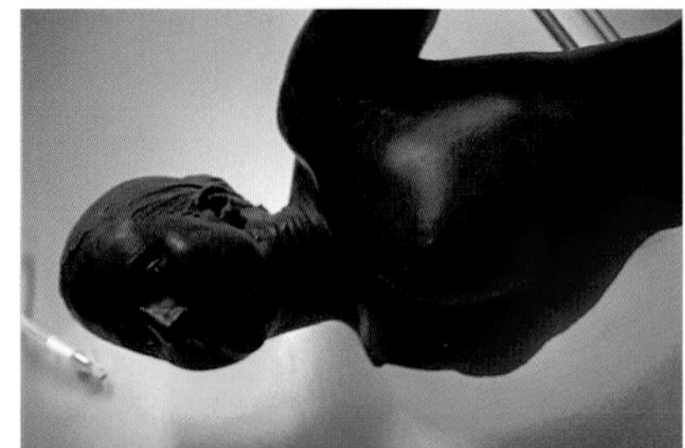

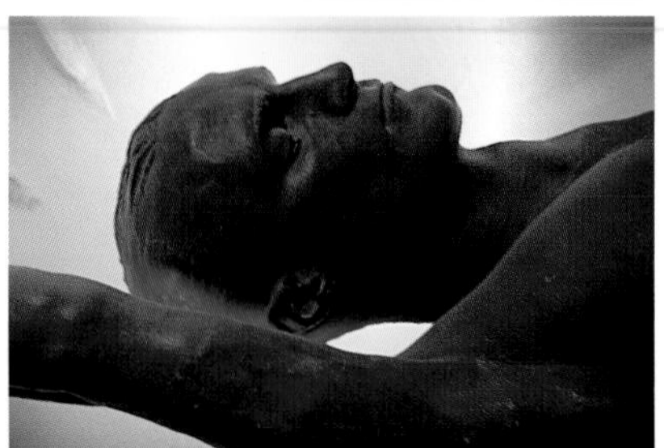

Untitled, private commission, 1999, life-size figures in bonded copper with neon Ellen Martin

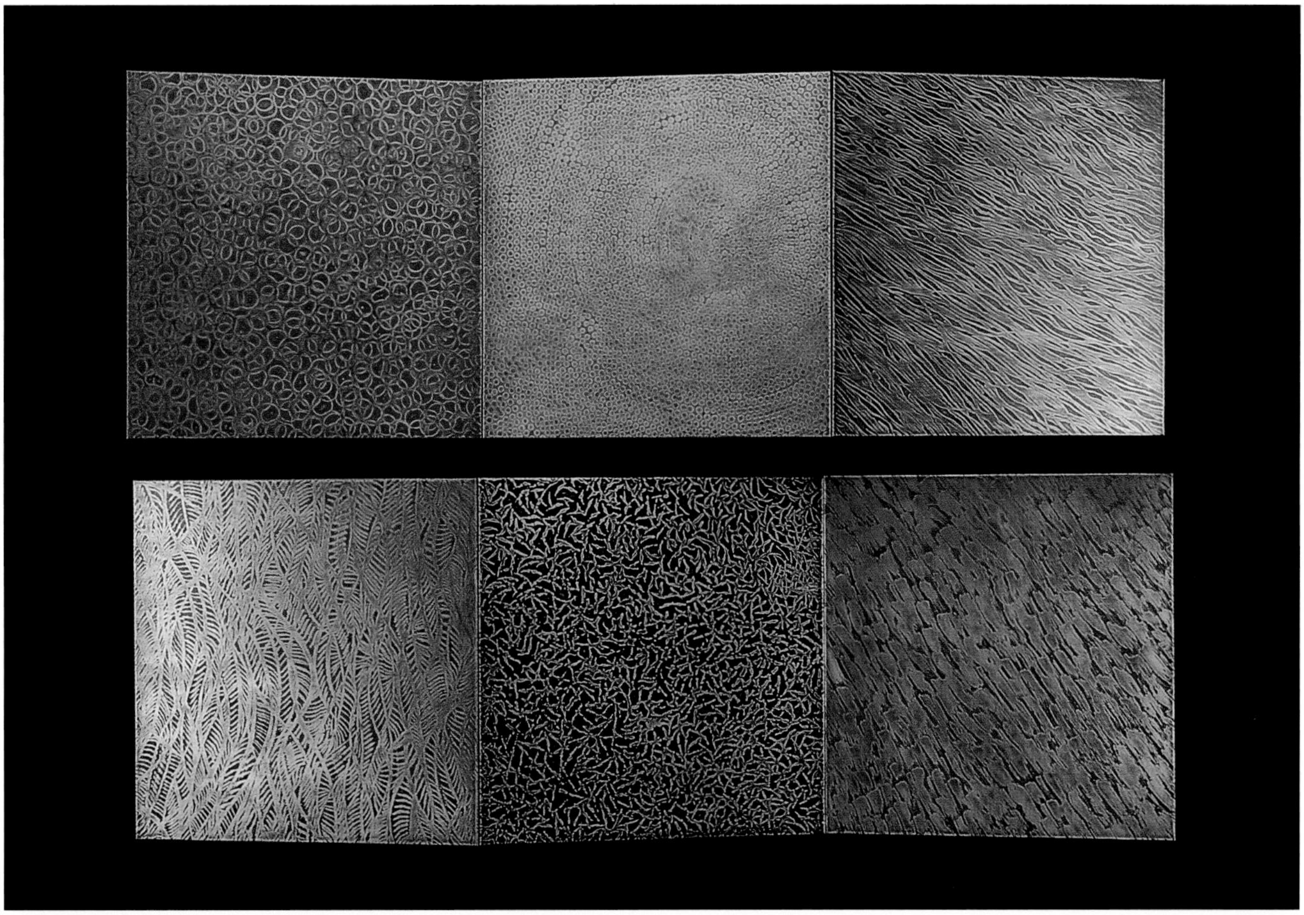

LINDA M. LEVITON

Patterns of Nature, 2001, copper, each three-square unit 14" x 42" x 3"

Jerry Anthony

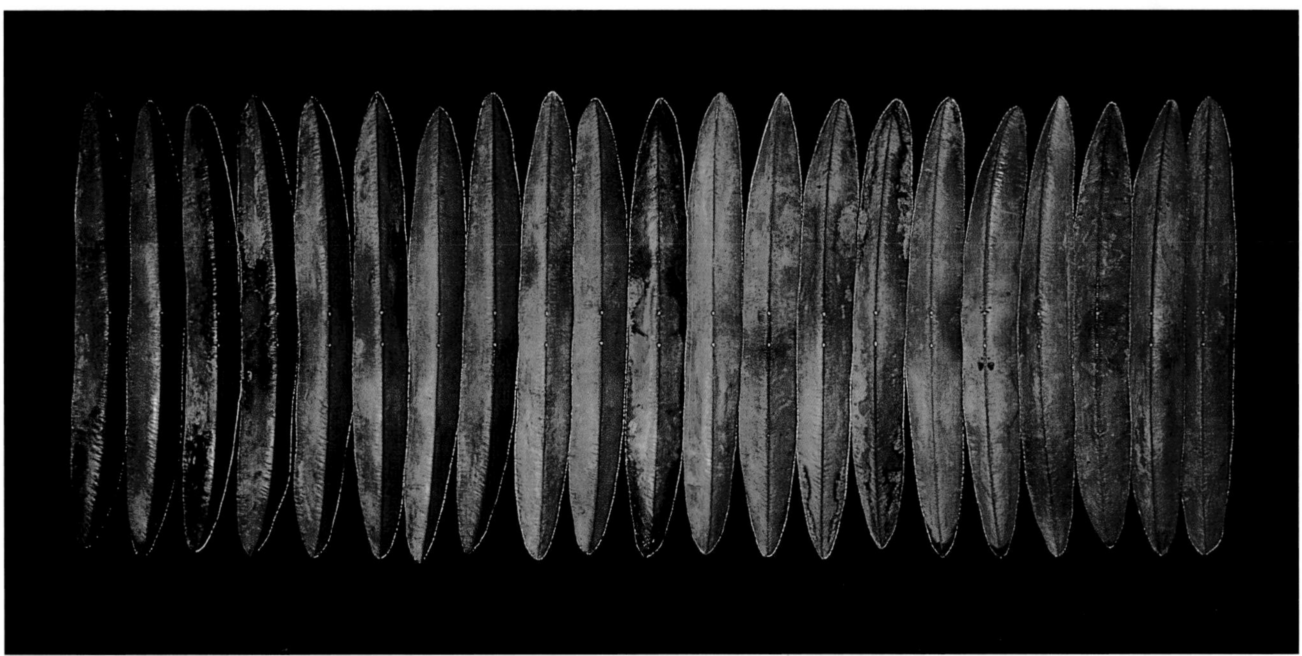

21 Forms, 1998, copper, 6' x 28" x 7"

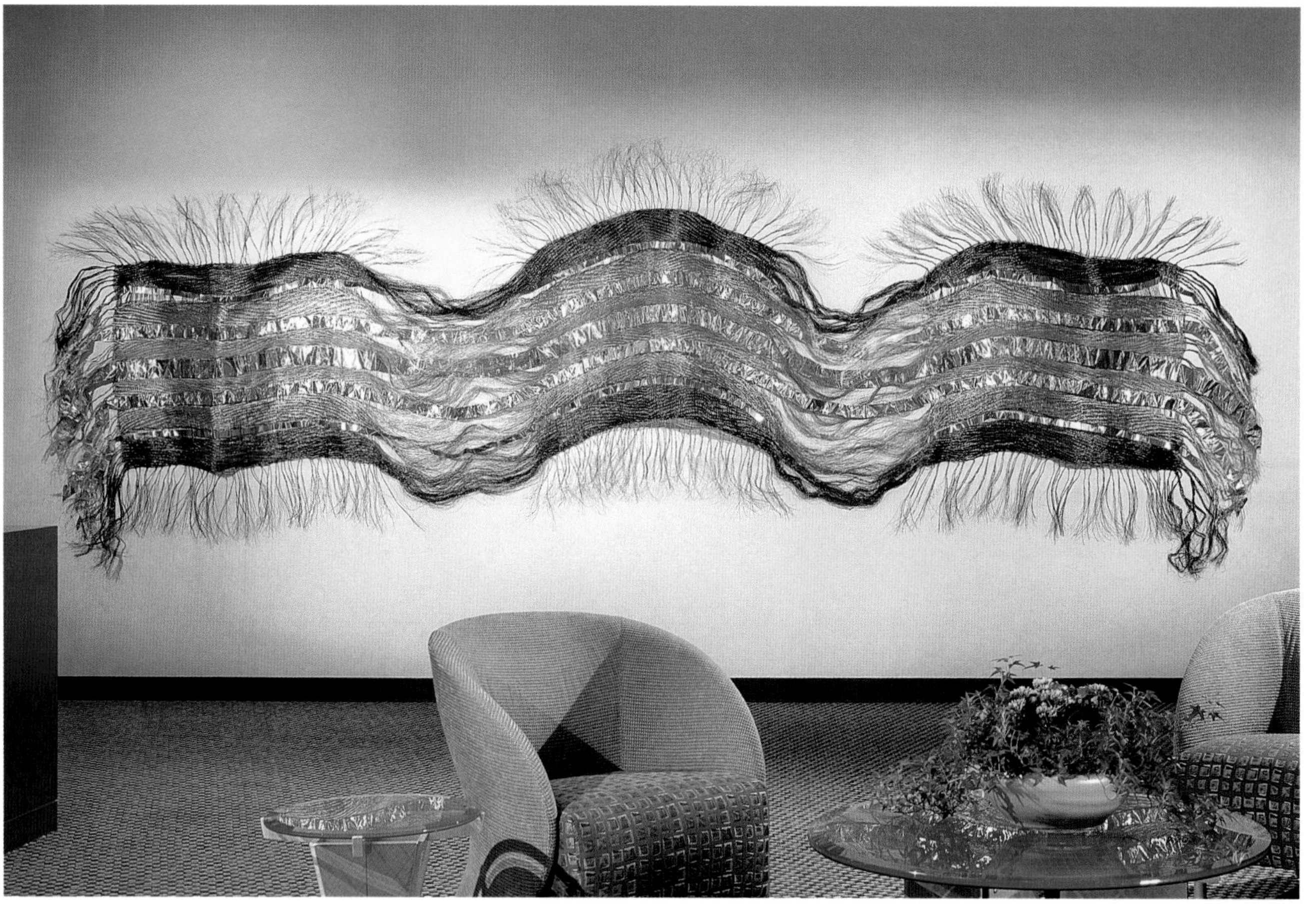

Nokia Corporation lobby, Burlington, MA, commissioned by Art Advisory/Boston, anodized aluminum wire and metal weaving — Edward Jacoby

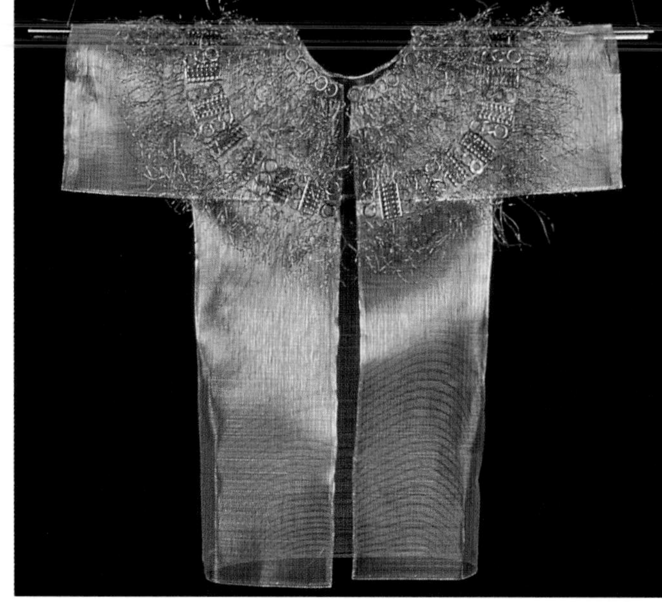

Serendipity Kimono, bronze screen embellished with wire and electronic findings, 36" x 36" — Andrew Neuhart

Evening Song Kimono, stainless screen embellished with wire and electronic findings, 13" x 13" — George Post

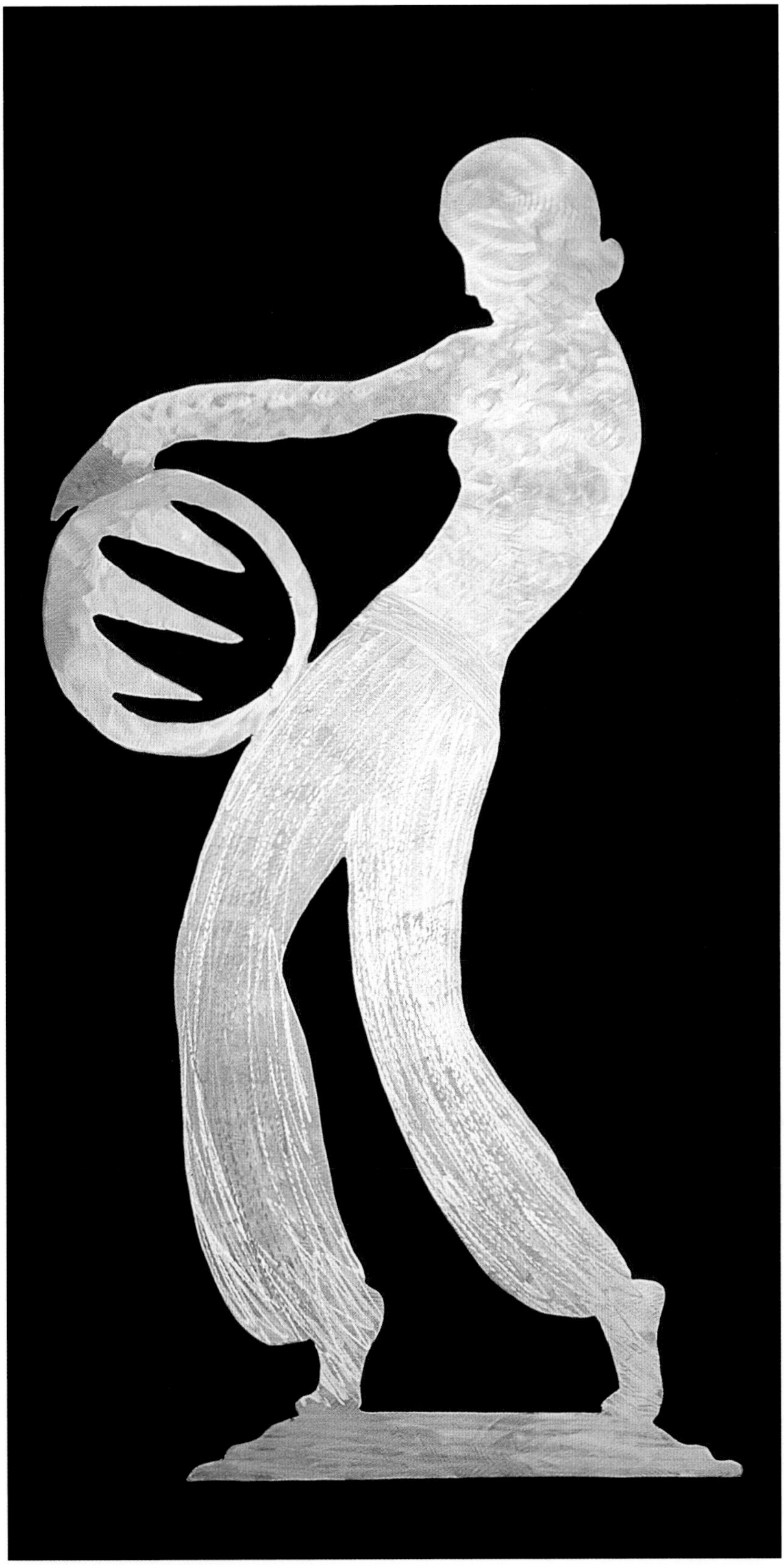

Harem Girl, 2001, stainless steel, 39" x 20" x 2"

Photos: Barry Michlin

Dancer, 2001, stainless steel, 29" x 21" x 2"

Adam and Eve, 1998, stainless steel door panels, 102" x 40" x 2"

PRISCILLA ROBINSON

Earth Beat, acrylic, handmade paper, fiberglass, 61" x 16" x 5"

Garden Series 70, acrylic, handmade paper, 19" x 19"

Portal, acrylic, handmade paper, 48" x 60"

30 Butterflies, acrylic, handmade paper and wood grid, 24" x 50"

27 Resting Butterflies, acrylic, handmade paper and wrought iron grid, 34" x 33"

Photos: Pat Pollard

Belize (detail), 2001, painted wood, 104" x 60"

SUSAN VENABLE

Spring Sunrise Samba, 4' x 9'

Shadowdance, 4' x 12'

Photos: William Nettles

Art for the Wall | Paper

Huli, diptych, private residence, Kapalula, Maui, hand-formed, painted paper, 10' x 11' and 10' x 6'
Inset: *Palm Draped Mountains,* hand-formed, painted paper, 66" x 38" x 4"

Kyle Rothenborg
Inset: Rob Ratkowski

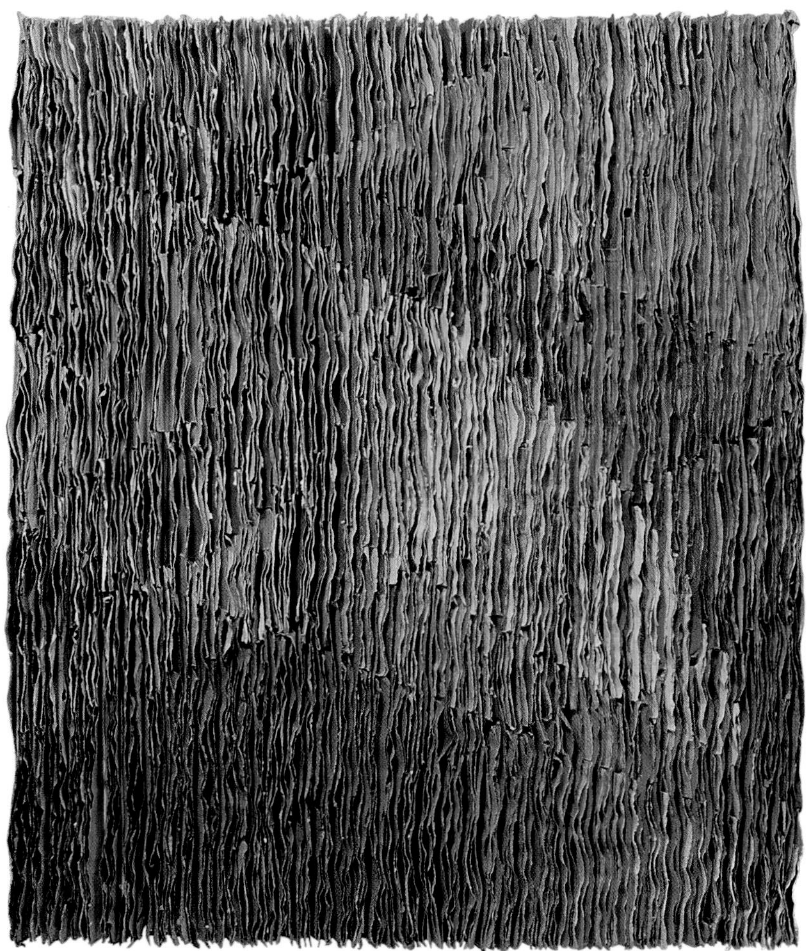

Light Under the Bridge, artist-made abaca paper, 50" x 55" x 5"

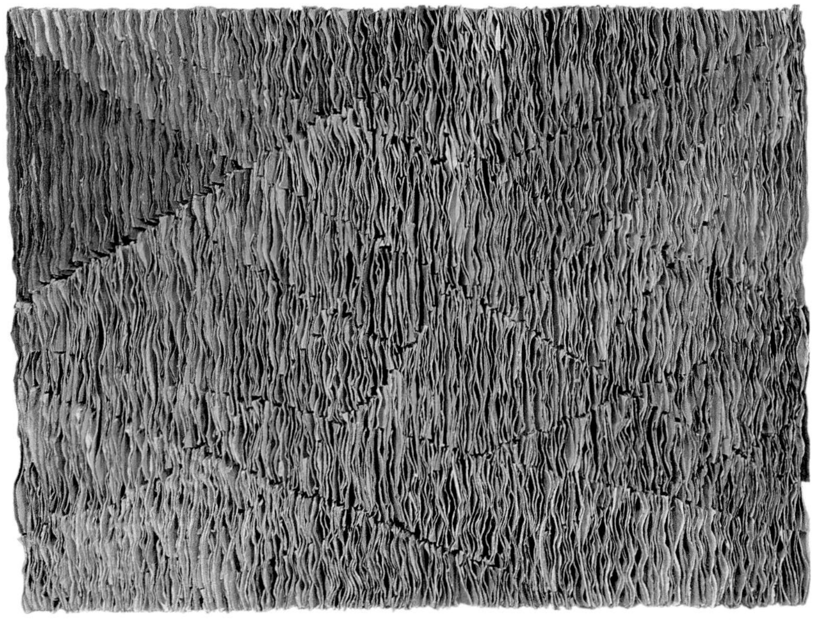

Wall Patches and Lines, artist-made abaca paper, 54" x 73" x 5"

Photos: PRS Associates

Violet Nastri, ASID, NCIDQ

Violet Nastri, owner of Creative Interiors in Orange, Connecticut, didn't start out in interior design. Her first career found her purchasing blade components for helicopters. So how does a contract administrator for a helicopter company end up owning her own interior design firm? ■ "I've always been artistic," Nastri explains, "but I had never considered making a living through art. Still, I had taken a lot of art courses; I drew and painted. Design was what I loved to do." ■ After her children were born, Nastri wanted more flexibility in her career. Feeling that she needed some credentials to be involved in design and decorating, she went back to school. ■ "I really wanted to be able to draft to scale," she recalls. "I got my degree and went into business for myself shortly thereafter. My first few projects were for friends, and my business still relies on word of mouth. People see my projects and I get referrals." ■ A recent commercial project for an office building featured the artwork of well-known photographer Marvin Wax, whom Nastri discovered through GUILD. ■ "There was a taupe-colored linen on the walls of the executive office," Nastri explains. "Since it was an environment where someone stays all day, I wanted the artwork to be soothing — not distracting, yet still pleasing to the eye." ■ She placed Wax's *Eureka Dunes* and *Death Valley Dunes* in the office. The executive was thrilled and told Nastri that everyone who comes into his office comments on the pieces. ■ "I've ordered another Wax photograph for the reception area," Nastri notes. Then she adds, "I may not get a referral from this next week, but at some point I will."

Mark Nastri

Sunrise Vista, 2001, handmade paper, each panel: 22" x 16", total: 22" x 48"

Facing South, Boston Public Gardens, 2001, handmade paper, 37" x 25"

Photos: Barry Kaplan

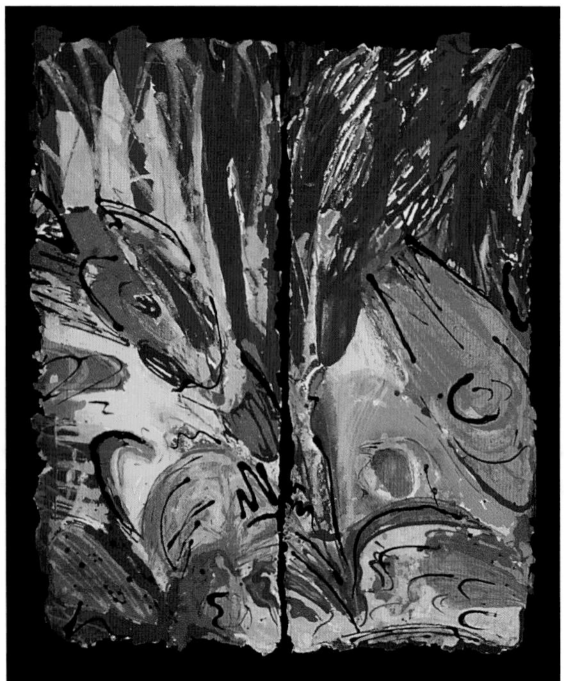

Tide Pool, 2001, pigmented handmade paper, 30" x 34"

Solar Circle, 2001, pigmented handmade paper, 29" x 32"

One Eye Open, 2001, pigmented handmade paper, 24" x 37"

Photos: Margo Geist, Albuquerque, NM

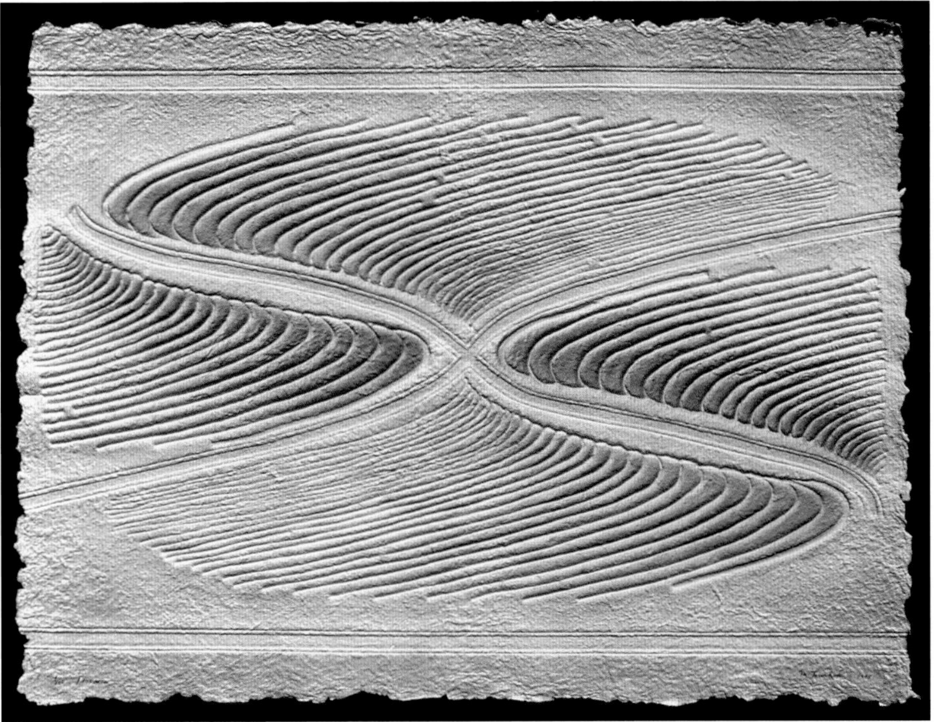

Terraces, 1998, embossed handmade paper, handcolored with airbrush, 25" x 36", edition of 100

Rolling Surf, 2001, embossed handmade paper, handcolored with airbrush, 36" x 50", edition of 100

Patricia Martin

Twenty years after Patricia Martin began teaching interior design at the college level, her life suddenly changed. Within a two-year period, both her father and her mother died of cancer. Then, incredibly, she too was diagnosed with cancer. After her recovery, Martin made the agonizing decision to leave her tenured teaching position and start her own interior design firm. ■ "I returned to my first dream," Martin says. "I loved teaching, and I think I was well respected. However, the death of your parents changes your focus on life. You say to yourself, 'Life is short. What should I be doing, since there are no guarantees about tomorrow?'" ■ Martin launched P.M. Consulting in 1994. The first few years were a struggle, but because she had taught courses in residential design, contract design and store planning, she felt comfortable taking on a variety of projects. "I had to know those subjects well to teach them," she notes. "I've been able to take on many interesting projects because of my teaching background. I also know when to search out the experts." ■ For experts in art, she turns to GUILD. Martin likes to browse through GUILD sourcebooks with her clients to get them thinking about artwork and to gain an understanding of their tastes and preferences. She believes that visual examples help her clients focus. ■ "Clients may not realize how significantly artwork can pull an environment together; art can enhance a space through pattern, harmony and balance. And a designer can be confident that artists represented in GUILD sourcebooks have met juried qualifications."

Bresnahan Studio

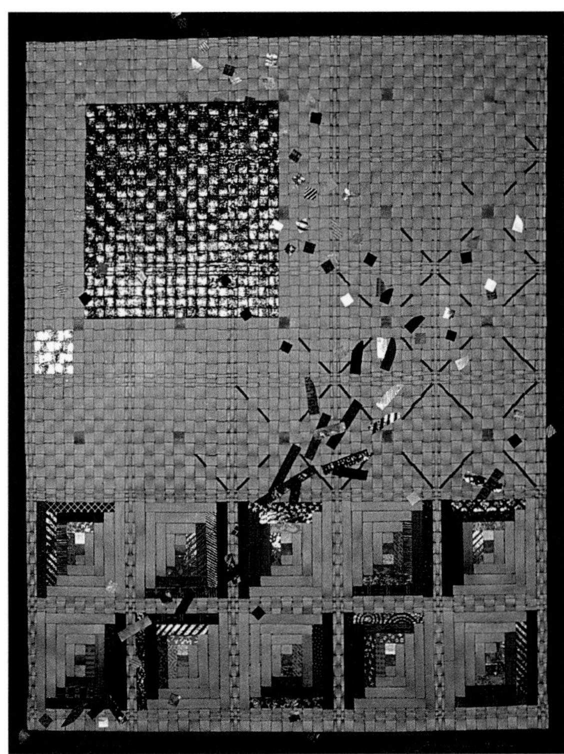

Log Cabin I, 2002, woven paper with paint, metallic foil, collage, 40" x 32"

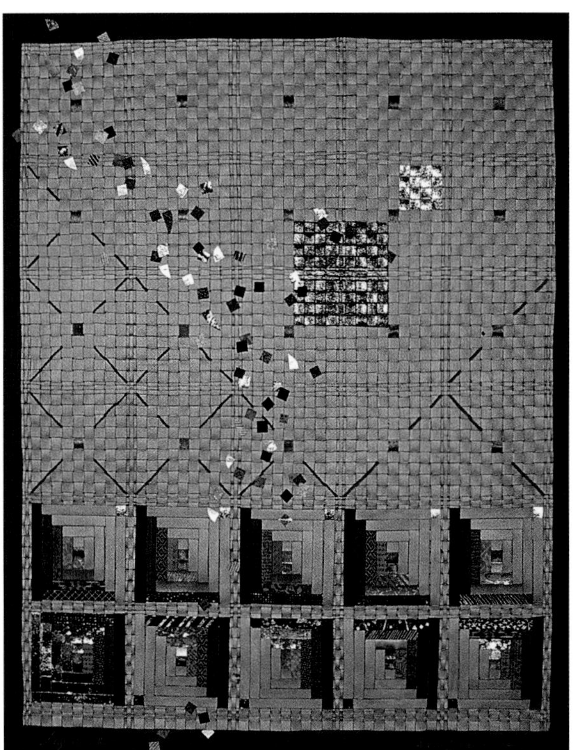

Log Cabin II, 2002, woven paper with paint, metallic foil, collage, 40" x 32"

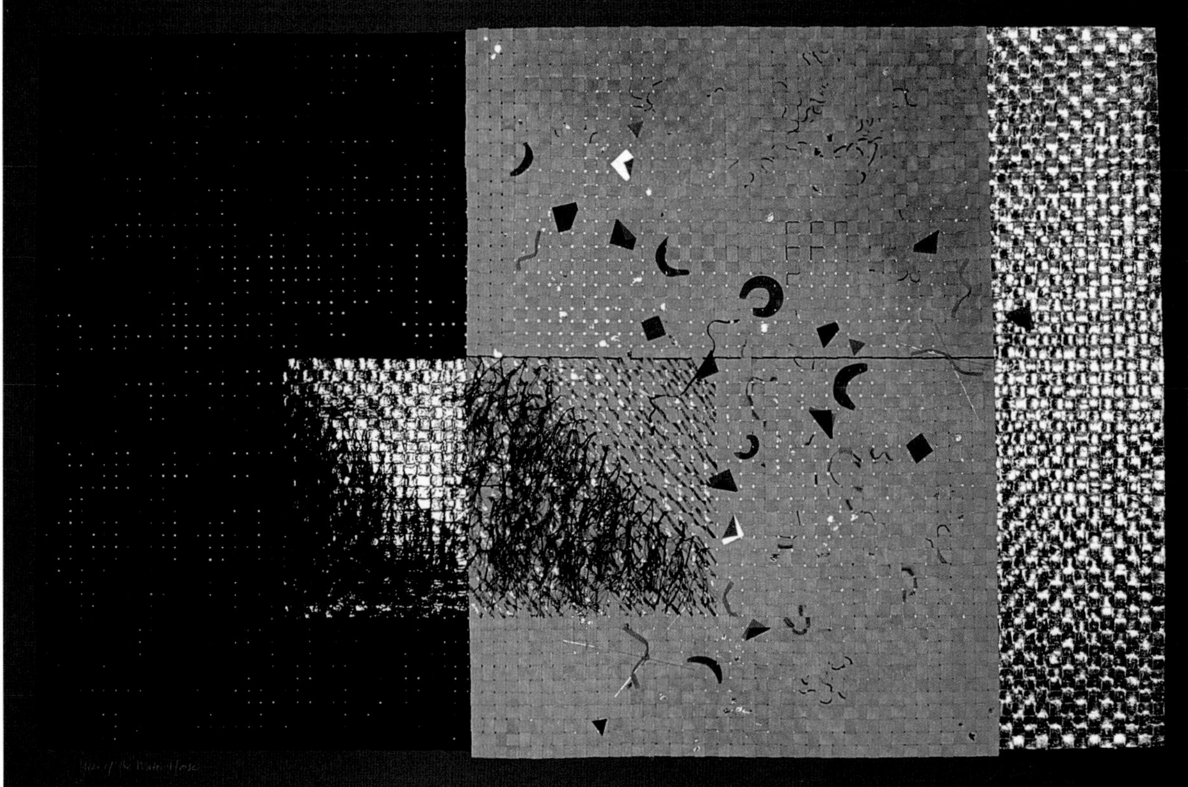

Year of the Water Horse, 2002, woven paper with paint, metallic foil, fibers, collage, 40" x 60" x 1"

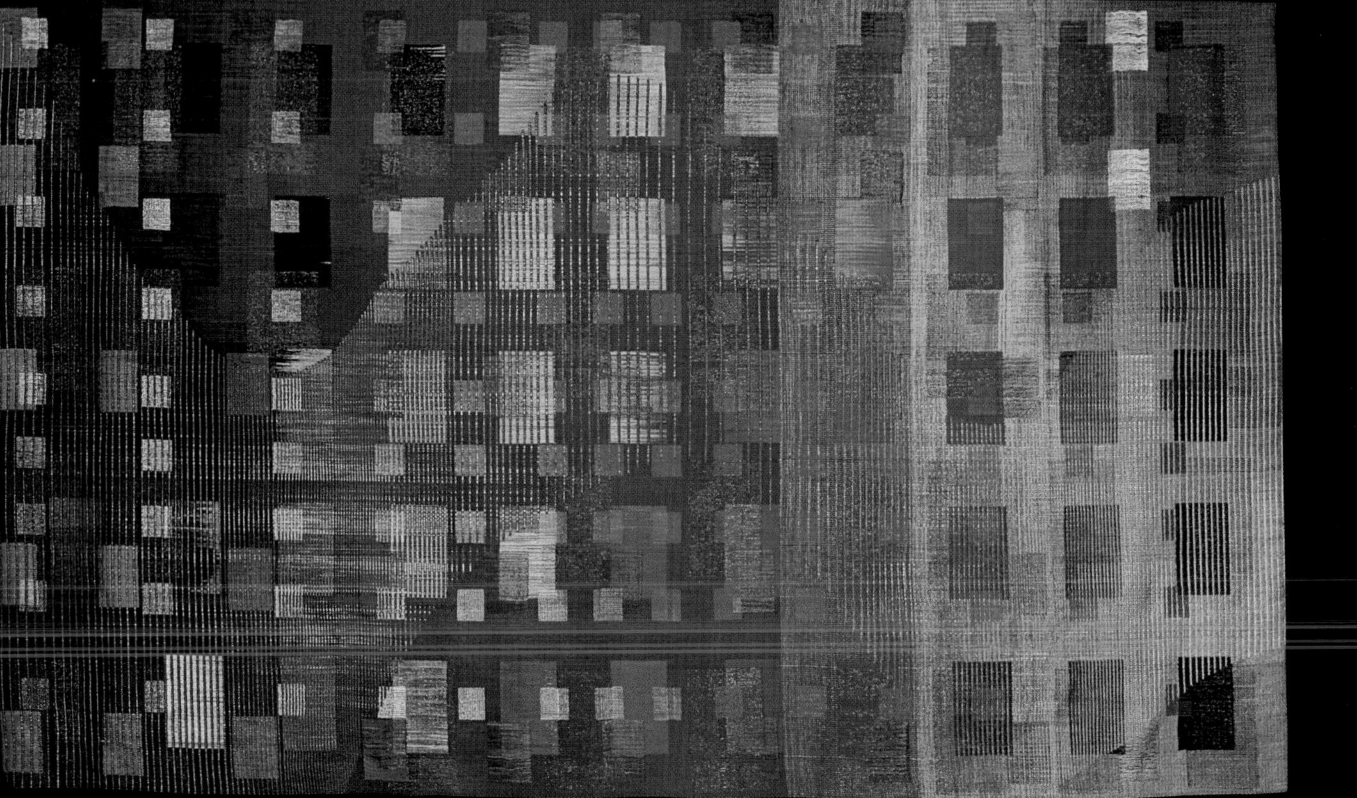

Art for the Wall | Fiber

LAURA MILITZER BRYANT

Chitawan Dreams, 2001, weaving on copper, 41" x 41"

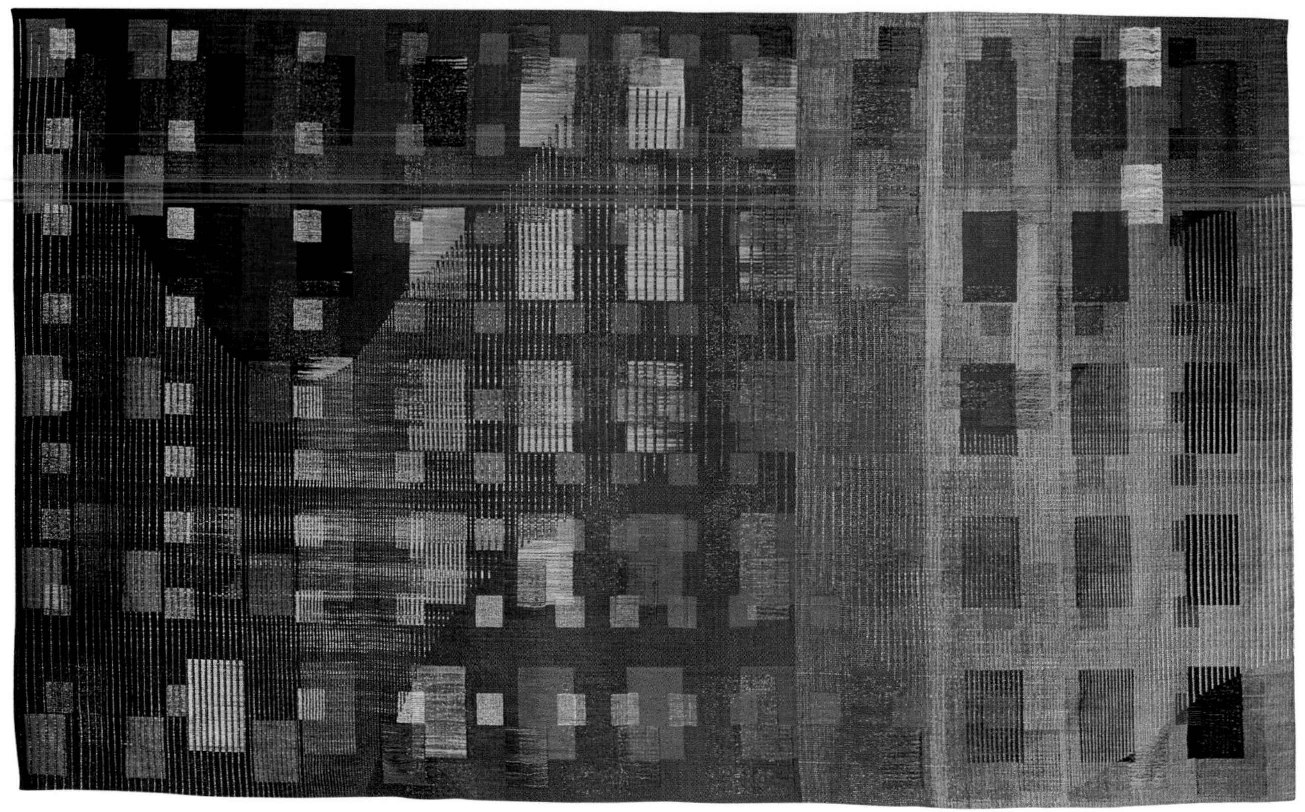

Wave Dance, 2001, weaving, 50.5" x 87.25"

Photos: Thomas Bruce

MYRA BURG

Quiet Oboes, (winter colors detail), 2001, wrapped fiber, 2" to 5"Dia., 2' to 12'H

Photos: Ron Luxemburg

Aladdinesque, 1998, wrapped fiber and burnished aluminum, 6' x 3' x 5"

Quiet Oboe installation, 1999, wrapped fiber, total: 15' x 12'

From the Deep, 1998, wrapped fiber and burnished aluminum, 8' x 3' x 5"

The Last Dance – Alaska Aspen, © 2001, handmade felt and paper, wrapping, wool and linen, 50" x 32" x 2"

Cindy Momchilov

Sidemen, 2001, cotton, silk, velvet, rayon and linen fabric; acrylic paint; mica powder; rayon, metallic and cotton thread; wool yarn; cotton batting, 61" x 60"

Hawthorne Studio

Life's a Square, 2000, pieced, appliquéd, quilted, woven and thread-painted cotton, 34" x 35"

Virgilia in the Forest, 2000, pieced, appliquéd, quilted and thread-painted cotton, organza and velvet, 35" x 84"

Photos: Neil Steinberg

Divertimento, silk, hand pieced and hand quilted, 57.5" x 17.25"

Fugue #2, silk, hand pieced and hand quilted, 58" x 35"

Fugue #1, silk, hand pieced and hand quilted, 50" x 19"

Photos: Karen Bell

Festival III, 1998, Booz-Allen & Hamilton, layered fabrics, 42" x 120"

Visual Poem I, 2001, private collection, layered fabrics, 84" x 36"

Tropical Snowdrops, private collection, layered silk, 56" x 37"

Early Morning, Vinh Binh Market, 2001, cotton warp, wool and novelty cotton weft, 28" x 36"

Benediction, 2000, private collection, cotton warp, wool, silk and linen weft, 24" x 30.5"

Moonrise, 1999, cotton warp, wool weft, 15" x 62"

Spirit Horse #2, silk art quilt, 26" x 22"H

Lady of the Lake, silk art quilt, 23" x 20"

Photos: Kim H. Ritter

July, 2001, pieced cotton, linen and silk, 63" x 77" Taylor Photo/Ross

Saint Basil's, 1996, pieced cotton, linen and silk, 67" x 68" William Taylor

River's End, 1997, pieced cotton, linen and silk, 58" x 64" William Taylor

Step Lightly, 2001, mixed-media collage quilt, 4' x 10'

Sorry, ... is no longer in service!

Step Lightly, detail

Photos: Sharon Risedorph

Redwrapping II, 2000, naturally dyed silk fiber and polymer, 53" x 40"

Midnight Grasses, 2001, naturally dyed silk fiber and polymer, 20" x 45"

Photos: Don Tuttle Photography

Artist Information

Artist Listings

The pages that follow provide important information on the artists featured in *The Sourcebook of Architectural & Interior Art 17.* ■ Listings in the Artist Information section are arranged in alphabetical order according to the heading on each artist's page. These listings include the artist's contact information, as well as details about materials and techniques, commissions, collections and more. References to past GUILD sourcebooks are also included so that you can further explore the breadth of a particular artist's work. The heading at the top of each listing includes a page reference to the artist's display within the book. ■ As you explore *The Sourcebook of Architectural & Interior Art 17,* use the Artist Information section to enrich your experience. If something intrigues you while perusing the sourcebook — a shape, a form, an exotic use of the commonplace — please give the artist a call. Serendipity often leads to a wonderful creation.

MARY LOU ALBERETTI
pp. 28

Alberetti Studios
16 Possum Drive
New Fairfield, CT 06812
TEL 203-746-1321
E-mail: mlalb@aol.com
Web: www.southernct.edu/~alberett/

Mary Lou Alberetti's hand-carved ceramic reliefs, inspired by the artist's studies in Italy, include images of architectural details for public, corporate or residential spaces throughout the United States. Sizes range from 12" x 12" x 12" to 72" x 20" x 4".

COMMISSIONS: Cultural Commission, City of New Haven, CT

COLLECTIONS: HBO World Headquarters, New York, NY; Reese, Lower Patrick & Scott, Ltd., Architects, Lancaster, PA; Fuller Museum of Art, Brockton, MA; Mint Museum of Art, Charlotte, NC

AWARDS: Master craftsperson, honorary lifetime member, Society of Connecticut Crafts

PUBLICATIONS: *Architectural Ceramics; Sculptural Clay*

GUILD SOURCEBOOKS: *Designer's 14, 15; Architectural & Interior Art 16*

RICHARD ALTMAN
pp. 82

Richard Altman Designs
974 East Divot Drive
Tempe, AZ 85283
TEL 480-831-0201
E-mail: ra@richardaltman.com
Web: www.richardaltman.com

Contemporary style, vivid colors, texture and dramatic design are the hallmarks of Richard Altman's glass art. Projects include wall panels, skylights, room dividers, wall sconces and sculptural elements. The glass can be mounted on walls, supported with custom metal stands for floor and table display or integrated into unique metal frameworks for very large-scale installations. Stunning visual effects are created using combinations of glass particles, poured glass shapes and kiln-forming techniques. Richard's work is well suited for custom residential projects as well as high-tech corporate environments and commercial projects, including retail, restaurants and resorts.

GUILD SOURCEBOOKS: *Architect's 14; Architectural & Interior Art 16*

DANIEL ALTSHULER
pp. 104

42 Blackburn Center
Gloucester, MA 01930
TEL 978-283-9128
E-mail: daltshuler@sculpturesales.com
Web: www.sculpturesales.com

Daniel Altshuler's work ranges from statuary to bas-relief tablets and medals to fountains. When making a bust, he works from life, photographs and videos. His works are made primarily in bronze and marble; other materials are considered for statuary and fountains. Most of his work is created on a commission basis, made on time and within budget.

RECENT PROJECTS: Presidential medal, American Embassy, Prague, Czech Republic; Louisa May Alcott bust, Orchard House, Concord, MA

COLLECTIONS: The White House, Washington, DC; McLean Hospital, Belmont, MA; Health South Headquarters, Birmingham, AL

EXHIBITIONS: New York Art Expo, with The Classical Gallery, 2002, NY; State of the Art Gallery, 2001, Gloucester, MA

AWARDS: Excellence in Classical Sculpture, 2000, National Academy of Design

MICHAEL ANDERSON
pp. 132

5121 North 13th Place
Phoenix, AZ 85014
TEL 602-279-6105
E-mail: arcform777@aol.com

Michael Anderson is most recognized for his gracefully soaring works in steel. Anderson aims high with his art. He says, "I believe creativity is a part of our God-given nature and should convey a high standard of excellence." His sculptures are in public and private collections around the world.

COMMISSIONS: City of Palm Desert, CA; City of Tempe, AZ; Wisconsin Manufacturers & Commerce, Madison, WI

EXHIBITIONS: Pierwalk, Navy Pier, Chicago, IL 1998, 1999, 2000

AWARDS: Tempe Beautification Award, Art in Private Development, 2000

GUILD SOURCEBOOKS: *Architect's 10, 11, 12, 13, 14*

ROBIN ANTAR
pp. 105

Antar Studios Incorporated
1485 East 5th Street
Brooklyn, NY 11230
TEL/FAX 718-375-5156
E-mail: antarstudios@msn.com
Web: www.robinantar.com

Robin Antar carves common American objects out of stone, "freezing" them in time and creating a visual record of our culture. The life-size stone carvings are highly realistic, confounding the eye and defying the viewer to discern the sculpture from the original object. Antar uses tints from custom-made stains and incorporates paints, plastics, gold leaf and other materials into her work.

RECENT PROJECTS: DIESEL Jeans show, 2002, Soho, NY

COMMISSIONS: Skechers Boots USA, Inc.; Chateau Haut-Brion

EXHIBITIONS: *The Really Big Shoe Show,* 2000, City Museum, St. Louis, MO; *More Artistic License,* 1999, Nabisco Corporate Gallery, East Hanover, NJ

GUILD SOURCEBOOKS: *Architect's 14, 15; Designer's 15*

ARCHIE HELD STUDIO
pp. 133

Archie Held
PO Box 70331
Point Richmond, CA 94807-0331
TEL 510-235-8700
FAX 510-234-4828
E-mail: archieheld@aol.com
Web: www.archieheld.com

Archie Held works mainly in bronze and stainless steel, and many of his works incorporate water. He enjoys using contrasting materials, surfaces and textures.

RECENT PROJECTS: Harrah's Resort Casino, Shreveport, LA; Howard Hughes Corporation, Las Vegas, NV; Bishop Ranch, San Ramon, CA; Tmimarlik, Istanbul, Turkey

EXHIBITIONS: International Exposition of Sculptural Objects and Functional Art, 2001, Chicago, IL; International Exposition of Sculptural Objects and Functional Art, 2001, New York, NY

ARCHITECTURAL GLASS ART, INC.
pp. 50

Kenneth F. vonRoenn, Jr.
815 West Market Street
Louisville, KY 40202
TEL 502-585-5421
FAX 502-585-2808
E-mail: info@againc.com
Web: www.againc.com

Architectural Glass Art, Inc. provides a complete range of services, from design to fabrication to installation, for a broad range of work (leaded, cast, laminated, printed and beveled). Kenneth vonRoenn's work is noted for its sympathetic integration with architecture and for his innovative application of new technologies.

GUILD SOURCEBOOKS: *THE GUILD 1, 2, 3, 4, 5; Architect's 6, 7, 8, 9, 10, 11, 12, 13, 14, 15; Architectural & Interior Art 16*

SHAWN ATHARI
pp. 208-209

14332 Mulholland Drive
Los Angeles, CA 90077
TEL 310-476-0066
FAX 310-4769-ART
Web: www.shawnathari.com

Whether embracing an environment to create a statement through her work or borrowing from history to create a contemporary form, Shawn Athari has developed the skills and talents to do both successfully. She has been in the glass field since 1975, and through her vision, she exemplifies good taste and sophistication. The work featured in this book is a continuation of her repertoire, which includes the creation of Disney figures for the Walt Disney Corporation, as well as synagogue panels in excess of 240 square feet. Her work can be seen in many prominent private and public collections and has been featured in many distinguished magazines and on television programs.

COLLECTIONS: GUILD.com; Adamm's Stained Glass, Santa Monica, CA; Cantoni, Dallas and Houston, TX and Irvine, CA; Latitudes South, Houston, TX; Lynch & Kennedy, Skagway, AK; Scanlon Gallery, Ketchikan, AK

ALLAN BAILLIE
pp. 260

29 Fifth Avenue, 3B
New York, NY 10003
TEL 212-477-0745

Allan Baillie's photographs have a warm, luminescent quality and a quiet simplicity. He works with Polaroid type 55, a 4x5-format film, deliberately choosing to show the film's borders in the finished sepia-toned prints. Each custom-printed photograph is provided using the highest quality materials and techniques. Orders can be shipped within a week or two weeks. Call for mural-sized print costs.

COLLECTIONS: Brooklyn Museum; Larry Aldridge Museum

EXHIBITIONS: Galerie Simone Berno, 2001, Paris, France; Palm Springs Desert Museum, 2000, CA

AWARDS: Artist in Residence at C-Scape Dune Shack, 2001, Princetown, MA

PUBLICATIONS: *Graphis,* 2002; *Flora,* 2002; *Black and White Magazine,* No. 7, 2000

GUILD SOURCEBOOKS: *Architect's 13, 14, 15; Architectural & Interior Art 16*

GARIN BAKER
pp. 222

Carriage House Art Studios
478 Union Avenue
New Windsor, NY 12553
TEL/FAX 845-562-7802
E-mail: gb@carriageart.com
Web: www.carriageart.com

Garin Baker's hand-painted murals and fine art commissions can be painted on site or in his studios. He works traditionally in oils on canvas, walls or any surface to which paint can be applied. Founded in the great traditions of the WPA-era muralist, his training and collaborative abilities transform flat walls into visions of depth and presence. He is well recognized for his skill and abilities to capture realistic visions of people, life, color and atmosphere. To his credit, his work has been exhibited widely throughout New York City and the Hudson Valley region. Garin's work has received many awards and his clients include Sony Theatres, Planet Hollywood and *New York Magazine,* as well as countless public, private and corporate assignments.

RECENT PROJECTS: Lobby interior, Rudolph & Slatten, Inc. corporate offices, Irvine, CA; interior mural, Gidney Avenue Children's Museum, Newburgh, NY

JAMES BARNHILL
pp. 186

206 South Chapman Street
Greensboro, NC 27403
TEL/FAX 336-275-7135

James Barnhill combines his skill of rendering the figure with the simplest of compositional elements. The work's quiet restraint and elegance result in a powerful visual impact.

COMMISSIONS: North Carolina A&T State University, 2001, Greensboro; North Carolina Symphony, 2000, Raleigh; TWA Flight 800 Memorial, 1999, Montoursville, PA; Patrick Beaver Memorial Library, 1998, Hickory, NC; City of Mountain Brook, 1997, AL; Mission Viejo Regional Medical Center, 1996, Mission Viejo, CA; Booker T. Washington National Monument, 1996, Burnt Chimney, VA

AWARDS: Leonard J. Meiselman Prize, National Sculpture Society, 1995, New York, NY; Jefferson D. Rubin Memorial Award, 1994, Loveland, CO; First place, James Wilbur Johnston Sculpture Competition for Figure Modeling, 1992, Lyme Academy of Fine Art, Lyme, CT and 1987, The Corcoran, Washington, DC

GUILD SOURCEBOOK: *Architect's 7, 8, 11, 13, 15; Architectural & Interior Art 16*

BARTEV
pp. 234

6590 Windflower Drive
Carlsbad, CA 92009
TEL 760-804-0810
TEL 800-804-1454
FAX 760-804-1610
E-mail: bartev@connectnet.com
Web: www.bartev.com

Bartev paints with oil on canvas. Using a unique painting style, enlivened with exciting colors, he takes the viewer to an event in progress, somewhere between the real world and fantasy. His signature technique is creating motion and a sense of action for a wide range of subjects. As a former interior designer, Bartev has an excellent understanding of projects and is very receptive to designers' requests.

PUBLICATIONS: *Art & Antiques,* 2002; *Art & Antiques,* 2001

MATTHEW A. BERG V
pp. 134

Berg Studios Inc.
1417 North Harding
Indianapolis, IN 46202
TEL 317-974-1844
FAX 317-974-0845
E-mail: matt@bergstudios.com
Web: www.bergstudios.com

Matthew Berg creates relationships between various media. He connects a rigorous visual exploration with the needs of a particular commission or space. Matt's sculptures are durable forms that infuse their environments with a sense of play, using light, color, texture and scale to achieve a powerful aesthetic experience.

RECENT PROJECTS: Franklin College Johnson Center of Fine Arts, 2002, Franklin, IN

COMMISSIONS: Eli Lilly & Co. Building 98, 2001, Indianapolis, IN; St. Vincent Hospitals, 2000, Indianapolis, IN; Kiwanis International Headquarters, 2000, Indianapolis, IN

EXHIBITIONS: Safeco Art Competition, 2001, Indianapolis, IN; White River State Park, 2001, Indianapolis, IN

GUILD SOURCEBOOKS: *Architectural & Interior Art 16*

SANDRA C. Q. BERGÉR
pp. 51

Quintal Studio
100 El Camino Real #202
Burlingame, CA 94010
TEL 650-348-0310
FAX 650-348-8733

Internationally exhibited and published, award-winning glass designer Sandra Bergér creates exceptional custom glass art and limited editions for corporate, public and private clients. Precision-engineered, each glass sculpture or installation is effectively designed and executed. Experienced and professional, worldwide service, timely delivery.

RECENT PROJECTS: "*All Seasons*," multi-colored heirloom screen

COMMISSIONS: Concert Theatre, Minot, ND; Tanforan Business Center, South San Francisco, CA; White House, Washington, DC; Thermo King Corporation, Minneapolis, MN; other public and private commissions

PUBLICATIONS: *Designing Interiors* textbook; *Women in Design International*; *Facets Magazine*

GUILD SOURCEBOOKS: *THE GUILD 1, 2, 3, 4, 5; Architect's 6, 7, 8, 10, 11; Designer's 8, 11, 13, 14, 15; Architectural & Interior Art 16*

MARC BERLET
pp. 138

Berlet Studio
5890 SW 50 Terrace
Miami, FL 33155
TEL/FAX 305-666-7481
E-mail: mberlet@aol.com

Art historians and critics recognize Marc Berlet for his "forceful capacity for creating aesthetic pleasure." His sculptures and paintings portray the ease with which he transforms various forms into works of art. Since 1989, he has collaborated with design professionals on numerous private and corporate commissioned art projects.

COMMISSIONS: Skylake Professional Plaza Building, Miami, FL; Royal Caribbean Cruise Line, USA

COLLECTIONS: Musee d'Art Moderne; Musee Des Beaux Arts; Chrysler Museum; President Perez-Balladares, Panama

EXHIBITIONS: Musee d'Art Moderne; Cordier-Warren Galerie; Signa Gallery; Galerie Breteau; Walter Chrysler Museum; Jaffe Baker Gallery

RITA BLITT
pp. 136

Rita Blitt, Inc.
8900 State Line, Suite 333
Leawood, KS 66206
TEL 913-381-3840
FAX 913-381-5624
E-mail: rita@ritablitt.com
Web: www.ritablitt.com

Rita Blitt, embracing a desire to respond to nature and music, creates drawings, paintings and monumental sculptures that are exhibited, collected and installed internationally.

RECENT PROJECTS: Gold Coast Regional Art Center, Surfers Paradise, Australia

COMMISSIONS: Compass Corporate Center, 2000, Overland Park, KS; Hilton-Tokyo Bay, 1998, Shiba, Japan;

COLLECTIONS: National Museum Art Gallery, Singapore; Brandeis University, Waltham, MA; John F. Kennedy Library, Boston, MA

PUBLICATIONS: *Rita Blitt: The Passionate Gesture*, 2000; *Sculpture*, Oct. 2001

GUILD SOURCEBOOKS: *Architect's 7, 8, 10, 11; Designer's: 11, 12, 13, 14; Architectural & Interior Art 16*

BLUE GENIE ART INDUSTRIES, INC.
pp. 272

Dana Younger
Kevin Collins
Rory Skagen
PO Box 684832
Austin, TX 78768
TEL 512-444-6655
FAX 512-926-6435
E-mail: mail@bluegenieart.com
Web: www.bluegenieart.com

With over 20 years of experience, the artists at Blue Genie are skilled in a variety of materials. Sculptures, design, murals, signage and architectural features are just a few of the many ways Blue Genie has enhanced the character or developed identities for various locations, events and businesses.

RECENT PROJECTS: Bob Bullock Texas State History Museum, GSD&M Advertising, Thinkwell.com, Sea World of Texas, Capstar Broadcasting, Schlotzsky's Restaurants

WILLIAM D. BOSWORTH
pp. 162

W.D. Bosworth Woodworking & Sculpture
59 Luther Warren Drive
St. Helena Island, SC 29920
TEL 843-838-9490
FAX 843-838-1187
E-mail: woodwork@hargray.com
Web: www.qualitywoodworking.com

The art of sculpting requires the finely tuned ability to visualize and the craftsmanship to bring forth this vision in the chosen medium. William D. Bosworth uses these same skills to create his original sculptures, as well as in creating commissioned pieces of enduring beauty. The illustrated sculptures are part of the *Endangered Marine Mammal* series created and used to educate children about the importance of the environment and its effects on marine life.

COMMISSIONS: Boys and Girls Club of the Low Country

PUBLICATIONS: "Modern Masters Series," HGTV; *The Majesty of Beaufort*, 2001; *Southern Accents; Classic American Homes; Country Living*

KATHY BRADFORD
pp. 52-53

North Star Art Glass, Inc.
142 Wichita Road
Lyons, CO 80540
TEL/FAX 303-823-6511
E-mail: kathybradford@webtv.net
Web: www.kathybradford.com

A variety of techniques employed for the illustrated commission at the Historic Stanley Hotel in Estes Park, CO, demonstrates Bradford's special abilities in creating lifelike imagery for nature's beauty. In addition, a 35' x 16" glass divider wall is also installed in the restaurant interior, including a babbling brook along the length, with natural flora and fauna from the Rocky Mountains.

COMMISSIONS: Centuria Health, 2001-2002, Denver, CO; City of Longmont, 2001-2002, CO; Marriott Hotels, 2001, Anaheim and San Mateo, CA

GUILD SOURCEBOOKS: *Architect's 12, 13, 14, 15; Architectural & Interior Art 16*

KATHY BRADFORD
pp. 52-53

North Star Art Glass, Inc.
142 Wichita Road
Lyons, CO 80540
TEL/FAX 303-823-6511
E-mail: kathybradford@webtv.net
Web: www.kathybradford.com

The Foothills Library of Glendale, AZ, had *The Magic Doors* installed with a matching transom. Bradford combined dichroic glass with 124mm lenses and deep sandblast carving to enchant the children using this story room.

The Bear Ballroom from the Russian Tea Room in New York, NY, includes ten panels of 5' x 10', each gracing the walls with half-inch-thick, sandcarved dancing circus bears. Bradford's sandcarving ability is demonstrated in the illustrated detail of one of the bears.

BOB BROWN
pp. 235

Bob Brown Studio
2725 Terry Lake Road
Fort Collins, CO 80524
TEL/FAX 970-224-5473
E-mail: bobbrown-artist@att.net

Bob Brown's colorful paintings highlight an area by bringing the bright outdoors to the inside. The thick texture, created with durable acrylic paint and a painting knife, provides an intriguing surface. Subjects are representational and mostly landscapes. Unframed paintings range from 16" x 20" to 36" x 48". A brochure is available.

COLLECTIONS: Prince Albert, Monte Carlo, Monaco; McGraw Hill Companies, New York

EXHIBITIONS: In galleries and public spaces in the United States, Monaco and France

GUILD SOURCEBOOKS: *Designer's 14, 15; Architectural & Interior Art 16*

GARY ALLEN BROWN
pp. 137

5420 West Del Rio Street
Chandler, AZ 85226
TEL 480-705-8300
FAX 480-785-7577
E-mail: baffin@cox.net
Web: www.garyallenbrown.com

Sculptor Gary Allen Brown works in wood, metal and stone, seeking a balance between organic and abstract forms. His work has a visual, tactile and structural integrity that makes it ideal for display in both private and public settings. For over 15 years, Gary owned a design firm specializing in custom architectural signage. This background gives him a unique perspective on the client-focused aspects of his art: a combination of art and engineering. Gary was chosen by *The Bulletin of Atomic Scientists* to produce the "Doomsday Clock." A portfolio is available upon request.

BRUCE R. BLEACH STUDIO
pp. 273

Bruce R. Bleach
146 Coleman Road
Goshen, NY 10924
TEL/FAX 845-294-8945
E-mail: brbleach@frontiernet.net

For the past 26 years, Bruce R. Bleach has been creating unique and exciting works for the wall. Listed in *Who's Who in American Art,* he is recognized internationally for his monoprints, etchings and paintings, as well as his dramatic, large-scale wall sculpture in etched bronze, aluminum and wood. All works are clear-coated, maintenance free and ready to hang. He has successfully collaborated with designers, consultants and architects to complete numerous corporate and residential commissions on schedule. Recent installations include an outdoor memorial sculpture for The International Association of Machinists & Aerospace Workers, MD, and two murals for the president's office at Montefiore Children's Hospital, NY. Selected collections include Motorola, Johnson & Johnson, Lockheed-Martin, Price Waterhouse, AOL, SmithKline Beecham, Xerox and IBM. Drawings, photos and color maquettes available upon request.

LAURA MILITZER BRYANT
pp. 298

2595 30th Avenue North
St. Petersburg, FL 33713
TEL 727-327-3100
FAX 727-321-1905
E-mail: knitlb@ix.netcom.com

Laura Militzer Bryant uses a variety of methods to create complex double weaves of wool and rayon. These mystical landscapes create a visually rich environment in both private and public spaces.

COMMISSIONS: Thermo King, 1999, Minneapolis, MN

COLLECTIONS: Mobil; Metropolitan Life, Indianapolis, IN; City of St. Petersburg, FL

EXHIBITIONS: *Octet,* 2001, Bradenton, FL; Florida Craftsmen Exhibition, 2001, Jacksonville, FL

AWARDS: Florida Individual Artist Fellowship, 1994-1995; National Endowment for the Arts Individual Artist Fellowship, 1990-1991

PUBLICATIONS: *American Craft,* 1994; *Fiberarts* magazine, 1992

GUILD SOURCEBOOKS: *Designer's 10, 11, 12, 13, 14, 15; Architectural & Interior Art 16*

MYRA BURG
pp. 299

6180 West Jefferson, Suite Y
Los Angeles, CA 90016
TEL 310-399-5040
FAX 310-399-0623
Web: www.myraburg.com

Somewhere between tapestry and jewelry, the "quiet oboes" and sculptural installations of Myra Burg adorn a space in a free-floating, peaceful way. All of the hand-wrapped fiber is combined with burnished metals to create the sculptural pieces. These most inspired pieces meet the clients' needs and wants within the requirements of the space. "The bigger the challenge, the more the fun." Collaborations are welcome.

RECENT PROJECTS: *Sleeves of a Kimono,* Cypress Point, Denver, CO; *Japonaise,* Universal, Japan; *Galactic Curve,* Universal, Japan; *Quiet Oboes,* Caribé Hilton, Puerto Rico

AWARDS: First place, Beverly Hills Affaire in the Gardens, 2001, 1999, 1998; Best of Show, Artfest of Scottsdale, 1999; Best of Show, ASID Conference, 1995

GUILD SOURCEBOOKS: *Architect's 14, 15; Designer's 10, 13, 14, 15; Architectural & Interior Art 16*

RIIS BURWELL
pp. 135

Riis Burwell Studio
3815 Calistoga Road
Santa Rosa, CA 95404
TEL/FAX 707-538-2676
E-mail: riisburwell@aol.com

A member of the International Sculpture Center, Riis Burwell has been creating elegant abstract sculpture for 22 years, primarily in stainless steel and bronze. Whether tabletop or large scale, his sculpture is inspired by the dynamic relationships between order and chaos, and growth and decay. Riis' exquisitely fluid sculptures are hand fabricated so that each piece is unique. His work is found in private, museum, public and corporate collections within the United States and abroad.

COMMISSIONS: Santa Rosa Convention Center, 2002, CA; Burbank Airport Plaza, 2001, CA; Congregation Beth Ami, 2000, Santa Rosa, CA

EXHIBITIONS: *Contemporary Constructions,* Los Angeles County Museum; Olive Grove Sculpture Gallery, Rutherford, CA; Sandy Carson Gallery, Denver, CO

GUILD SOURCEBOOKS: *Architect's 13, 14, 15; Architectural & Interior Art 16*

BRIDGET BUSUTIL
pp. 236

Busutil Impressions, LLC
120 Ralph McGill Boulevard
Studio 906
Atlanta, GA 30308
TEL 404-875-9155
FAX 404-875-9750
E-mail: bmbart@attglobal.net
Web: bridgetbusutil.com

Bridget Busutil works with oil, acrylics and encaustics on both canvas and board. Her passion for landscapes has led to her creation of enticing horizons that have magical depths and luminosity. Perhaps what makes these landscapes so attractive is the wondrous sense of escape they offer the minds of those who immerse themselves in them.

COMMISSIONS: The Windsor Condominiums, Atlanta, GA; The Hilton, Aruba, Caribbean; Banque National de Paris, Basel, Switzerland

EXHIBITIONS: Walter Wickiser Gallery, 2001 & 2000, New York, NY; Gallery La Maison Francaise (French Embassy), 2000, Washington, D.C

GUILD SOURCEBOOKS: *Architectural & Interior Art 16*

JEFFREY TRAVIS BUTLER
pp. 106

Water Street Studio
2406 Ainsworth Street
Portland, OR 97211
TEL 203-853-7757
FAX 203-853-3260
E-mail: mail@waterstreetstudio.com
Web: www.waterstreetstudio.com

Butler holds an architecture degree from the University of Oregon, where he also studied sculpture, furniture making and silversmithing. He was recently commissioned to create a large sculpture of a dragonfly (the state insect of Washington). The sculpture utilizes etched copper with a stainless steel supporting structure. It will be mounted on a new building in Vancouver, WA, in 2002. Butler's sculpture is designed for exterior and interior spaces. He works with all metals, wood and stone.

KAREN BRUSSAT BUTLER
pp. 255

Water Street Studio
169 West Norwalk Road
Norwalk, CT 06850
TEL 203-853-7757
FAX 203-853-3260
E-mail: mail@waterstreetstudio.com
Web: www.waterstreetstudio.com

Butler has created her own distinctive style that combines vibrant color, faultless line, an innate sense of design and considerable humor. She is a storyteller. Her paintings and commissioned work have found their way into leading restaurants and food businesses both here and abroad. Butler's paintings have received numerous honors and awards from national arts organizations, including the National Academy of Design. She also won the first International Artist in Watercolor competition held in London, England.

BARBARA CADE
pp. 300

262 Hideaway Hills Drive
Hot Springs, AR 71901
TEL 501-262-4065
E-mail: cade@ipa.net

Collectible rocks, luscious vegetation, textured trees and dramatic skies: two- and three-dimensional sculptural landscape elements inspired by your geographic location, maybe using your favorite photograph. Use elements together or individually. Barbara Cade continues to be inspired by themes in nature, translating her photographs into tapestries of woven and felted wool, often incorporating other fiber techniques.

COMMISSIONS: The Kraft Center, 1997, Paramus, NJ

COLLECTIONS: Weyerhaeuser Company, Tacoma, WA; Tacoma Art Museum, Tacoma, WA

EXHIBITIONS: *Reality Check,* Ohio Craft Museum, 2001, Columbus, OH

GUILD SOURCEBOOKS: *Designer's 8, 9, 10, 11, 12, 15*

RENO CAROLLO
pp. 139

1562 South Parker Road, Suite 336
Denver, CO 80231
TEL 303-695-6396
FAX 303-695-8560
E-mail: rcar173278@aol.com

As an artist, Reno Carollo loves the process of creating. He is constantly pursuing new designs, new combinations of materials and new ideas for the human figure. Carollo's current work combines metal and stone in an abstract figurative form. For him, creativity occurs in pushing and pulling the space of the figure, creating new possibilities while connecting the viewer with the essence of the human form. Carollo's formal education includes a B.A. from the University of Northern Colorado in Greeley and the Academy of Fine Arts in Florence, Italy.

RECENT PROJECTS: Art Expo, 2002, New York, NY

COMMISSIONS: George and Barbi Benton Gradow, 2001, Aspen, CO; Michael and Sheila Martin Stone, 1996, Oakdale, CA

WARREN CARTHER
pp. 54

Carther Studio Inc.
80 George Avenue
Winnipeg, MB R3B 0K1
Canada
TEL 204-956-1615
FAX 204-942-1434
E-mail: warren@cartherstudio.com
Web: www.cartherstudio.com

Glass artist Warren Carther explores light in varied and unusual ways, manipulating the quality of light as it is filtered through the complex layers of his work. His respect and understanding of the structural capabilities of glass, combined with his interest in working sculpturally within the architectural environment, lead him to produce unique work that crosses the boundaries between art and architecture. Innovative techniques in structure, abrasive blast carving, laminations and color application distinguish his often large-scale work. Numerous commissions and publications throughout the world have earned him an international reputation.

COMMISSIONS: Canadian Embassy, Tokyo, Japan; Swire Group, Hong Kong; Charles de Gaulle Airport, Paris, France; Anchorage International Airport, AK

JOSEPH L. CASTLE III
pp. 140

Castle Sculpture
331 Bay Horse Road
Bellevue, ID 83313
TEL 208-788-1305
FAX 208-788-2519
E-mail: joscastle@aol.com

For over 15 years, Joseph Castle has been exploring the circle and the reverse curve. The connection between the physical and metaphysical intrigues him. Organic shapes, as well as the contrast between subtle, soft arcs and crisp edges, capture his attention. His simple designs demand exacting attention to proportion and are extraordinarily sensitive to the slightest alteration. With minimal line, outside influences are removed and the tender teardrop or bird emerges.

RECENT PROJECTS: Group show, 2002, Anne Reed Gallery, Ketchum, ID; 14th Annual Outdoor Sculpture Exhibition, 2001, Lawrence, KS; commission, 2001, Mr. and Mrs. James Yarnell, Philadelphia, PA

COMMISSIONS: Secretary and Mrs. Donald Rumsfeld, 2000, Taos, NM; City of Redlands, 1993, CA

GUILD SOURCEBOOKS: *Architect's 12, 13*

JILL CASTY
pp. 92

Jill Casty Design
494 Alvarado Street, Suite D
Monterey, CA 93940
TEL 831-649-0923
FAX 831-649-0713
E-mail: jillcdesign@hotmail.com
Web: www.jillcastydesign.com

Jill Casty's exuberant, graceful art, while inventive and personal, is always sensitive to a site's spirit and spaces as well as to the vision of client and architect. Her aerial pieces — from joyful atrium mobiles to innovative, large-scale hanging art programs — and her festive abstract standing sculptures (up to 30 feet high) employ diverse materials such as Plexiglas, metals, and glass.

RECENT PROJECTS: City of Montclair, CA; SuperMall of the Great Northwest, Auburn, WA; Northwest Plaza, St. Louis, MO

GUILD SOURCEBOOKS: *Architect's 10, 11, 12, 13, 14, 15; Architectural & Interior Art 16*

CHARLES L. MADDEN — SCULPTURES IN BRONZE
pp. 189

21 Conwell Drive
Maple Glen, PA 19002-3310
TEL 215-646-1599
FAX 215-643-7272
E-mail: charleslmadden@aol.com

Charles L. Madden sculpts in monumental forms of bronze and mosaic. His clients include Pope John Paul II, the U.S. Department of State, and corporations and churches worldwide.

RECENT PROJECTS: 11' bronze, the shore of the Sea of Galilee, Pope John Paul II; 30' arch mosaic, Charleston, SC, diocese; bronze of St. Augustin for the Augustinian Community, Malvern, PA; bronze, Foreign Ministry Building, Jerusalem, Israel

AWARDS: Papal Gold Medal, 2000, Pope John Paul II

GUILD SOURCEBOOKS: *Architect's 14*

LAURIE REGAN CHASE
pp. 237

1255 California Street
San Francisco, CA 94109
TEL 415-203-2676
E-mail: laurie@lauriechase.com
Web: www.lauriechase.com

Heralded as a leader in contemporary realism, Laurie Chase is one of the most exciting artists to emerge in recent years. Chase captures the simple, untarnished charm of coastlines and landscapes from around the world. Her paintings masterfully combine detailed brushwork with the soft, impressionist-influenced use of the palate knife, creating images radiant with intense color and rich textures.

RECENT PROJECTS: Marriott Hotel and Resort, Ft. Lauderdale, FL; St. Rose Dominican Hospital-CHS, Las Vegas, NV

COMMISSIONS: Catholic Healthcare West; Patriot Cruise Line; Princess Cruise Line

COLLECTIONS: St. Rose Dominican Hospital, Las Vegas, NV

PUBLICATIONS: *LA Times*, 2001; *U.S. Art*, August, 2000 and November, 1999; *Coast Magazine*, 1998

MARK D. CHATTERLEY
pp. 107

231 Turner Road
Williamston, MI 48895
TEL 517-655-4012
E-mail: mark@chatterley.com
Web: www.chatterley.com

Mark Chatterley deals with large-scale sculptural ceramic pieces. He focuses primarily on the figure. Each piece is unique, the surface a crusty texture reminiscent of rusted metal or weathered stone. Bronze castings are available. Inquiries welcome.

COLLECTIONS: Aruba Radisson; Hocheng Cultural and Educational Foundation, Taiwan; JINRO, Seoul, Korea; Milton Keynes, United Kingdom; James Wallace Arts Trust, Auckland, New Zealand; Michigan State University; Lake Forest Library, IL; Plymouth Community Arts Council, Plymouth, MI

IONE CITRIN
pp. 239

2222 Avenue of the Stars #2302
Los Angeles, CA 90067
TEL 310-556-4382
FAX 310-556-1664
E-mail: icitrin@aol.com
Web: www.artbyione.com

Ione uses only one name but a variety of styles to soothe her wild imagination. A native of Chicago, she is a former television star and commercial voice-over artist. Now she wins awards and sells her creativity through her hands. Ione is a gold medal winner in the Nielson Bainbridge-Armstrong Art Show and a Grand Winner in the *Art Calendar* magazine Crabbie contest. Her studio boasts a host of other art awards, alongside the paintings and sculptures she has in progress. She works from her soul and wants to fill the world with love and beauty. Please contact the artist for prices. Slides and photographs are available upon request.

CITY GLASS SPECIALTY, INC.
pp. 56

Richard Hollman
2124 South Calhoun Street
Fort Wayne, IN 46802
TEL 260-744-3301
FAX 260-744-2522

City Glass Specialty is a family-owned business that has been in operation since 1944. City Glass operates as a glazing contractor, tailoring to the needs of the commercial and residential sectors. The art glass studio is a multi-faceted studio featuring commissioned work as well as restoration. The studio offers stained, leaded, engraved, molded, beveled, etched and faceted glass. These forms of art glass have been commissioned and installed in various types of architectural styles and applications.

JEREMY R. CLINE
pp. 141

Incline Glass
768 Delano Avenue
San Francisco, CA 94112
TEL 415-469-8312
FAX 415-469-8463
E-mail: jc@jeremycline.com
Web: www.jeremycline.com

The *Birds of Paradise* series illustrates Cline's interest in hand working molten glass to create an object of inherent movement and flexibility. Each piece, with its sensitive color palette and subtle undulating form, creates an ever-changing expression of the vessel as organic, suggesting both flower and bird. Cline's goal as a glassblower is to challenge himself to constantly improve his skills. As a result, his works express an ever-searching passion for an elusive perfection. In addition to the *Birds of Paradise* series, he accepts commissions.

PUBLICATIONS: *Contemporary Glass,* 2001; *Beautiful Things,* 2000

CLOWES SCULPTURE
pp. 93

Jonathan and Evelyn Clowes
PO Box 274
Lynn Hill Road
Acworth, NH 03601
TEL/FAX 603-835-6441
E-mail: jon@clowessculpture.com
Web: www.clowessculpture.com

Jonathan and Evelyn Clowes are a husband and wife team who create lyrical sculpture for public and private spaces. With 25 years of experience collaborating with clients, architects and engineers, they specialize in site-specific designs. Power and elegance mark the Clowes' sculptural work. Organic shapes and flowing curves speak of serene seas, soft winds and gracious gestures. The counterpoint of strong lines formed in wood, metals and composites – with the colors of blown glass, stone and other materials – compose balanced, graceful forms, fugues in motion.

COMMISSIONS: Hilton Hotel International, Tokyo, Japan; Royal Caribbean International, Miami, FL; Indianapolis Museum of Art, IN; Monadnock Paper Inc., Bennington, NH; Manchester District Courthouse, Manchester, NH; Visalia Convention Center, Visalia, CA

GRETCHEN LEE COLES
pp. 274

The Great Circle Press
PO Box 456
Glen Ellyn, IL 60138-0456
E-mail: gcoles@claypeople.org

Cartographer and sculptor Gretchen Lee Coles constructs one-of-a-kind, three-dimensional maps using various appropriate materials, such as paper, fabric, wood and ceramic. Her maps express the physical and ephemeral spirit of a place, and range from geographic realism to playful abstraction. With more than 20 years of professional experience, Coles honors traditional map making by welcoming teamwork in designing unique maps of real places. Please contact the Great Circle Press for a map list and prices.

EXHIBITIONS: Elmhurst Art Museum, 2001, Elmhurst, IL

AWARDS: Purchase Prize, College of DuPage, 1997, Glen Ellyn, IL

GUILD SOURCEBOOKS: *Designer's 14, 15; Architectural & Interior Art 16*

PAMELA COSPER
pp. 240

4439 Rolling Pine Drive
West Bloomfield, MI 48323
TEL 248-366-9569
E-mail: pamelacosper@hotmail.com
Web: http://go.to/pcosper

Pamela Cosper has traveled extensively, and her paintings are influenced by a wide variety of architectural, cultural, historical and natural designs. She enjoys the challenge of expressing the personality and interests of her clients in her work. She accepts commission work for projects of any size.

RECENT PROJECTS: 5' x 9' painting commission for private residence

EXHIBITIONS: *Swingtime at the Fisher,* 2001, Detroit, MI; *Animal/Vegetable/Mineral,* 2001, University of Michigan-Dearborn

GUILD SOURCEBOOKS: *Architectural & Interior Art 16*

LINDA DABEAU
pp. 187

Dabeau Studio
PO Box 10126
Albuquerque, NM 87184
TEL/FAX 505-898-2227
E-mail: ldabeau@swcp.com
Web: www.ldabeau.com

Linda Dabeau has been awarded both national and international commissions. Her positive personal energy, combined with prodigious hand skills and her comprehension of the roots of Christianity, enable her to become a conduit for the vision of the parish, church authority and architect. Through her highly disciplined work, Dabeau acts as a catalyst to create a bond within the whole community. Her materials are selected and utilized to create the best and most unique total visage of spirituality in the physical form.

DALLERIE & ASSOCIATES: HIGH PLAINS SCULPTORS' GUILD
pp. 108-109

Dallerie Davis
302 Main Street
Rapid City, SD 57701
TEL 605-342-3926 or 605-347-3752
FAX 605-343-8900
E-mail: dallerie@mato.com
Web: www.dallerie.com

Involved in the production of public art from Palm Springs to Washington, DC, the team at Dallerie & Associates has worked together in varying combinations since 1985. In 1999 Dallerie selected this team to create 43 life-size bronzes of the American presidents for downtown street corners in Rapid City, SD. Artists native to South Dakota make up the "Dream Team": Edward E. Hlavka, Lee Leuning, Sherri Treeby, John Lopez and James Michael Maher.

RECENT PROJECTS: World War II Memorial, State Capitol, Pierre, SD; Pro Rodeo Hall of Fame, Colorado Springs, CO; Sacred Heart Monestary, SD; James Madison University, VA

COLLECTIONS: The White House, Washington, DC; St. Louis University, MO; High Plains Heritage Center Museum, Spearfish, SD

DAVID WILSON DESIGN
pp. 55

David Wilson
202 Darby Road
South New Berlin, NY 13843-2212
TEL 607-334-3015
FAX 607-334-7065
E-mail: mail@davidwilsondesign.com
Web: www.davidwilsondesign.com

Renowned for his successful collaborations with architects on large-scale works for both public and private buildings, David Wilson pursues the goal of designing glass that adds to and enriches architecture. Emphasizing the importance of harmony in the built environment, his designs are the result of reducing forms to their simplest solution.

COMMISSIONS: Corning Incorporated offices, 2000, New York, NY; Kowitz apartment, 2000, New York, NY; College of the Holy Cross, 2002, Worcester, MA; Spirit of Christ Catholic Church, 2002, Arvada, CO

GUILD SOURCEBOOKS: *THE GUILD 1, 2, 3, 4, 5; Architect's 6, 7, 8, 9, 11, 13, 14, 15; Architectural & Interior Art 16*

KAREN DAVIDSON
pp. 288

3290 Waileia Place
Kihei, HI 96753
TEL 808-879-8819
FAX 808-879-6009
E-mail: davidson@maui.net
Web: www.karendavidson.net

The work of Maui-based artist Karen Davidson is an ethereal interpretation of the elements. Although some of her collages fill an entire wall, the effect is light and airy. Clouds seem to float, luminescent, above the mountains, and the sea leaps and rolls provocatively. The unique work is made by sculpting handmade paper and using custom-blended paints. Davidson's art can be found in prominent corporate and private collections, as well as in galleries. Refer to the website for specific project and collection information.

ALONZO DAVIS
pp. 275

2080 Peabody Avenue
Memphis, TN 38104
TEL 901-276-9070
FAX 901-276-0660
E-mail: artalonzo@aol.com
Web: www.alonzodavis.com

Alonzo Davis creates bamboo constructions embellished with burned-in patterned designs and wrappings of rawhide, canvas, rubber and copper.

RECENT PROJECTS: Plaza Club, Memphis, TN; Main Library, Memphis, TN

COMMISSIONS: Soulsville Gateway Project, Memphis, TN; Peter Formanek, Memphis, TN

COLLECTIONS: Federal Reserve Bank, Philadelphia, PA; Alabama State Bar Association, Montgomery, AL; Kaiser Permanente, CA

EXHIBITIONS: Memphis College of Art, TN; Thomas Hall Gallery, Dallas, TX; Southside Gallery, Oxford, MS; Louisiana Technical University, Rustin, LA; Sande Webster Gallery, Philadelphia, PA

ANN L. DELUTY
pp. 110

12 Randolph Street
Belmont, MA 02478
TEL/FAX 617-484-0069
E-mail: anndel@aol.com
Web: www.ann-deluty.ws

Ann Deluty strives to express the essence of natural objects in stone and wood. Her work ranges from abstract to extremely realistic. Her mastery of textures and carving techniques gives an air of realism to any object. A graduate of the School of the Museum of Fine Arts, she is also known for her portraits of people and pets in bronze, clay and cold-cast bronze. Deluty has numerous works in private collections, and commissions are welcome. Because of the variety of colors available in alabaster, she can carve to match any color scheme.

RECENT PROJECTS: Neon sculpture for dentist office, Lawrence, MA

GUILD SOURCEBOOKS: *Architect's 15; Designer's 15; Architectural & Interior Art 16*

JOSEPH DeROBERTIS
pp. 163

DeRobertis Designs
PO Box 1851
New London, NH 03257
TEL 603-768-3994

From small-scale sculpture and jewelry to large-scale public art, Joseph's fabricated stainless steel sculptures reflect nature with wildlife, feathers and abstract images. The feathers, made from stainless steel, are unique in that their fragility is represented in a hard material. Joseph also creates other types of work, including lighted sculpture, abstract sculpture and functional artwork.

RECENT PROJECTS: Public art commission for New Hampshire Technical Institute library and career center, Concord

AWARDS: Silvermine Community Association Award, 1998, Silvermine Art Guild, New Cannan, CT, juried by the curator of the Metropolitan Museum of Art, New York, NY

ROLAND DesCOMBES
pp. 241

Architectural Artworks, Inc.
163 East Morse Boulevard
Winter Park, FL 32789
TEL 407-644-5356
FAX 407-644-1016
E-mail: roland@arch-art.com
Web: www.rolanddescombes.com

"Roland DesCombes' work suggests an artistic vision that is both immersed in the complexity of the natural world and one that aspires to a kind of preternatural clarity. The artist's recurring subject has been the landscape of Florida's rivers. When we consider DesCombes' still lifes and interiors, we see similar concerns explored on the domestic level. Here again is the careful respect for the reality of things, the way they exist visually in the world."

John Mendelsohn

EXHIBITIONS: Florida Department of State, Supreme Court, 2002, Tallahassee, FL; The Disney Nature Conservancy, 2002, Orlando, FL

AWARDS: First prize, *The Real Show*, Grand Central Gallery, New York, NY

JOHN J. DeVLIEGER
pp. 223

John J. DeVlieger, Artist LLC
PO Box 203
Drexel Hill, PA 19026
TEL 610-246-1372
FAX 610-446-2426
E-mail: john@muralmaster.com
Web: www.muralmaster.com

John DeVlieger's technical acumen extends effortlessly from figures to marble to tapestries and beyond. His murals and paintings grace many private estates and commercial establishments throughout North America and abroad. John welcomes commissions, finding that collaboration adds a dynamic and intriguing dimension to his work. Commissions are available as on-site creations or as works on canvas to be installed.

RECENT PROJECTS: Vassar Design House, Philadelphia, PA; Restaurant Primavera, Philadelphia, PA; pool murals, private residences

PUBLICATIONS: *Romantic Home* magazine, 2002; "Modern Masters," 2002, Home and Garden Television

GUILD SOURCEBOOKS: *Designer's 11, 12, 13, 14*

JAMES F. DICKE II
pp. 242

Haines Galleries
405 Lafayette Avenue
Cincinnati, OH 45220
TEL 513-559-1405
FAX 513-651-0860
E-mail: HainesGalleries@aol.com
Web: www.jamesfdicke.com

James Dicke's process employs mixed-media oil on canvas. He seeks to build on the development of art in America over the last century with images that are abstract and representational. He seeks to engage the viewer in what they are viewing and with the levels of meaning and information contained therein. If the art lover sees a work of beauty that is "of nature" and contains emotional components of our time, then the artist has reached his goal.

COLLECTIONS: NASA, Washington, DC; Eli Wilner collection, New York, NY; National Museum of American Art, Washington, DC

EXHIBITIONS: 57 North Fine Art Gallery, Washington, DC, 2001; Cincinnati Art Galleries, Cincinnati, OH, 2001; Ralls Collection, Washington, DC, 1999

AWARDS: National Academy of Design honoree, 1999

JUDY DIOSZEGI
pp. 94

Judy Dioszegi, Designer
1295 Margate Lane
Green Oaks, IL 60048
TEL 847-433-2585
E-mail: jdiox2@aol.com
Web: www.jdioszegi.com

Judy Dioszegi specializes in designing and fabricating banners, tapestries and mobiles for corporate, residential, liturgical and public spaces. Collaborating with clients, she produces site-specific creations that enhance environments through color, shape and attention to architectural surroundings. Materials range from richly textured silks in tapestries to durable, vibrant nylon for mobiles and atrium pieces.

AWARDS: Design Award, 1998 and 1994, Industrial Fabrics Association International; Two Outstanding Achievement Awards, 2001, Industrial Fabrics Association International

GUILD SOURCEBOOKS: *Architect's 8, 10, 12, 14*

EILEEN DOUGHTY
pp. 302

Doughty Designs
9701 Rhapsody Drive
Vienna, VA 22181
TEL 703-938-6916
E-mail: quilter@doughtydesigns.com
Web: www.doughtydesigns.com

The tactile nature of quilts is explored and celebrated in the art of Eileen Doughty. She incorporates unique fabric layering and manipulations and a variety of nontraditional materials. Details are added with "thread painting." A favorite theme of Doughty's quilts is the positive and negative interactions we have with our environment. Doughty has been creating distinctive fiber art for public, corporate and private clients since 1991.

COMMISSIONS: White House Ornament Collection, Washington, DC; City of Greeley, Colorado (gifted to the city of Moriya, Japan); Red Cross, Washington, DC

EXHIBITIONS: Annapolis State House, MD; Virginia Quilt Museum, Harrisonburg, VA; Schweinfurth Memorial Art Center, Auburn, NY; Clayton Street Gallery, Athens, GA

WILLIAM F. DUFFY
pp. 164

Duffy & Associates
2220 East Fairmount Avenue
Baltimore, MD 21231
TEL 410-522-2747
FAX 410-522-2747
E-mail: bill-duffy@worldnet.att.net
Web: www.williamduffy.com

Widely recognized for his urbane sculpture compositions for public and private collections, Duffy works most often in bronze, stainless steel and granite to create works designed to withstand time, weather and human contact. He believes that art and its surroundings are part of a cultural whole and rejects the notion that sculpture is a decorative afterthought. Collaborating with landscape professionals, Duffy incorporates water in many of his compositions.

RECENT PROJECTS: Gaithersburg Concert Pavilion, 2001, MD; Ashburton Elementary School, 2000, Baltimore, MD; Kashiwa Public Gardens, 1999, Japan

EXHIBITIONS: Ogunquit Museum of American Art, 2001, Ogunquit, ME; Wolfarth Galleries, 1998, Provincetown, MA; Hunter Museum, 1995, Chattanooga, TN

NICK EDMONDS
pp. 142

Nick Edmonds, Sculptor
29 Summit Avenue
Sharon, MA 02067
TEL 781-784-4531

Nick Edmonds' images are inspired by the landscape and often utilize figures and man-made objects as counterpoints to nature. The primary material used is carved wood, which is then covered with coats of lacquer and acrylic paint and protected with varnish. The idea of making large, jointed-wood sculpture came from the study of demountable wood structures in Japan. For outdoor commission work, the carved wood forms are cast in bronze.

RECENT PROJECTS: *Nick Edmonds: A Natural World,* retrospective exhibition, February – March, 2002, 808 Gallery, Boston University, MA. Catalog available.

COMMISSIONS: Veronica Smith Senior Center, 1989, Brighton, MA

COLLECTIONS: Boston Public Library, MA; New Britain Museum of Art, New Britain, CT; State University of New York, Courtland, NY

AWARDS: The Orville Lance Prize for Sculpture, National Academy of Design, 2001

ELLEN MANDELBAUM GLASS ART
pp. 57

Ellen Mandelbaum
39-49 46th Street
Long Island City, NY 11104-1407
TEL/FAX 718-361-8154

Since 1981, Ellen Mandelbaum has been creating extraordinary glass art that attracts professionals working in the fields of art, architecture and religion. There is a rare and unique element of spontaneity and openness that Mandelbaum manages to achieve in a medium that traditionally projects great weight and formality. The beauty of stained glass's color and light remain at the heart of her work.

AWARDS: Ministry and Liturgy Magazine "Bene" Best of Show; AIA-IFRAA Award of Excellence, 1997

GUILD SOURCEBOOKS: *GUILD 1, 2, 3, 5; Architect's 6, 8, 9, 10, 11, 12, 13, 14, 15; Architectural & Interior Art 16*

ELVIS CRUZE FURNITURE
pp. 200

55 Waverly Drive, Suite 105
Pasadena, CA 91105
TEL 626-793-1010
FAX 626-793-1236
E-mail: elvis@elviscruze.com
Web: www.elviscruze.com

America has a rich pallet of cultures to draw inspiration from. The furniture of Elvis Cruze feels familiar because the styles are reminiscent of the classics, but Cruze's painted designs and finishes are undeniably 21st century. The team at Elvis Cruze draws inspiration from what is happening now. As artists, they are driven to reflect contemporary culture in their designs. The mission of their creativity is to leave a lasting impression on future generations.

CAROLYN EVANS
pp. 243

Evans Arts
38 Eliot Hill Road
South Natick, MA 01760
TEL 508-655-9102
FAX 508-653-0192
E-mail: evansarts@attbi.com
Web: www.evansartstudio.com

Carolyn Evans' paintings evolve from the first washes through layers of thin, thick, scraped and manipulated paint to find solutions that satisfy all criteria of classical painting. The act of painting drives the work into provocative compositions where objects take on their own lives. Evans is a painter working to compose a poetic view of the world we live in.

COLLECTIONS: Allan Stone, New York, NY; Wellington Management, Boston, MA; Royal Sonesta, Key Biscayne, FL; United States Banker Collection, Cos Cob, CT; North American Petroleum, Greenwich, CT

EXHIBITIONS: Clark Gallery, 2002, Lincoln, MA; Allan Stone Gallery, 2001, New York, NY; Munson Gallery, 2001, Santa Fe, NM; Lowe Gallery, 2001, Atlanta, GA

AWARDS: Provincetown Art Association and Museum National Competition Finalist

TOM FERDERBAR
pp. 262

Tom Ferderbar, Photographer
1905 Hillside Drive
Delafield, WI 53018
TEL 262-646-8441
FAX 262-646-8451
E-mail: tomferd@wi.rr.com

Tom Ferderbar has been photographing Route 66, the former "Main Street of America" for over 20 years and is in the process of producing a book on the mother road. Ferderbar's photography captures the haunting beauty and loneliness of the decaying homes, businesses — and indeed, of the road itself. His prints are archival giclee prints, available in a variety of sizes.

His work appears in the Ansel and Virginia Adams collection at the Center for Creative Arts at the University of Arizona, Tucson, and the Milwaukee Art Center.

EXHIBITIONS: Franklin Mint Gallery, 2000, Philadelphia, PA

AWARDS: Numerous advertising photography awards, 1954-1995

STEVE FEREN
pp. 165

Feren Studios
2601 Highway MM
Oregon, WI 53575
TEL 608-273-0911
FAX 608-273-0988
E-mail: sfferen@facstaff.wisc.edu

Steve Feren has been creating sculpture for public places since 1980. The artist's projects have included cast glass relief murals, fiber optics with blown and cast glass, concrete and glass outdoor environments, and mosaic sculpture and floors.

RECENT PROJECTS: Wilson Performing Arts Center, Brookfield, WI; Marriott Hotel and Office Building, Milwaukee, WI; Neurosurgery Center, Santa Fe, NM; Oceanside Library, Oceanside, CA

COMMISSIONS: Rutgers University, New Brunswick, NJ; Lopes Veterans Nursing Home, Land O' Lakes, FL; Milwaukee Public Library, Milwaukee, WI; Bellfaire School, Cleveland, OH

BRUCE PAUL FINK
pp. 40-41

Pole Bridge Studio/Foundry
90 Pole Bridge Road
Woodstock, CT 06281
TEL 860-974-0130
E-mail: bpfink@artmetal.com
Web: www.artmetal.com/bpfink

Since 1961, Bruce Paul Fink's more than 895 internationally collected works have been illustrated, updated and technically discussed on the web at www.artmetal.com, as well as under any web engine search for "bpfink." In his private studio/foundry, bronze and cast metals, steel, fiber, polyester resins and stone are commonly used. Architectural doors, walls, area entries and sculptures are often site-commissioned and have included some Participatory Works and Community Creativity Sculpture with special needs children and elderly groups. Currently, Fink is the part-time State Artist in Residence in Lana'i, Hawaii. He has received over 54 first place awards for his sculpture creations.

BRUCE PAUL FINK
pp. 40-41

Pole Bridge Studio/Foundry
90 Pole Bridge Road
Woodstock, CT 06281
TEL 860-974-0130
E-mail: bpfink@artmetal.com
Web: www.artmetal.com/bpfink

COMMISSIONS: Hawaii State Foundation on Culture and the Arts; Connecticut Commission on the Arts; Connecticut Quinebaugh Valley Prevention Council; Rhode Island Substance Abuse Prevention Task Force Association

GUILD SOURCEBOOKS: *Architect's 8, 9, 11, 12, 14, 15; Architectural & Interior Art 16*

CAROL FLEMING
pp. 144

Terra Nova Studio
4 Whitfield Lane
St. Louis, MO 63124
TEL 314-692-7800
FAX 314-692-7801
E-mail: ladueclay@carolfleming.com
Web: www.carolfleming.com

Since 1988, Carol Fleming has been a full-time studio artist, selling large ceramic sculptures. She makes nine-foot, slab-built stoneware columns and three-foot eggs of coiled clay. She specializes in site-specific projects, working with architects and private clients. Fleming's work includes fountains, seating, tables and garden focal points. Her artwork is durable and waterproof and will enhance any site.

COLLECTIONS: Daum Museum of Contemporary Art, Sedalia, MO; First Hawaiian Bank, Honolulu; The Private Bank, Brentwood, MO; Windermere Real Estate, Mercer Island, WA

EXHIBITIONS: *Sculptural Clay Invitational*, Daum Museum, Sedalia, MO; The Sheldon Galleries, St. Louis, MO; Wood Street Gallery, Chicago, IL; The John McEnroe Gallery, New York; NY

FLUX
pp. 201

Denni and Karen Boger
20202 Beaver Dam Road
Lewes, DE 19958
TEL/FAX 302-945-3176
E-mail: djboger@verizon.net
Web: www.thisisflux.com

Flux is a husband-and-wife team dedicated to the designing and making of contemporary furniture. The Bogers work in steel, hardwood, stone and glass in a small studio to create custom mixed-media pieces and limited-production runs. Their furnishings are uniquely styled and critically made in order to meet the needs, tastes and surroundings of every client.

RECENT PROJECTS: Private residence, Ocean City, NJ, wall unit of 20' and two free-standing cabinets composed of steel, mahogany and birdseye maple

EXHIBITIONS: Philadelphia Furniture & Furnishings Show, 2001 and 2002, Philadelphia, PA; Fine Furnishings Providence Show, 2001, Providence, RI; Designer Arts at the Armory, 2000, New York, NY

STEVE FONTANINI
pp. 42-43

Steve Fontanini Architectural and
Ornamental Blacksmithing
PO Box 2298
Jackson, WY 83001
TEL 307-733-7668
FAX 307-734-8816
E-mail: sfontani@wyoming.com

The confluence of the Snake and Hoback rivers is where Steve Fontanini and company produce metalwork of all kinds. Stair railings, gates and chandeliers are made to your design, or they will be happy to create a design to fit your needs. Projects are built by forging hot metal and joining the pieces with traditional methods such as rivets, collars and mortise-and-tenon joints. Fontanini's work is found throughout the United States.

AWARDS: Silver award, forged interior railings, 2002, National Ornamental and Miscellaneous Metals Association (NOMMA)

PAUL FRIEND
pp. 58

Paul Friend Architectural Glass & Design, Inc.
1916 Old Cuthbert Road, Studio B19
Cherry Hill, NJ 08034
TEL 856-428-9100
FAX 856-428-1199
E-mail: info@paulfriendartglass.com
Web: www.paulfriendartglass.com

Paul Friend is noted for his distinctive design of architectural stained and leaded glass for site-specific applications. With over 25 years of design experience, Paul Friend has fabricated installations for some of the most prestigious corporations and liturgical institutions in the United States. From stained glass to limited-edition sculptures, Paul Friend transforms open areas into spaces of immense artistic impact.

RECENT PROJECTS: National competition winner, New Mexico State Council of the Arts Award for Art in Public Spaces program; glass sculpture created for Temple Emmanuel, Cherry Hill, NJ

COMMISSIONS: New Mexico Military Institute, Roswell, NM; Our Lady of Mount Carmel, Camden, NJ

GUILD SOURCEBOOKS: *Architect's 8, 10, 12, 15*

STEPHANIE GASSMAN
pp. 276

Villa Rosa
4219 Miriana Way
Sarasota, FL 34233
TEL 941-341-0721
FAX 941-342-9541

Stephanie Gassman creates commissioned, site-specific paintings and wall reliefs. Her work can be found in public, corporate and residential environments around the United States. She enjoys the challenge of making an original statement for a client or a community, using a variety of materials. A diverse portfolio reflects her ability to handle both large and small projects, logos and established color schemes, while maintaining a contemporary visual excitement. A commission list, slides and pricing are available upon request.

GUILD SOURCEBOOKS: *Designer's 13, 14, 15; Architectural & Interior Art 16*

GEORGE PETERS AND MELANIE WALKER / AIRWORKS, INC.
pp. 99

815 Spruce Street
Boulder, CO 80302
TEL/FAX 303-442-9025
E-mail: airworks@concentric.net

As a collaborative team, Geroge Peters and Melanie Walker create works that address contemplation and celebration. Their site-specific sculptures and mobiles enliven, illuminate and soften architectural spaces with elegant simplicity and lightness. Both artists are proficient in a wide range of materials and processes, incorporating their unique visions into works that inspire kinetic and poetic play in aerial atrium spaces.

RECENT PROJECTS: University of Central Florida, Orlando; University of Colorado, Health Sciences Center, Denver; University of Arizona, Special Collections Library, Tucson

COMMISSIONS: Tokyo Bay Hilton, Japan; Univeristy of Colorado-Colorado Springs; Shriners Hospital for Children, Boston, MA; Desert Sage Library, Phoenix, AZ; Colorado Department of Education, Denver

GUILD SOURCEBOOKS: *Architect's 13, 14, 15; Architectural & Interior Art 16*

MARY GILLIS
pp. 145

2650 Oldepointe Drive NE
Grand Rapids, MI 49525
TEL 616-516-8194
TEL 616-942-5360
E-mail: gillisstudio@cs.com
Web: www.marygillis.com

Mary Gillis works primarily in glass, granite, steel and aluminum. Numerous commissions and exhibitions have earned her international recognition.

COMMISSIONS: RDV Sportsplex, Orlando, FL; Radisson Plaza Hotel, Kalamazoo, MI; McDermott, Will & Emery, New York, NY; Baan Inc., Oakbrook Terrace, IL; Central Wesleyan Church, Holland, MI

COLLECTIONS: Daimler Chrysler; Standard Federal Bank; Davis, Polk and Wardwell, New York, NY; Young & Rubicam, Detroit, MI

EXHIBITIONS: Burnaby Gallery, Bermuda; Gensler, New York; Germans van Eck, New York; Palazzo Grassi, Venice, Italy

GODDARD & GIBBS STUDIOS LTD.
pp. 59

Maureen Martin-Crowell
12 Priscilla Avenue
Scituate, MA 02066
TEL 781-545-7589
FAX 781-545-7233
E-mail: gandgstudiosusa@aol.com
Web: www.goddard.co.uk

Designers and manufacturers of decorative glass for corporate and private buildings. The studios provide both traditional and contemporary artworks for internal and external locations.

RECENT PROJECTS: Decorative glass skylight for a conference center, Salt Lake City, UT; stained glass dome, UAE Chancery, Washington, DC; complete window scheme for Boston Temple, Boston, MA; complete window scheme for Lubbock Temple, TX

AWARDS: Washington Building Congress Craftsmanship Award, 2001

DANIEL GOLDSTEIN
pp. 95

Goldstein Studio
224 Guerrero Street
San Francisco, CA 94103
TEL 415-621-5761
FAX 415-863-1778
E-mail: danieljgoldstein@yahoo.com

Daniel Goldstein has successfully collaborated with architects and designers for more than 25 years. His suspended sculptures of glass and steel, as well as his mobiles and wall-hung sculptures of expanded aluminum, have been commissioned for numerous public, corporate and residential environments.

RECENT PROJECTS: BART Station, Colma, CA; Norcal Headquarters, San Francisco, CA; Alcoa Aluminum Corporate Headquarters, Pittsburgh, PA

COLLECTIONS: Chicago Art Institute, IL; Brooklyn Museum, Brooklyn, NY; Berkeley University Art Museum, CA

GUILD SOURCEBOOKS: *Architect's 7, 8, 10, 11, 12, 13, 14*

LYNN GOODPASTURE
pp. 26-27

10753 Weyburn Avenue
Los Angeles, CA 90024
TEL 310-470-2455
FAX 310-470-4257
E-mail: lgoodpast@aol.com

Lynn Goodpasture designs, fabricates and installs site-specific art (including large-scale clocks) in collaboration with architects for integration with architecture. Materials include stone and glass mosaic; art glass; metal.

Public art commissions include *The Children's Clock,* 12' diameter, to be completed January 2003, Center for Early Education, West Hollywood, CA.

RECENT PROJECTS: Three mosaic murals, 663 square feet, *Explorer of the Seas,* Royal Caribbean Cruise Line; 243-square-foot art glass window and 715-square-foot mosaic mural, Children's Therapy Unit, Good Samaritan Hospital, Puyallup, WA; Station Clock, Glendale Transportation Center, Glendale, CA

SUSAN GOTT
pp. 85

Phoenix Glass Studio
811 East Knollwood Street
Tampa, FL 33604
TEL 813-237-FIRE
FAX 813-238-7864
E-mail: gottglass@msn.com
Web: www.gottglass.com

Susan Gott has worked in glass for over 20 years and specializes in casting to create architectural glass and large-scale sculpture. Her public artworks are significant to the community while reflecting her own aesthetic interests in mythology, symbolism and ancient traditions.

COMMISSIONS: Port Tampa Library, FL; HARTline, University Transit Center, Tampa, FL; St. Petersburg City Hall & Municipal Services Center, FL; University of Central Florida, Orlando

EXHIBITIONS: Solo exhibition, Polk Museum of Art, Lakeland, FL

JIM GRAY
pp. 84

The Carving Workshop
4562 East 2nd Street, Unit K
Benicia, CA 94510
TEL 707-747-6918
FAX 707-747-6958
E-mail: jg@carvingworkshop.com
Web: www.carvingworkshop.com

The Carving Workshop specializes in custom-carved architectural decoration and sculptural works that blend the rich elegance of classical designs with the individual expression of the client. Working in the mediums of limestone, marble, wood and bronze, Jim Gray creates fireplaces, mirror frames, marble mosaics, sculptural pieces, arched doorways, fountains, sconces, furnishings and more. His work can be seen in *Architectural Digest, Northern California Home & Design, Fine Woodworking* and *Designer's Illustrated.* Please visit his website.

NANCY GRAY
pp. 44

Gray Studio
508 East Fourth Street
Lampasas, TX 76550
TEL 512-525-1963
FAX 512-556-3608
E-mail: nancy@graystudio.net
Web: www.graystudio.net

Figurative and nonrepresentational paintings were hallmarks of Nancy Gray's art until she moved from the city to settle in rural central Texas. The area's rugged environment fueled a passion for landscape painting. Design decisions for her new country house and studio also inspired the award-winning artist to explore new applications for her work. She now paints her bold, romantic landscapes on trifold screens and designed metal gates that feature stylized representations of native flora.

RECENT PROJECTS: Set of double-entry gates to span a driveway; freestanding metal sculpture using metal techniques from Gray's own garden gates

GRETEMAN GROUP
pp. 166

Sonia Greteman
1425 East Douglas
Wichita, KS 67211
TEL 316-263-1004
FAX 316-263-1060
E-mail: sgreteman@gretemangroup.com
Web: www.gretemangroup.com

Specializing in environmental graphics, public art, signage, branding and way-finding for stadiums, public spaces, historical sites, parks, zoos and malls.

RECENT PROJECTS: Pittsburgh Steelers' Heinz Field, PA; Lawrence-Dumont Stadium, Wichita, KS; Hamilton Place, Chattanooga, TN; Provo Towne Centre, UT

MARK ERIC GULSRUD
pp. 60, 167

Architectural Glass/Sculpture
3309 Tahoma Place West
Tacoma, WA 98466
TEL 253-566-1720
FAX 253-565-5981
E-mail: markgulsrud@aol.com

Primarily site-specific, commissions range internationally and include public, private, corporate and liturgical settings. Media include custom hand-blown leaded glass; sand carved, laminated and cast glass; handmade ceramic; stone and carved wood. Encouraging professional collaboration, the artist is personally involved in all phases of design, fabrication and installation, and is primarily concerned with a sympathetic integration of artwork with environment.

GUILD SOURCEBOOKS: *GUILD 3, 4; Architect's 7, 8, 9, 10, 11, 12, 13, 14, 15; Architectural & Interior Art 16*

JEFFERY L. HALL
pp. 111

Jeff Hall Studios
39331 Rodeffer Road
Lovettsville, VA 20180
TEL 540-822-5398
FAX 540-822-9110
Web: www.jeffhallstudio.com

Jeff Hall began his career in art as a fantasy illustrator, and he currently explores fiction through figurative sculpture. His works are surreal in that he does not concern himself with scale within a piece. While the human body itself is beautiful, it is the mind that affects body language. The figure is not just a body in motion, but a mind at work. Jeff's experience with a wide range of materials allows him to create with purpose.

RECENT PROJECTS: Portrait bust of Dan Quayle, Capitol Building, Washington, DC; conservation and reconstruction of Frederick Hart's *Ex Nihilo,* Washington National Cathedral, Washington, DC

EXHIBITIONS: American Craft Council Winter Show, 1999-2002, Baltimore, MD; Washington County Museum, 1998-2001, Hagerstown, MD

WILLIAM HANSON
pp. 112

535 West Carpenter Lane
Philadelphia, PA 19119
TEL 215-843-4242
FAX 215-843-4544
E-mail: hansonwg@aol.com

When done well, a portrait captures not only a likeness but some of the spirit of a person, and a portrait in bronze makes that spirit tangible for generations.

COLLECTIONS: The Patrons' Museum, Gloucester, MA

EXHIBITIONS: With Philadelphia Sculptors at *Grounds For Sculpture,* 1998, Hamilton, NJ; National Sculpture Society Annual, 1995, New York, NY

AWARDS: Pietro & Alfrieda Montana Award, Hudson Valley Art Association, 1999, Hastings-on-Hudson, NY; Greg Wyatt Award, Hudson Valley Art Association, 1998, Hastings-on-Hudson, NY; Anna Hyatt Huntington Award, American Artists Professional League, 1994, New York, NY

JOAN ROTHCHILD HARDIN
pp. 29

Joan Rothchild Hardin Ceramics
393 West Broadway #4
New York, NY 10012
TEL 212-966-9433
FAX 212-431-9196
E-mail: joan@hardintiles.com
Web: www.hardintiles.com

Hardin's award-winning art tiles, installed or hung as paintings, add a jewel-like richness to residential, corporate and public settings. Layered glazes create abstract and representational paintings on ceramic tile.

COMMISSIONS: Veterinary hospitals, 2000, New York, NY

COLLECTIONS: American Art Clay Company, Indianapolis, IN

EXHIBITIONS: *Artists' Tiles: Beyond Tradition,* 2001, Pence Gallery, Davis, CA

AWARDS: Architecture Award, Fourth Silverhawk Competition

PUBLICATIONS: *Ceramic Art Tile for the Home,* 2001

GUILD SOURCEBOOKS: *Designer's 14, 15; Architectural & Interior Art 16*

YOSHI HAYASHI
pp. 244

255 Kansas Street
San Francisco, CA 94103
TEL 415-552-0755/415-924-9224
FAX 415-552-0755
E-mail: yoshihayashi@att.net

Yoshi Hayashi was born in Japan and learned the rigorous techniques of Japanese lacquer art from his father. Hayashi carries the spirit, history and inspiration of this process with him today as he reinterprets the ancient lacquer traditions for his screens and wall panels. Hayashi's designs range from delicate traditional 17th-century Japanese lacquer art themes to bold and contemporary geometric designs. By skillfully applying metallic leaf and bronzing powders, he adds both illumination and contrast to the network of color, pattern and texture.

Recent commissions include works for private residences in the United States and Canada.

GUILD SOURCEBOOKS: *THE GUILD 3, 4, 5; Designer's 6, 7, 8, 9, 10, 11, 12, 13, 14, 15; Architectural & Interior Art 16*

HEARTSMITH ENTERPRISES
pp. 86

Biruta Akerbergs Hansen
111 Barner's Road
Liverpool, PA 17045
TEL 717-444-3682
FAX 717-444-7483
E-mail: hrtsmith@pa.net
Web: www.natureandart.com

Cast glass bas-relief in an architectural setting has the unique quality of capturing colors of the background in ever-changing patterns. As a result it is not a static sculpture, but one that retains a constant element of surprise and delight. Molten glass poured to produce a negative image is capable of revealing exquisite detail — even against a dark background — with minimal lighting. Wall elements are sculpted to a maximum dimension of 16" x 16" x 2" and can be combined to form a continuous wall. Biruta Akerbergs Hansen has had an award-winning artistic career in various media. Making the most complicated or disturbing subject matter drawn from nature or the human condition compelling to the viewer is as important as creating a work of beauty. Partial list of clients and exhibits: National Geographic Society, National Wildlife Federation, Smithsonian Institution.

CHRISTIAN HECKSCHER
pp. 45

Lift Design Architectural Details & Etching
PO Box 1380
123 Main Street
Vineyard Haven, MA 02568
TEL/FAX 508-696-6284
E-mail: liftdesignhda@earthlink.net
Web: www.liftdesignetching.com

Christian Heckscher has been creating and producing a unique range of etched metal artwork since 1971. Whether a one-of-a-kind piece for public space or a large series suited for corporate spaces, his work provides original details for any environment. His craftsmanship embraces many styles suitable for elevator or entry doors, murals and furnishings such as conference or dining room tables. Working on the East and West Coasts, Christian welcomes collaboration with architects and interior designers on major residential and commercial projects.

COMMISSIONS: Starrett Lehigh Building, New York, NY; Mirage Hotel and Casino, Las Vegas, NV; Hyatt Park Tower, Chicago, IL; MGM Hotel and Casino, Las Vegas, NV; Sitmar Cruise, Fairsea & Fairwind Cruise Ships; Mandrian Oriental Hotel, Miami, FL; Transamerica Tower, San Francisco, CA

STEVE HEIMANN
pp. 245

196 Stefanic Avenue
Elmwood Park, NJ 07407
TEL 201-797-5434
E-mail: steve@steveheimann.com
Web: www.steveheimann.com

Like icons in their simplicity, Heimann's works employ few elements. He creates images that seek to engage the viewer into a feeling of resonance, much the way religious icons seek to elicit that response in believers. Heimann's distinctive style is featured in corporate collections and extends to an international audience through numerous commissions for postage stamps. Countries that have commissioned stamps include the British Virgin Islands, Grenada, Sierra Leone, Uganda, Tanzania, Dominica and Antigua/Barbuda. In 1999, seven paintings were featured in "Extreme Homes," a production of the Home & Garden network. Catalog available upon request.

GUILD SOURCEBOOKS: *Designer's 15; Architectural & Interior Art 16*

HELAMAN FERGUSON, SCULPTOR
pp. 143

Helaman Ferguson
10512 Pilla Terra Court
Laurel, MD 20723
TEL 301-604-4270
FAX 301-776-0499
E-mail: helamanf@helasculpt.com
Web: www.helasculpt.com

Helaman Ferguson's sculpture celebrates science and mathematics in granite, marble and bronze.

COLLECTIONS: Clay Mathematics Institute, Cambridge, MA; Maryland Science and Technology Center, Bowie, MD; Institute for Defense Analyses, VA; University of St. Thomas, St. Paul, MN; American Center for Physics, MD; Smith College, MA; National Council of Teachers of Mathematics, VA; Mathematical Sciences Research Institute, University of California, Berkeley; Weisman Art Museum, Minneapolis, MN; Mathematical Association of America, Washington, DC; American Mathematical Society, RI

MARILYN HENRION
pp. 303

505 LaGuardia Place #23D
New York, NY 10012
TEL 212-982-8949
FAX 212-979-7462
E-mail: oetzi@mindspring.com
Web: www.marilynhenrion.com

Henrion's abstractions are pieced in vibrant silks and animated by hand-quilted surfaces, transforming geometric elements into metaphorical images with strong graphic impact.

COLLECTIONS: American Craft Museum, New York, NY; Lucent Technologies, Avaya Communications, Kaiser Permanente, Denver, CO; Dana Farber Cancer Institute, Boston, MA

EXHIBITIONS: Thirteen Moons Gallery, Santa Fe, NM, 2001 (solo); Noho Gallery, New York, NY, 2000 (solo)

PUBLICATIONS: *Women Designers in the U.S.A. 1900-2000,* 2001; *The Art Quilt,* 1997

GUILD SOURCEBOOKS: *Designer's 9, 11, 13*

KAREN HEYL
pp. 31

907 Sonia Place
Escondido, CA 92026
TEL 760-489-7106
E-mail: Heylstone2@aol.com

1310 Pendleton Street, Suite 101
Cincinnati, OH 45210
TEL 513-421-9791

Karen Heyl's award-winning limestone mural relief sculpture combines Old World stone carving techniques with contemporary design, lending itself to a variety of architectural applications, monumental and small. Using varied textural surfaces, Heyl creates aesthetic sophistication with simplified sensual forms. Collaborating with architects, art consultants and interior and landscape designers, she has received commissions from hospitals, corporations, universities, parks, churches, cities and private collectors. Her works have gained regional and national recognition. Pricing upon request.

GUILD SOURCEBOOKS: *Designer's 9, 12, 13, 14, 15; Architectural & Interior Art 16*

CLAUDIA HOLLISTER
pp. 32

PMB 158, 333 South State Street, Suite V
Lake Oswego, OR 97034-3691
TEL/FAX 503-636-6684
Web: www.guildtrade.com

Utilizing hand-built colored porcelain, Claudia Hollister creates site-specific architectural wall pieces for public, corporate and residential environments. Her work is highly textured and richly colored. She creates a distinctive style by combining the intricate techniques of inlaying, embossing and hand carving three-dimensional elements on tiles.

RECENT PROJECTS: Nike, Beverton, OR; Humana Medical Center, Cincinnati, OH; Maxtor Corporation, Longmont, CO; BGT, West Conshohocken, PA

GUILD SOURCEBOOKS: *Designer's 8, 11, 13, 14, 15; Architectural & Interior Art 16*

AI QIU CHEN HOPEN
pp. 146

Chen Hopen Art International
227 Main Street, Suite B
Sutton, WV 26601
TEL 800-872-8578 (within U.S.)
TEL 304-765-5611 (international)
Web: www.aiqiuhopen.com
E-mail: sculptureinternational@yahoo.com

Ai Qiu Chen sculptures are like songs in space, consummately crafted in stainless steel. Graceful and light, yet powerful and moving, they are engineered to withstand the winds of a typhoon and endure with lasting beauty in the harshest environments. Ai Qiu's fountain and plaza works have been widely commissioned in China, but are now being created and placed in the U.S. and Europe.

Shown in this book are *Bat in Sunshine,* located in downtown Shanghai, and the one-meter tall scale model for a 10-meter work in progress for a science and performing arts center in the U.S.

The artist invites you to call or write her directly to begin the design process for a work in your space. Six months is the average time it takes to complete a project, from beginning to installation. Prices range from $50,000 to $400,000.

BILL HOPEN
pp. 188

Hopen Studio Inc.
227 Main Street, Suite A
Sutton, WV 26601
TEL 800-872-8578 (within U.S.)
TEL 304-765-5611
E-mail: hopen@access.mountain.net
Web: www.aagg.com/hopen

Scores of churches, hospitals and universities throughout the U.S. have commissioned Bill Hopen to create beautiful and meaningful works that symbolize the spirit of their space. Hopen's true strength is his ability to listen, and intuitively understand, what a congregation wishes to express. That intuited spiritual expression, mingled with the clay, gives his figures a unique radiance. Featured in this book are two works portraying St. Joseph the worker. The earliest was commissioned by the Sisters of St. Joseph for St. Joseph's Hospital of Parkersburg, WV, in 1988. The Sisters of St. Joseph commissioned Hopen again in 2000 to create a much larger bronze work (twice life-size) for placement above the portico of their newly constructed wing.

GUILD SOURCEBOOKS: *Architect's 9, 10, 11, 12, 13, 15; Designer's 12; Architectural & Interior Art 16*

HOPEN STUDIO INC.
pp. 113

Bill Hopen
227 Main Street, Suite A
Sutton, WV 26601
TEL 800-872-8578 (within U.S.)
TEL 304-765-5611
E-mail: hopen@access.mountain.net
Web: www.aagg.com/hopen

Hopen Studio Incorporated has created, cast and installed nearly two million dollars in bronze sculpture throughout the U.S. in the last 15 years. *Three Stags,* featured in this book, is a restoration work created for historic Boldt Castle and was commissioned by the Thousand Island Bridge Authority of New York/Canada. *Sisters in Learning* is shown as a clay in progress for the bronze commissioned by Benedictine College in Atchison, KS.

Hopen Studio's reputation for sensitive work accomplished quickly, reasonably and beautifully is reported by a long list of clients. Hopen Studio will design and create, cast and finish, deliver and install a sculptural work for one quoted bottom-line price. Simply call or e-mail if you are interested in discussing your project. Typical commissions are completed in six months to a year from the first call.

PAUL HOUSBERG
pp. 61

Glass Project, Inc.
875 North Main Road
Jamestown, RI 02835
TEL 401-560-0880
E-mail: housberg@glassproject.com
Web: www.glassproject.com

Paul Housberg creates site-specific works in glass. Central to his work is the use of light, color and texture to shape and define a space. Housberg is a graduate of the Rhode Island School of Design and a Fulbright Scholar in architectural glass.

The artist welcomes inquiries regarding any planned or contemplated project.

RECENT PROJECTS: William J. Nealon Federal Building, Scranton, PA; BankRI, Providence, RI; Peninsula Hotel, Chicago, IL; Dreyfus Corporation, New York, NY; Pfizer Inc., Groton, CT

PUBLICATIONS: *Stained Glass Quarterly,* 2000; *The Art of Glass: Integrating Architecture and Glass,* 1998; *Glass Art Magazine,* 1996

GUILD SOURCEBOOKS: *Architect's 6, 7, 8, 9, 10, 11, 13, 15; Architectural & Interior Art 16*

BRUCE HOWDLE
pp. 33

225 Commerce Street
Mineral Point, WI 53565
TEL 608-987-3590
E-mail: bhowdle@chorus.net
Web: www.brucehowdle.cjb.net
Web: www.artstop.com

Bruce Howdle has been a ceramic sculptor since 1976. He has produced work ranging from thrown forms up to 6 feet in height to 30-foot relief murals utilizing 9 tons of clay.

He fires with a sodium process that melts the clay surface, preserving the integrity of the media and creating a very durable piece.

His work is suitable for freestanding or installed wall locations; pieces are in large public institutions, banks, corporations, private offices and homes. Prices range from $1,500 to $150,000. Howdle collaborates closely with his clients and provides detailed drawings of his proposed projects.

GUILD SOURCEBOOKS: *Architect's 7, 9, 10, 11, 12, 13, 14, 15; Architectural & Interior Art 16*

GORDON HUETHER
pp. 62

101 South Coombs Street, Suite X
Napa, CA 94559
TEL 707-255-5954
FAX 707-255-5991
E-mail: mail@gordonhuether.com
Web: www.gordonhuether.com

Gordon Huether brings 23 years of experience to his creation of artwork for all types of architectural settings, ranging from large public installations to smaller, autonomous works for private collections. Huether leads a studio of 25 skilled artisans and project managers who have successfully fabricated large-scale projects all over the country and around the world. Please visit the website for more information.

HURSTIN STUDIO GLASS AND METAL
pp. 202

Mark Robert Hursty
176 Willow Street
South Hamilton, MA 01982
TEL/FAX 978-468-0626
E-mail: hurstin@aol.com
Web: www.hurstin.com

Mark Hursty's passion is to bring the freedom of painting to typically static materials, such as glass and metal. He strives in both his cast glass installations and in his blown glass artworks to balance the luminous and textural aspects of glass in daring, yet lyrical, ways. Using color and abstraction ranging from lavish to sparse, Hursty invites the viewer to enjoy the play of changing light on his unique works.

EXHIBITIONS: *Emerging Artist Annual,* 2002, Marta Hewett Gallery, Louisville, KY; RISD Alumni Show, 2001, Kälin Gallery/Trinity Communications, Boston, MA; *Second Nature,* 2001, Gallery 5 North, Boston, MA; *Chroma,* 2001, Gallery 5 North, Boston, MA; RISD Alumni Exhibition, 2000, Gallery 5 North, Boston, MA

PUBLICATIONS: *Louisville Eccentric Observer,* February, 2002

MARIE-LAURE ILIE
pp. 304

Marilor Art Studio
106 Via Sevilla
Redondo Beach, CA 90277
TEL/FAX 310-375-4977
E-mail: marilorilie@earthlink.net

Ilie's large abstract compositions achieve rich painterly effects by combining layers of sheer mesh with painted polyester fabric lightly coated with a special varnish. This technique ensures exceptional colorfastness, durability and easy maintenance. Ilie is also known for her sophisticated layered silk wall hangings.

For the past 25 years, Ilie has exhibited extensively in the United States and Europe. She has created many commissions for residential and corporate collectors.

GUILD SOURCEBOOKS: *THE GUILD 4, 5; Designer's 7, 8, 9, 10, 11, 12, 13, 14*

HUBERT J!
pp. 263

Photos As Art
PO Box 9657
Marina Del Rey, CA 90295
TEL 310-398-9444
FAX 310-398-0035
E-mail: hubertj@photosasart.com
Web: www.PhotosAsArt.com

Hubert J! is a practicing radiologist and Doctor of Nuclear Medicine. As a photographer, his global quest for images is reflected in extensive archives, including Antarctica's thousands of penguins, exotic Chinese cormorant fishermen, native people worldwide and landscapes ranging from dramatic to soft, watercolor-like scenes. Special collections and sizes available. Photographic and Iris prints.

COLLECTIONS: UCLA Medical Center, Westwood, CA

EXHIBITIONS: Republique D'Elegance Gallery, 2000, Santa Monica, CA; Fara Fina Collection, 1999, Marina Del Rey, CA

PUBLICATIONS: National Geographic Traveler Calendar, 1996

SUSAN MARIE JOHNSON
pp. 277

1695 18th Street, Studio 310
San Francisco, CA 94107
TEL 415-643-3970
FAX 415-553-4182
E-mail: dave@reification.com

Susan Marie Johnson has been creating artwork for more than 30 years. She uses lines and repeated elements to create innovative and poetic images.

Commissions are available.

COMMISSIONS: Bistro Ralph, Healdsburg, CA

COLLECTIONS: M.H. de Young Memorial Museum, San Francisco, CA (promised gift)

EXHIBITIONS: Oakland Museum Sculpture Court, Oakland, CA; *10th International Biennial of Tapestry,* Lausanne, Switzerland; Gallery/Gallery, Kyoto, Japan; Museum of Contemporary Crafts, New York, NY; House of Culture, Nevers, France

MARIAN JONES
pp. 261

4527 Tremont Lane
Corona Del Mar, CA 92625
TEL 949-760-6575
FAX 949-760-9471
E-mail: mj1s@adelphia.net

Using combined images, close-up views and abstraction to create an altered awareness and connection, Marian Jones focuses on the interconnection, beauty and strangeness of nature's many forms. She works in color and black and white photography. Limited editions.

EXHIBITIONS: The Studio Galleries, Santa Fe, NM and San Diego, CA; Circle Fine Arts, Chicago, IL and Denver, CO; *Art, Design and Barbie: The Evolution of an Icon,* New York, NY

PUBLICATIONS: *Leg,* 1997

TED JONSSON
pp. 168

Humongous Arts
805 NE Northlake Way
Seattle, WA 98105
TEL 206-547-4552

When using less to achieve more, a refined simplicity of form, devoid of unintentional ambiguity, requires elegant crafting and fastidious finishing. Jonsson achieves these results through a conceptual design process combining the skills of sculptor, engineer and architect to design, fabricate and install site-specific sculpture and fountains. He has over 38 years of experience, with major commissions in national, state, corporate and private collections. Contemporary, distinctively innovative, durable sculptures range in scale from gallery to fountain to monumental.

COMMISSIONS: Federal Reserve Bank of San Francisco, Seattle Branch, 1991; Fair Oaks Center, 1980, Arlington, VA; Manoogan Collections, Marley Station, 1987, Glen Burnie, MD; Alaska Council on the Arts, 1976, University of Alaska, Anchorage; Jon and Mary Shirley, 2001, Medina, WA

BJ KATZ
pp. 66-67

Meltdown Glass Art & Design
PO Box 3850
Chandler, AZ 85244
TEL 480-633-3366
FAX 480-633-3344
E-mail: bjkatz@meltdownglass.com
Web: www.meltdownglass.com

Kiln-cast glass is the new frontier in art glass. Using this method, glass is molded and, at times, colored and shaped in large industrial kilns at temperatures up to 1600 degrees. Artwork can be fired multiple times until the desired effect is achieved. The creative process of BJ Katz is spontaneous. She begins with an overall concept and design for each work of art, but the nuances of each piece happen at the time of creation. Her artwork is "in process" until it feels fully evolved.

RECENT PROJECTS: QVC Store, Mall of America, Minneapolis, MN; Phelps Dodge Corporate Headquarters, Phoenix, AZ; Desert Ridge Marketplace, Phoenix, AZ; Texas Children's Hospital, Houston; public art project, Phoenix Children's Hospital, AZ

GUILD SOURCEBOOKS: *Architect's 14, 15; Designer's 14, 15; Architectural & Interior Art 16*

BJ KATZ
pp. 66-67

Meltdown Glass Art & Design
PO Box 3850
Chandler, AZ 85244
TEL 480-633-3366
FAX 480-633-3344
E-mail: bjkatz@meltdownglass.com
Web: www.meltdownglass.com

COMMISSIONS: Numerous private collections

EXHIBITIONS: One-person show, 2002, West Valley Art Museum, Surprise, AZ

AWARDS: Regional Craftsmanship Award, Southwest Region, 2000, Construction Specifications Institute

PUBLICATIONS: "Modern Masters" television special on women artisans in America, 2002, HGTV

GUY KEMPER
pp. 65

Kemper Studio
190 North Broadway
Lexington, KY 40507
TEL/FAX 859-254-3507
E-mail: kemperstudio@juno.com
Web: www.kemperstudio.com

Poetry of light and line, color and form. Only beauty matters. Guy Kemper's strength lies in quiet listening – to the architect, the client and the space itself. The right questions must be asked with an open, quiet mind to hear the correct answers. As an architectural glass artist, Kemper is concerned with creating the most beautiful work possible, regardless of the cost of the materials or the amount of time involved. He strives for a harmonious design that will outlast fashion and rest tranquilly in its setting. He guarantees his work for his lifetime.

ELLEN MEARS KENNEDY
pp. 289

6500 Broxburn Drive
West Bethesda, MD 20817
TEL 301-320-9014
FAX 301-320-9044
E-mail: emearskenn@aol.com

Ellen Mears Kennedy's artwork is constructed of hundreds of double-sided papers, all handmade in her studio from pigmented pulp. Each paper has a left and right side that displays a unique shade. When the paper is folded, one color shows on the left side and a second color shows on the right. As viewers walk past each construction, the colors subtly change as they see alternating sides of the design.

GUILD SOURCEBOOKS: *Architectural & Interior Art 16*

LISA KESLER
pp. 246

Lisa Kesler Fine Art
9250 15th Avenue NW
Seattle, WA 98117
TEL 206-782-3730
FAX 206-784-3304
E-mail: lisa@lkesler.com
Web: www.lkesler.com

Lisa Kesler's mixed-media works on paper and canvas integrate printmaking, collage and painting. She continually experiments with techniques and materials, and it is this act of experimentation that inspires her as an artist. She is intrigued by the possibilities of repetition and attributes her attraction to the patchwork in the quilts and farmland of her childhood. In her art, she stylizes forms into simpler geometric shapes and juxtaposes bold colors in fanciful compositions. Contrasts between light and dark are central to her art. Kesler's work can be found in private and corporate collections throughout the country. Unframed images on paper or canvas range from 6" x 6" to 6' x 8'. Commissions welcome. A color catalog of her work is available.

COLLECTIONS: Riversoft Corporation, San Francisco, CA: Alexis Hotel, Seattle, WA; Microcrafts, Redmond, WA

RAIN KIERNAN
pp. 147

94 Birch Hill Road
Weston, CT 06883
TEL 203-226-5045
FAX 203-227-3187
E-mail: rain@rainkiernan.com
Web: www.rainkiernan.com

Rain Kiernan creates sculpture in marble, bronze, stainless steel and alternative media, including fiberglass and cement. Her abstracts include both large-scale outdoor works and smaller interior sculpture. Kiernan's forms are both free-form and derivative and are characterized by her unique style, which features powerful but sensuous curves, relieved by supporting planes. The artist has won several awards of merit for sculpture and is represented in various U.S. galleries. Kiernan, who has been showing her sculpture professionally since 1990, works with architects, designers and art consultants to create work for public parks, commercial property and private residences.

COMMISSIONS: Bristol Community College, Fall River, MA; Waveny Public Park, New Canaan, CT; private homes and businesses in New York City, Atlanta, Palm Beach, Greenwich, CT, and Southampton, NY

STEPHEN KNAPP
pp. 63, 97

74 Commodore Road
Worcester, MA 01602-2792
TEL 508-757-2507
FAX 508-797-3228
E-mail: sk@stephenknapp.com
Web: www.stephenknapp.com

Stephen Knapp is internationally renowned for his large-scale works of art in public, corporate and private collections, collaborating with architects and designers here and abroad. He is known for his complex walls in kiln-formed art glass, his sculptural light paintings and his carved slate and mosaic tile installations. Working in kiln-formed, cast and dichroic glass, he has combined steel, glass, wood and stone for furniture, sculpture and lighting. Having researched materials for public art for many years, he frequently writes and lectures on architectural art glass, the collaborative process and the integration of art and architecture. He is the author of *The Art of Glass* (1998), "A Guide to Architectural Art Glass" (*Architectural Record,* May 1995) and "Architectural Art Glass" (*Glass Magazine,* May 1995).

GUILD SOURCEBOOKS: *Architect's 8, 9, 10, 11, 12, 13, 14, 15; Architectural & Interior Art 16*

STEPHEN KNAPP
pp. 63, 97

74 Commodore Road
Worcester, MA 01602-2792
TEL 508-757-2507
FAX 508-797-3228
E-mail: sk@stephenknapp.com
Web: www.stephenknapp.com

Mr. Knapp's work has appeared in countless international books and publications, including *Architectural Glass Art, Artisans Glass, Art & Antiques, Architectural Record, Honoho Geijutsu, Identity, Interior Design, Interiors, Nikkei Architecture, Progressive Architecture* and *The New York Times.*

RECENT PROJECTS: Walter Reed Army Institute of Research; Florida Department of Health; Love Library, University of Nebraska; Sam Nunn Federal Center, Atlanta, GA; Worcester Public Library; Arpeggio, Pasadena, CA; Worcester Medical Center; Women and Babies Hospital, Lancaster, PA

COMMISSIONS: Kilroy Airport Center, Long Beach, CA; Fox Chase Cancer Institute, Philadelphia, PA; Sprint, Washington, DC; Dana Farber Cancer Institute, Boston, MA; CNA Insurance Companies, Chicago, IL; Royal Caribbean Cruise Lines

KORYN ROLSTAD STUDIOS
pp. 98

Bannerworks, Inc.
2610 Western Avenue
Seattle, WA 98121
TEL 206-448-1003
FAX 206-448-1204
E-mail: koryn@krstudios.com
Web: www.krstudios.com

Koryn Rolstad established her internationally recognized business in Seattle in 1975. Working with architects and designers, she creates projects to soften hard architectural lines, diffuse light in various settings, and incorporate color and form to fill large spaces. Her studio facilitates design, engineering and fabrication (using metal, textiles, mixed media and higher computer technologies), as well as construction installation for all projects.

PUBLICATIONS: *This Way: Signage Design for Public Spaces,* 2000

CRAIG KRAFT
pp. 278

Kraft Studio
931 R Street NW
Washington, DC 20001
TEL 202-588-9655
FAX 202-588-1012
E-mail: neonman454@aol.com
Web: www.craigkraftstudio.com

Craig Kraft has gained national recognition as a Smithsonian presenter and National Endowment for the Arts recipient from the District of Columbia. He combines the dynamism of the human figure with the vitality and versatility of neon light. By fabricating his own neon tubing, he is able to simultaneously incorporate light into his copper life-cast figures.

COMMISSIONS: Private residence, 1999, West Virginia; Rhode Island School of Design, 1998, Providence, RI; Citibank, 1997, Washington, DC

COLLECTIONS: French Consulate, New Orleans, LA; Museum of Neon Art, Los Angeles, CA

GUILD SOURCEBOOKS: *Architect's 12, 15*

SILJA TALIKKA LAHTINEN
pp. 247

Silja's Fine Art Studio
5220 Sunset Trail
Marietta, GA 30068
TEL 770-993-3409
FAX 770-992-0350
E-mail: pentec@mindspring.com
Web: www.artmarketing.com/gallery/lahtinen/lahtinen.html

Silja Lahtinen's work draws from the myths, landscape, folk songs and textiles of her native Finland. She is especially inspired by Lapland Shamanism in her paintings, collages, wall panels, prints and drums.

COLLECTIONS: Chattahoochee Valley Museum of Art, La Grange, GA; Mukkulan Koulu, Lahti, Finland; Santa Barbara Museum of Art, CA

AWARDS: State of Georgia Award for Women in the Visual Arts, 1997

EXHIBITIONS: Galleria ARS ARRAKOSKI, 2000, Padasjoki, Finland; *Women's Caucus of Art,* 2001, Barbara Archer Gallery, Atlanta, GA

GUILD SOURCEBOOKS: *Gallery 1, 2, 3; Designer's 9, 10, 11*

TUCK LANGLAND
pp. 114

12632 Anderson
Granger, IN 46530
TEL/FAX 574-272-2708
E-mail: tuckandjan@aol.com

Tuck Langland specializes in figurative bronze sculptures for gardens and public spaces. His work is available from his catalog or by commission. Tuck is a fellow in the National Sculpture Society and a member of the National Academy of Art.

RECENT PROJECTS: *Circle of Life,* four, ten-foot figures representing creation, life, transformation and dormancy, Bronson Hospital, Kalamazoo, MI; *Herman B Wells Plaza* at Indiana University; five seven-foot figures for Hillman Cancer Center, Pittsburgh, PA; entry archway dedicated to educators, Mishawaka, IN

COLLECTIONS: Smithsonian Collections, Midwest Museum of American Art, Minnesota Museum of American Art, Weisman Museum

GUILD SOURCEBOOKS: *Architect's 8, 9, 10, 11, 12, 13, 14; Architectural & Interior Art 16*

LAUREN CAMP, FIBER ARTIST
pp. 301

25 Theresa Lane
Santa Fe, NM 87507
TEL 505-474-7943
E-mail: lauren@laurencamp.com
Web: www.laurencamp.com

Lauren Camp creates original fiber works with the soul of jazz and the joy of color. She works intuitively, combining texture and pattern to design vibrant, abstract studies. Exceptional handwork, glorious hand-dyed and digitally printed fabric and dense machine quilting define her signature style. Her award-winning pieces have been exhibited internationally.

COLLECTIONS: Sherwin Miller Museum of Jewish Art, Tulsa, OK; Sheriff's Substation & Communications Center, Albuquerque, NM; Vista Grande Community Center, Sandia Park, NM

GUILD SOURCEBOOKS: *Designer's 15; Architectural & Interior Art 16*

MARLENE LENKER
pp. 248

28 Northview Terrace
Cedar Grove, NJ 07009
TEL 973-239-8671

Lenker Fine Arts
13 Crosstrees Hill Road
Essex, CT 06426
TEL 860-767-2098 (Studio)
E-mail: lenkerart@prodigy.net
Web: www.guild.com

Marlene Lenker is a painter, layerist and colorist, working on canvas and paper in transparent and opaque layers. Her brushstrokes and marks are unique, intuitive expressions of energy and spirit. Her monotypes and collages are evocative abstract layers of mixed media.

COLLECTIONS: American Airlines, Lever Bros., Arthur Young, PepsiCo, Kidder Peabody, Union Carbide, Pfizer, Warner-Lambert, Vista Hotels, Hoffman-LaRoche, Merrill Lynch

PUBLICATIONS: *Bridging Time and Space*, 1999; *Layering*, 1991; *Who's Who in America; Who's Who of American Artists; Who's Who of Women Artists; Who's Who of World Women*

GUILD SOURCEBOOKS: *Designer's 10, 12, 13, 15; Architectural & Interior Art 16*

LEPOWORKS, INC.
pp. 170-171

David Lepo and Robert Lepo
4640 Allentown Road
Lima, OH 45807
TEL 419-339-5370
E-mail: dlepo@woh.rr.com
Web: www.lepoworks.com

LepoWorks is composed of a family of artists who use their individual talents to create work that reveals the studio's one-of-a-kind philosophy. For 30 years, LepoWorks has designed private, public and corporate art to match a client's particular aesthetic preferences. The studio enhances interior and exterior architectural elements and spaces, offering artistic solutions while meeting budget and deadline demands. LepoWorks expresses its diversity through a multitude of materials used in traditional and contemporary styles.

GUILD SOURCEBOOKS: *Architect's 8, 9, 10, 11, 12, 13; Architectural & Interior Art 16*

LINDA M. LEVITON
pp. 279

Linda Leviton Sculpture
1011 Colony Way
Columbus, OH 43235
TEL 614-433-7486
E-mail: lindaleviton@columbus.rr.com

Linda Leviton creates modular wall sculpture that evokes the color and texture of nature. Her designs are executed in modules that can be hung to form one large piece or mounted as separate units. Using etchings, dyes, patinas and metal-forming techniques, Linda creates artwork that is flexible and easy to hang. Please contact Linda for color reproductions of her work.

RECENT PROJECTS: Profiled on HGTV's "Modern Masters"

COMMISSIONS: Northwest Airlines, Detroit, MI; Longmont Clinics, CO; WICHE, Inc., Boulder, CO; State of Ohio, Columbus, OH

AWARDS: Cheongju International Craft Biennale, Korea

PUBLICATIONS: *Color on Metal*, 2001; *Niche Magazine*, Autumn 2001

GUILD SOURCEBOOKS: *Designer's 15, Architectural & Interior Art 16*

JOYCE P. LOPEZ
pp. 264

Joyce Lopez Studio
1147 West Ohio Street #304
Chicago, IL 60622-5874
TEL 312-243-5033
FAX 312-243-7566
E-mail: joycelopez@aol.com
Web: joycelopez.com

Photography: In series of black-and-white or color prints. Sculpture: Interior wall-hung works, French thread, chrome steel tubes.

COLLECTIONS: Nokia Collection; City of Chicago; Health South; Sony Corporation

EXHIBITIONS: Riga, Latvia, 2001; International Tapestry Exhibition, Beijing, China, 2000; San Diego Art Institute, 2000

PUBLIC ART: Washington State; Art in Architecture, State of Illinois

PUBLICATIONS (cover art): College math textbook, Pearson Education; College math textbook series (four titles), Harper Collins; *Made in Illinois*

GUILD SOURCEBOOKS: *THE GUILD 1, 2, 3, 4, 5; Designer's 6, 7, 8, 9, 10, 11, 12, 13, 14, 15; Architectural & Interior Art 16*

LUKE DAVID SCULPTURE
pp. 148

Luke David
325 Odense
Buellton, CA 93427
TEL 805-252-8864
FAX 253-399-7647
E-mail: lukedavid@earthlink.net
Web: www.lukedavidsculpture.com

Luke David sculpts with silicon bronze and stainless steel for public or private commissions. He also makes large-scale complex fountains and site-focused water sculptures. Beginning with the stylization of recognizable forms, Luke David creates with technical excellence, resulting in breathtaking work that relates to individual and universal themes. Luke David brings into the world works that express a sense of purpose beyond ornamental status. Ascending to a level of visual poetry, his sculptures have depth beyond their inherent elegance and beauty.

Luke David welcomes commissions for public and private spaces.

LYON SPIRO GLASS
pp. 64

Jacqueline Spiro Balderson
17283 Hwy 82
Carbondale, CO 81623
TEL/FAX 970-963-8535
E-mail: jacq@sopris.net
Web: www.lyonglass.com

Lyon Spiro Glass specializes in hot-cast glass panels as architectural elements. They hand carve each resin-bonded sand mold to create unique castings, which can be up to 48" x 48" and from 1" to 4" thick. Each panel displays a high relief design that mates with adjacent panels to create windows, doors, walls, floors, furnishings and more. Lyon Spiro Glass works with architects, contractors and designers to create original, dynamic architectural components. The artists' work can be found nationally in private, corporate and public spaces. To view recent commissions, please visit the website at www.lyonglass.com. Brochures are available upon request.

ELIZABETH MacDONALD
pp. 35

Box 186
Bridgewater, CT 06752
TEL 860-354-0594
FAX 860-350-4052
E-mail: epmacd@earthlink.net
Web: www.garden-art.com/sculpture/macdonald/elizabeth.html

Elizabeth MacDonald produces tile paintings that suggest the patinas of age. These compositions are suitable for in- or out-of-doors and take the form of freestanding columns, wall panels or architectural installations.

COMMISSIONS: Conrad International Hotel, Hong Kong; St. Luke's Hospital, Denver, CO; Department of Environmental Protection, Hartford, CT (Percent for Art)

EXHIBITIONS: New Arts Gallery, 2001, Litchfield, CT; The Works Gallery, Philadelphia, PA

AWARDS: State of Connecticut Governor's Arts Award, 1999

GUILD SOURCEBOOKS: *THE GUILD 1, 2, 3, 4, 5; Architect's 6, 7, 8, 9, 10, 11, 12, 13, 14, 15; Designer's: 6, 8, 9, 10, 11, 12, 13, 14, 15; Architectural & Interior Art 16*

ANNE MARCHAND
pp. 249

Marchand Studio
1413 Seventeenth Street NW
Washington, DC 20036
TEL 202-265-5882
FAX 202-265-0232
E-mail: foster99@ix.netcom.com
Web: www.annemarchand.com

From private commissions to site-specific murals, Anne Marchand's vibrant cityscapes are colorful expressions of "joie de vivre." Combining architectural geometry with lyricism, her oil and acrylic techniques reflect the vitality of American cities. Marchand achieves a richness of color and surface texture, bringing a new, tactile dimension to her paintings.

COMMISSIONS: Westminster Playground mural, 2002, Washington, DC; Richards, Spears, Kibbe & Orbe, 2001, Washington, DC

COLLECTIONS: Alabama Power Company; AT&T Broadband; DC Commission on the Arts and Humanities; Kennedy Center; U.S. Trust

PUBLICATIONS: *Object Lessons,* 2001

GUILD SOURCEBOOKS: *Designer's 13, 14, 15; Architectural & Interior Art 16*

CORK MARCHESCHI
pp. 169

192 Connecticut
San Francisco, CA 94107
TEL 650-738-2932
FAX 650-355-3249
E-mail: corkmarch@earthlink.net
Web: www.corkm.com

Cork Marcheschi's work is about formality and fun. He uses a variety of materials that are well suited for light play. In the day they reflect light and in the evening they glow from an internal light source. Frequently, the light is animated and the effect is a very natural changing of intensity and position. The pieces are designed to function well in daylight and at night, as well as in all climates.

RECENT PROJECTS: New Jersey Transit, 2002; San Jose Repertory Theatre, 2001; Anchorage School for the Deaf, 2000; Singapore, Millennium Walk, 1999

EXHIBITIONS: Museum of Neon Art, Los Angeles, CA, 2002; Braunstein Quay Gallery, San Francisco, CA, 2000 and 2002 (solo show)

GUILD SOURCEBOOKS: *Architect's 8, 11*

CORK MARCHESCHI JAMES NOWAK
pp. 215

192 Connecticut
San Francisco, CA 94107
TEL 650-738-2932
FAX 650-355-3249
E-mail: corkmarch@earthlink.net

Cork Marcheschi and James Nowak produce, design and engineer illuminated glass fixtures. Blown forms, as well as flat glass and castings, are illuminated with neon and halogen sources. Neon tubes and transformers fit into blown glass forms, giving a very saturated and even light; there is never a hot spot. The mechanical support systems are designed to be very durable and subtle. The effect is one of familiar comfort with something you have never seen before.

COMMISSIONS: Monterey Bay Aquarium, 2002; San Jose Repertory Theatre, 2001; Auroras Café, 1998; Carroll Studios, Seattle, WA, 1999

MARK HOPKINS SCULPTURE, INC.
pp. 115

Mark Hopkins
21 Shorter Industrial Boulevard
Rome, GA 30165
TEL 706-235-8773
FAX 706-235-2814
E-mail: markhopkinsbronze@earthlink.net
Web: www.markhopkinssculpture.com

From children, to wildlife, to western subjects and more, Mark Hopkins is known for his diversity and unique ability to capture the essence of any theme he sculpts. "Bronze in motion" is a trademarked term often used to describe Hopkins' beautiful and flowing style.

RECENT PROJECTS: Alabama Sports Hall of Fame, Chicago Bulls, City of Atlanta, Coca-Cola Corporation, Merrill Lynch

PUBLICATIONS: *Southwest Art, Wildlife Art, Traditional Building*

GUILD SOURCEBOOKS: *Architectural & Interior Art 16*

WELLS MASON
pp. 203

Ironwood Industries
204/206 Commerce Street
Coupland, TX 78615
TEL 512-856-1186
FAX 512-856-2186
E-mail: wells@ironwoodindustries.com
Web: www.ironwoodindustries.com

Mean what you build. For Wells Mason, this idea is at the heart of every commission. Wells is the owner of Ironwood Industries, a custom woodworking and metal-working studio. He's also the designer and chief craftsman. He believes that strong design is just as important as superb craftsmanship. His specialty is combining seemingly disparate materials, like exotic wood veneer and wrought steel, to create works that are uniquely dynamic. Please feel free to contact the artisan directly if you'd like to discuss a project.

MOLLIE MASSIE
pp. 47

Myers Massie Studio, Inc.
PO Box 30073
8602 Granville Street
Vancouver, BC V6P 6S3, Canada
TEL 604-266-5009
FAX 604-266-8431
E-mail: mollie@myersmassiestudio.com
Web: www.myersmassiestudio.com

Mollie Massie works with architects, interior designers and individual clients to create one-of-a-kind, site-specific artistic metalwork. She tells her clients "the sky's the limit — if you can imagine it, I can most likely create it for you." Massie's metalwork includes tables, chairs, gates and chandeliers, as well as fireplace screens and tools, mirror frames and custom cabinet pulls.

COMMISSIONS: Grouse Mountain Resort; Vail Resort; Four Seasons Resorts; Fairmont Hotels; private homes

PUBLICATIONS: *Metropolitan Home, Architectural Digest, Log Home Living, Log Home Design Ideas, Canadian House & Home, Syle At Home, Better Homes & Gardens*

GUILD SOURCEBOOKS: *Architectural & Interior Art 16*

R.W. McBRIDE
pp. 116

R.W. McBride Studio
80 North Roop Street
Susanville, CA 96130
TEL 530-257-3985
FAX 530-257-7999
E-mail: ron@rwmcbridestudio.com
Web: www.rwmcbridestudio.com

Ron McBride's love for nature has driven him to become an accomplished wildlife sculptor. Working with hand-forged metal, chiseled stone and other elements, McBride brings his sculptures to life with texture and metal dye finishes. By incorporating both hot and cold forging in his fabricated sculptures, McBride creates one-of-a-kind interior and exterior pieces for private, corporate and public commissions. A professional artist for more than 30 years, McBride knows the importance of quality, price and timely delivery. He has developed the skills and understanding to work well in collaborative efforts. Sculptures range from pedestal to monumental.

GUILD SOURCEBOOKS: *Architect's 14; Architectural & Interior Art 16*

McCONNELL-COLLINS GLASS STUDIO
pp. 68

Vivienne McConnell and Valerie Collins
71B Pearl Street
Schuylerville, NY 12871
TEL 877-369-1818
TEL 518-695-4062
E-mail: mccglass@aol.com

McConnell-Collins Glass Studio has chosen their medium for love of light. Art and craft unite to fuse glass and light into work with a luminous life of its own. Since 1980, the McConnell-Collins Studio has created site-specific stained and cast glass panels for public and private, indoor and outdoor spaces. Their art glass is unique in design and specifically suited to clients' needs.

RECENT PROJECTS: Property and Facilities Management Center, City of Durham, NC; First Reformed Church, Schenectady, NY; Crowfoot Valley Coffee Company, Castle Rock, CO; Randy Smith Middle School, Fairbanks, AK

COMMISSIONS: Oregon State University, 1998, Corvallis, OR; Mirror Lake Middle School, 1997, Chugiak, AK; Nesbett Federal Courthouse, Anchorage, AK

GUILD SOURCEBOOKS: *Architect's 13, 14, 15*

SUSAN McGEHEE
pp. 280

Metallic Strands
540 23rd Street
Manhattan Beach, CA 90266
TEL 310-545-4112
FAX 310-546-7152
E-mail: susan@metalstrands.com
Web: www.metalstrands.com

Susan McGehee produces two bodies of work: woven metal weavings and sculptural wire kimonos. Applying traditional textile techniques, she weaves wires and metals into striking forms that seem to float on the wall. The kimonos are created from bronze or stainless steel screening, then embellished with scraps of wire from the weavings and recycled electronic remnants. Even though the pieces use late 20th-century recycled materials, they have a look and feel of previous centuries. These lightweight, easily installed and maintained pieces complement both residential and commercial settings.

GUILD SOURCEBOOKS: *Designer's 12, 13, 14, 15; Architectural & Interior Art 16*

NOELLE McGUIRE
pp. 305

Taipéis Safan
497 Reis Avenue
Oradell, NJ 07649
TEL 201-261-5336
FAX 201-261-3154
E-mail: noellemcguire@worldnet.att.net
Web: www.e-noelle.net

An interior designer for 29 years, Noelle has found in hand-woven tapestries a technique that truly expresses her vision. She combines her love of painting with the tactile qualities of textiles to reflect the diversity of the world around her. Highly regarded for her ability to design and create custom work to suit specific client needs, she can express many different styles and cultural motifs. Prices range from $95 to $145 per square foot with pieces available from stock or as commissions.

EXHIBITIONS: Fall Arts, 2000 and 1999, Franklin Lakes, NJ; Edgewater Arts Festival, 1998, Edgewater, NJ

GUILD SOURCEBOOKS: *Architect's 15; Designer's 15*

TRENA McNABB
pp. 225

McNabb Studio, Inc.
PO Box 327
Bethania, NC 27010
TEL 336-924-6053
FAX 336-924-4854
E-mail: trena@tmcnabb.com
Web: www.tmcnabb.com

Trena McNabb's *Painted Stories* are created by juxtaposing images transparently, one over the other, telling the story of a facility or company in pictures. Her work usually consists of large geometrically shaped configurations of canvas panels, sometimes with Plexiglas or suspended from ceilings.

Major installations of her work are represented in permanent collections for public buildings, corporations, a half-dozen hospitals across the U.S., a museum, a factory in China and a company in Japan.

GUILD SOURCEBOOKS: *Architect's 6, 7, 8, 9, 10, 11, 12, 13, 14, 15, 16; Designer's 8, 14*

MEAMAR
pp. 226

37338 Fowler Street
Newark, CA 94560
TEL 510-435-4152
Web: www.meamar.com

For Meamar, each work is as individual as the client. He goes to great lengths to reveal the appropriate feeling for the piece, transforming any interior environment with a magical depth. The results are breathtaking.

Meamar's expertise is the result of years of study under the masters in Italy as well as personal experience. He also works in other mediums, including modern sculpture and relief.

COMMISSIONS: Disney Co., Los Angeles, CA; E-Trade mansion, San Francisco Bay area

PUBLICATIONS: *Sunset Magazine*

GUILD SOURCEBOOKS: *Architectural & Interior Art 16*

JOHN MEDWEDEFF
pp. 172-173

Medwedeff Forge & Design
695 Future Lane
Murphysboro, IL 62966
TEL 618-687-4304
FAX 618-687-5220
E-mail: jmedwedeff@aol.com

Metal heated in the forge and hammered, or cold-formed under pressure, assumes plasticity that can be manipulated to mimic qualities of growth, movement and rigidity. Inspired by his direct experience with botanical, aquatic and atmospheric phenomena, John Medwedeff has developed a visual vocabulary with which he explores the natural world in relation to architecture. Master craftsmanship and aesthetic considerations result in finished work that fully integrates the concept and function of the sculptural form.

COLLECTIONS: Minneapolis Institute of Art; Illinois State Museum; National Ornamental Metal Museum, Memphis, TN; City of Memphis, TN; State of Illinois; Christ Church Cathedral, St Louis, MO; City of Clarksville, TN; Shakespeare's Globe Theatre, London, England

MEG BLACK HANDMADE PAPER PAINTINGS
pp. 291

Meg Black
48 Prospect Street
Topsfield, MA 01983
TEL/FAX 978-887-8670
E-mail: mblack86@aol.com
Web: www.megblack.com

Meg Black's landscape, seascape and garden paintings are created exclusively from fibrous paper pulp; no paint of any kind is used on the surface. Each pulp painting is pigmented with 100% pure, non-fading, acid-free pigments and is carefully treated so that it may be hung with or without glass. The unique process and masterful craftsmanship provide a seductive, textured surface that lends itself to the natural subject matter of Black's artwork.

COLLECTIONS: Fidelity Investments, Harvard University

GEORGE THOMAS MENDEL
pp. 265

PO Box 13605
Pittsburgh, PA 15243
TEL 412-563-7918
Web: www.photo-now.com
Web: www.guild.com

George Thomas Mendel, a location/freelance and fine art photographer, has been working with the medium for more than 20 years. In this time he has produced a variety of portfolios, which include architecture, waterscapes and humanitarian projects.

Primarily working in black and white as an art form, limited-edition prints are produced by way of traditional fiber-based gelatin silver (cold or warm tone per request).

His creative use of light and composition is matched by his master craftsmanship in the darkroom, producing the highest level of quality and archival stability. Project portfolios are available for view on his website gallery, and commissioned project and documentation services are available by request.

PUBLICATIONS: *Beautiful Things,* 2000

GUILD SOURCEBOOKS: *Designer's 15; Architectural & Interior Art 16*

AMOS MILLER
pp. 251

5741 SW 84th Street
Miami, FL 33143
TEL 305-668-3536
E-mail: amiller1307@earthlink.net

Amos Miller's work exhibits brash spontaneity and verve in its sweeping linear brushstrokes and vivid color, indicative of a neo-fauvism. His compositions of striving figures occupy stark environments with explosive tension, challenging and confronting while eliciting empathy. Paint, emotion and method mirror the subject depicted, transfixing the viewer to the canvas and demanding visual participation in the unfolding event.

COMMISSIONS: Private collectors: Asheville, NC; Atlanta, GA; Cleveland, OH; Miami, FL

COLLECTIONS: Constitutional Court of South Africa, Johannesburg, South Africa; Masur Museum of Art, Monroe, LA; Progressive Corporation, Cleveland, OH

AWARDS: Best of Show, 28th Annual Juried Competition, 2001, Masur Museum of Art, Monroe, LA

BRIDGETTE MONGEON
pp. 117

Sculptor, Bridgette Mongeon
610 Heidrich
Houston, TX 77018
TEL/FAX 713-699-1739
E-mail: bridgette@creativesculpture.com
Web: www.creativesculpture.com

For 20 years, Bridgette Mongeon has breathed life into clay and bronze. She strives to capture the spirit and essence of individuals and works with clients in a collaboration of creativity to make commissions personal and intimate. Ms. Mongeon creates memorials, architectural elements, garden art, furniture, planters and fountains in bronze, clay, concrete, resin and other media. Her vast knowledge of different casting and reproduction techniques helps serve the individual needs of each client. Her work is collected by individuals for their homes and gardens and also appears in parks and churches. Ms. Mongeon, and her work, have been featured in numerous publications and on television shows.

COLLECTIONS: Hevrdejs art collection; Kipper Mease Sports Park; B.B. King; Willie Nelson; Bill Monroe; Nolan Ryan; Harry Sheppard

WILLIAM AND RENEE MORRIS
pp. 217

The William Morris Studio
1716 Ellie Court
Benicia, CA 94510
TEL/FAX 707-745-3907
E-mail: william@williammorrisstudio.com
Web: www.williammorrisstudio.com

William and Renee Morris handcraft lamps of hardwood and mica by allowing natural beauty to dictate final form. William uses only select fine woods, including mahogany and fallen redwood, in handcrafting each base. Renee accents art shades with hand-collected leaves and hand-cut motifs. Together they create table, desk and floor lamps, which radiate elegance and quality in corporate and private settings.

COMMISSIONS: Edmonds Community College Library, Lynnwood, WA

AWARDS: The Rosen Group's Niche Award, 1997 and 1996

JAMES C. MYFORD
pp. 149

320 Cranberry Road
Grove City, PA 16127
TEL/FAX 724-458-9672

James C. Myford's sculptures are found in corporate, museum, university, public and private collections throughout the United States and internationally. Myford's cast and fabricated aluminum sculptures, reflect a subtle inner strength and spirit that expand and interact gracefully with space.

RECENT PROJECTS: Medical College of Wisconsin; Aluminum Company of America Awards of Excellence

COMMISSIONS: Soffer Organization, 2000, Pittsburgh, PA; Tracewell Systems, 2000, Columbus, OH

COLLECTIONS: University of Michigan, Ann Arbor; British Airways, Pittsburgh International Airport, PA

EXHIBITIONS: Associated Artist of Pittsburgh, Museum of Art, 2001 and 2000, PA; Westmoreland County Museum of Art, 2001, Greensburgh, PA

GUILD SOURCEBOOKS: *Architect's 9, 10, 11, 12, 13, 14, 15; Architectural & Interior Art 16*

JAMES C. NAGLE
pp. 252

James C. Nagle Fine Art
1136 East Commonwealth Place
Chandler, AZ 85225-5716
TEL 480-963-8195
FAX 480-857-3188 (call first)
E-mail: extraice@msn.com
Web: www.jcnaglefineart.com

Since the mid-1970s, James C. Nagle has performed a Herculean task: to continually change his view of life and express it through the dual arts of sculpture and painting. Nagle's abstract paintings are charged with complexity and sensuous color. Commissions are welcomed.

GUILD SOURCEBOOKS: *Architect's 15; Designer's 15; Architectural & Interior Art 16*

MARLIES MERK NAJAKA
pp. 253

241 Central Park West
New York, NY 10024
TEL 212-580-0058
E-mail: najaka@att.net
Web: www.watercolorart.com

Marlies Merk Najaka's watercolor paintings are reproduced as limited-edition giclée prints. The giclées are printed on a heavy-weight archival watercolor paper. Each print is signed, numbered and has a certificate of authenticity. Custom sizes and commissions are welcome. Her work has been nationally exhibited and is included in many corporate and private collections. To view additional paintings and biographical information, please visit the website. Brochure and price list are available upon request.

GUILD SOURCEBOOKS: *Designer's 14, 15; Architectural & Interior Art 16*

NATIONAL SCULPTORS' GUILD
pp. 174-175

2683 North Taft Avenue
Loveland, CO 80538
TEL 970-667-2015
FAX 970-667-2068
E-mail: nsg@frii.com
Web: www.columbinensg.com

Since 1992 The National Sculptors' Guild (NSG) has specialized in the placement of limited-edition and site-specific sculptures in bronze, stone and stainless steel. Headed by a team of designers, including director John W. Kinkade, NSG has installed monumental-scale work by Guild members in public and private collections throughout the world. Guild members are: Gary Alsum, Kathleen Caricof, Chapel, Tim Cherry, Dee Clements, Jane DeDecker, Lincoln Fox, Carol Gold, Bruce Gueswel, Denny Haskew, Tuck Langland, Mark Leichliter, Herb Mignery, Gino Miles, Leo E. Osborne, Rosetta, Sandy Scott, Sharles, Shirley Thomson-Smith, Kent Ullberg and C.T. Whitehouse.

GUILD SOURCEBOOKS: *Architect's 9, 10, 11, 12, 14, 15; Architectural & Interior Art 16*

NEW WORLD PRODUCTIONS
pp. 227

Skip Dyrda
253 South Links Avenue
Sarasota, FL 34236
TEL/FAX 941-366-5520
E-mail: painterskip@emurals.com
Web: www.emurals.com

New World Productions is owned and operated by Skip Dyrda, whose artistic knowledge and creativity can be found on furniture, *objets d'art,* walls, ceilings and just about any surface you can imagine. His eye for detail and originality are especially evident in his area of specialty, trompe l'oeil.

Dyrda's commissions can be found around the world from St. Armand's Circle to Buenos Aires.

RECENT PROJECTS: The Crisp Building mural, Sarasota, FL, 62' x 92'

EXHIBITIONS & AWARDS: "Best mural in town," The Crisp Building, Sarasota, FL, *Weekly Planet* readers award; "Best of public art in Sarasota 2000," *Sarasota Herald Tribune*

GUILD SOURCEBOOKS: *Architect's 15; Architectural & Interior Art 16*

NICHOLAS SIMILE FURNITURE
pp. 204

Nicholas Simile
PO Box 511
Rosendale, NY 12472
TEL/FAX 845-658-3662

Nicholas Simile's work begins with references to fine art and design history. He uses restraint to accentuate the color and warmth of wood tone and grain pattern. In the finished piece, the form is pure and the function clear. All work is custom built and made to order. Nicholas Simile often collaborates with interior designers on room-specific pieces.

COMMISSIONS: Table bases and entertainment consol, 2001, private residence, Ulster County, NY; *Nile Cabinet* and *Night and Day Table*, 2001, private residence, Philadelphia, PA

COLLECTIONS: Private collections in Buenos Aires, Argentina; New York, NY; Jamesport, NY; Ulster County, NY

EXHIBITIONS: Frederick Williams Showroom, 2001, New York, NY; Neotu Gallery, New York, NY; Archetype Gallery, 1990-1995, New York, NY

PUBLICATIONS: *Object Lessons*, 2001; *Home* magazine, 1993; *Interni Magazine* (Italy), 1991

BRUCE A. NIEMI
pp. 176

Niemi Sculpture Gallery
13300 116th Street
Kenosha, WI 53142
TEL 262-857-3456
FAX 262-857-4567
E-mail: sculpture@bruceniemi.com
Web: www.bruceniemi.com

Bruce's sculptures range in size from tabletop interior pieces to site-specific public art. He also creates wall sculptures suitable for both interior and exterior locations. Niemi's welded stainless steel and bronze sculptures emanate aesthetics, balance, energy and structural integrity.

RECENT PROJECTS: Niemi Sculpture Gallery, representing over 20 sculptors with styles ranging from abstract to realism. Located on a 20-acre parcel with seven acres currently displaying outdoor works. Interior works may also be viewed on site.

GUILD SOURCEBOOKS: *Architect's 9, 10, 11, 14, 15; Architectural & Interior Art 16*

NANCY EGOL NIKKAL
pp. 257

22 Dogwood Lane
Tenafly, NJ 07670
TEL 201-568-0159
FAX 201-568-0873
E-mail: nancy@nikkal.com
Web: www.nikkal.com

Nancy Egol Nikkal's two-dimensional wall pieces in paint, collage and print media are included in private and public collections both nationally and internationally. Imagery is abstract, often figurative, with an emphasis on color, pattern and texture. Recent projects include giclee (Iris) prints for solo exhibitions and commissions.

RECENT PROJECTS: Two-person show, 2001, Berlex Laboratories Corporation Center, Montville and Wayne, NJ; solo exhibition, 2000, The Lippman Gallery, Congregation B'nai Jeshurun, Short Hills, NJ; solo exhibition, 2000, Clinical Center Galleries, National Institutes of Health, Bethesda, MD

COLLECTIONS: Cablevision, Pfizer, Hewlett Packard

GUILD SOURCEBOOKS: *Designer's 13, 15; Architectural & Interior Art 16*

JUDY NORDQUIST
pp. 120

Judy Nordquist Studio, Inc.
Sculptures in Bronze
5939 Lone Peak Drive
Evergreen, CO 80439
TEL 303-674-4559 or 800-234-0290
FAX 303-674-5640
E-mail: info@judynordquist.com
Web: www.judynordquist.com

From tabletop pieces to site-specific public art, Judy Nordquist has established the precedent for excellence in equine art. Her love and passion for the magnificent horse is revealed in breathtaking bronze sculptures where the exciting spirit of the horse comes alive! "Nature accomplishes a perfection that man is unable to achieve, but Nordquist is one of the few living sculptors who comes close to the achievement." (Robert Vavra, author, *Equus.*)

COMMISSIONS AND SALES INCLUDE: Monument, 1 1/5 life-size, Telluride, CO; Arabian Horse Foundation; Houston Livestock Show and Rodeo; His Majesty King Hassan II, King of Morocco

EXHIBITIONS: North American Sculpture Exhibition; American Academy of Equine Art; Western Academy of Women Artists

PAM MORRIS DESIGNS EXCITING LIGHTING
pp. 216

Pam Morris
14 East Sir Francis Drake Boulevard
Studio D
Larkspur, CA 94939
TEL 415-925-0840
FAX 415-925-1305
E-mail: lighting@sonic.net

Pam Morris, owner of EXCITING LIGHTING, is a distinguished design innovator. Her clients encompass top restaurants, hotels and private collectors, including Wolfgang Puck, Sugar Ray Leonard, Georgio Armani and the Hong Kong Regent Hotel. "In my work, I create highly original and evocative illuminated pieces. I use light, together with blown, slumped or cast glass and forged or cast metal, to create art pieces that reflect a special sense of place."

GUILD SOURCEBOOKS: *Architect's 12, 13, 15*

PANTE STUDIO
pp. 190-191

Michael Demetz
Minert 7
Ortisei, Italy 39046
TEL 011-39-0471-796514
FAX 011-39-0471-797523
E-mail: info@pantestudio.it
Web: www.pantestudio.it

Pante Studio combines the centennial tradition of wood sculpting with the demands of contemporary design. The studio's goal is to unite the profound beliefs of Christian faith — and/or the demands of public art —with the creativity of architects and artists. The studio develops statues, ornaments, altars, fountains and more, starting from the sketch board. Different woods, bronze, stones and fiberglass are used for liturgical and secular works.

RECENT PROJECTS: Holy Apostles Catholic Church, Meridian, ID; St. Francis Hospital, Milwaukee, WI; St. Conrad Catholic Church, Hohenems, Austria; Plan de Corones-Skiresort, Brunico, Italy

PEARL RIVER GLASS STUDIO, INC.
pp. 69

Andrew Cary Young
142 Millsaps Avenue
Jackson, MS 39202
TEL 601-353-2497
FAX 601-969-9315
E-mail: prgs@netdoor.com
Web: www.prgs.com

Pearl River Glass Studio is committed to pursuing the craft of stained glass as an art form. They work in a broad range of styles and employ a wide variety of methods. Central to their mission is the principle of applying creative solutions to complex problems where thoroughness and quality count.

AWARDS: Governor's Award for Excellence in the Arts, State of Mississippi, 2002

PUBLICATIONS: *The Stained Glass Association of America Sourcebook,* 1998, 1999, 2000, 2001

GUILD SOURCEBOOKS: *Architect's 15; Architectural & Interior Art 16*

CITY ARTS / G. BYRON PECK
pp. 229

Peck Studios
1857 Lamont Street NW
Washington, DC 20010
TEL/FAX 202-331-1966
E-mail: byronpeck@earthlink.net
Web: www.peckstudios.com
Web: www.cityartsdc.org

Full service studios for the production of public art, murals and mosaics for large-scale artwork or intimate private murals. Their studios have 25 years of experience working with architects, designers and organizations to create solutions for any environment.

RECENT PROJECTS: 1,500' mosaic on the Potomac River waterfront, Washington, DC; 100' mural for the city of Los Angeles, Cultural Affairs Department; two murals for the newly built visitors center at historic Mt. Vernon, VA; 60' mural for main subway station, Washington, DC

COLLECTIONS: The Kennedy Center for the Performing Arts; Chamber of Commerce, Washington, DC

GUILD SOURCEBOOKS: *Architect's 6, 7, 8, 9, 10, 11, 12, 13, 14, 15; Architectural & Interior Art 16*

PETER COLOMBO ARTISTIC MOSAICS
pp. 36

Peter Colombo
600 Huyler Street
South Hackensack, NJ 07606
TEL 201-641-7964
FAX 201-641-5884
E-mail: pcmosaic@worldnet.att.net
Web: www.petercolomboartisticmosaics.com

Peter Colombo is a graduate of the School of Visual Arts in New York City. The artist uses glass, handmade ceramic tile and natural stone to create site-specific mosaics in both public and private environments.

These media combine durability and low maintenance, while allowing full color and flexibility in design and style. The studio offers original or collaborative designs, fabrications from artwork and on-site installations.

GUILD SOURCEBOOKS: *Architect's 9, 10, 11, 12, 13, 14, 15; Architectural & Interior Art 16*

CHRISTOPHER PETRICH
pp. 266-267

CoolPhoto
3741 North 29th Street
Tacoma, WA 98407
TEL 253-752-4664
FAX 253-276-0116
E-mail: cpetrich@coolphoto.com
Web: www.CoolPhoto.com

Christopher Petrich's pictures possess a beauty, high and light, like the works in silver of the ancient Irish. Within his photographs, a simple line can swell to a great size and a looming mass can disappear in movement. Passion always informs his work, exposing darkness rimmed with humor. His art is fierce and exact and his ideas are cool.

"I force my compositions to resonate, to shudder. My pictures emerge as a moving surface to my eye, like wind on water."

Christopher Petrich

RECENT PROJECTS: *Two days in San Francisco with a No. 2 Folding Cartridge Hawk-Eye Model B; LumenAria: In the Key of Light; CoolPhoto Guide to Puget Sound Lighthouses*

CHRISTOPHER PETRICH
pp. 266-267

CoolPhoto
3741 North 29th Street
Tacoma, WA 98407
TEL 253-752-4664
FAX 253-276-0116
E-mail: cpetrich@coolphoto.com
Web: www.CoolPhoto.com

COLLECTIONS: Gordon Bowker, Seattle, WA; Catholic Community Services, Seattle, WA; Kathleen Flynn, AIA, Southport, CT; Franciscan Sisters, Portland, OR; Rick Gottas, Tacoma, WA; James Hauer, San Francisco, CA; James McGowan, Edinborough, Scotland; Phil Raymer, Redmond, WA; Alan Ross, Santa Fe, NM; Tacoma Public Library; Kirk Weller, Portland, OR; Morgan Stanley, Tacoma, WA

EXHIBITIONS & AWARDS: Tahoma Center Gallery, Tacoma, WA, 2000, 1996; GUILD.com, 1999; Borders Books, 1997; American Art Company, Tacoma, WA, 1993; Handforth Gallery, Tacoma, WA, 1993; Canon USA, Los Angeles, CA, 1985; Downtown Gallery, Tacoma, WA, 1984; Sandpiper Gallery, 1984; Grand Prize, Tacoma Art Museum, 1983; Tacoma Art Museum, Annual Photography Exhibit, 1975-83; Silver Image Gallery, 1974

ROBERT PFITZENMEIER
pp. 100

Metalmorphosis
111 First Street #1-3A
Jersey City, NJ 07302
TEL 201-659-7629
FAX 201-659-4203
Web: www.metalmorphosis.org

Pfitz designs his work with a sparseness and delicacy that transcends the limited space it occupies. These geometric abstractions enliven spaces with an elegant, upbeat spirit. Complex kinetics and a wide use of polychromed or anodized color support this atmosphere. Anodized zirconium responds to light, yielding a full spectrum of colors that vary with changing light conditions. For 25 years, Pfitz has been constructing sculpture and suspended installations for public, private and corporate clients.

GUILD SOURCEBOOKS: *THE GUILD 5; Architect's 6, 9, 11, 12, 13, 14, 15; Architectural & Interior Art 16*

BINH PHO
pp. 210

Wonders of Wood
48W175 Pine Tree Drive
Maple Park, IL 60151
TEL 630-365-5462
FAX 630-365-5837
E-mail: toriale@msn.com
Web: www.wondersofwood.net

Binh Pho is a Chicago-based artist who works primarily with wood. He combines lathe work, sculpting, airbrush and piercing techniques to create commanding primitive art forms.

COMMISSIONS: Honeywell Corporation, Cupertino, CA; Olympia Network, St. Louis, MO; Frontier Development, Denver, CO

COLLECTIONS: The White House, Washington, DC; Union Planters Bank, St. Louis, MO; Prudential, Brighton, MI

EXHIBITIONS: SOFA, 2002, New York, NY and Chicago, IL; Challenge VI, 2002, Indianapolis Museum of Art, IN

AWARDS: Niche Award Finalist, 2002; Best Design in Wood, Midwest Salute the Masters Art Festival, 1999

GUILD SOURCEBOOKS: *Designer's 15; Architectural & Interior Art 16*

LYN PIERRE
pp. 292

Zimbrelyn Paperworks
301 Adams NE
Albuquerque, NM 87108
TEL 505-256-7185
E-mail: lpierre@tvi.cc.nm.us

Most of Lyn Pierre's images evoke a sense of movement through abstraction, shapes and color. Each handmade paper piece is formed by painting, pouring or collaging pigmented pulp until her desired image is achieved. Each piece she creates is one of a kind.

COMMISSIONS: Artist Circle Gallery, Potomac, MD

EXHIBITIONS: *Magnifico, Art of Albuquerque*, NM, 1997

AWARDS: Annual Distinguished Teaching Award, 1993, Stephens College, Columbia, MO; Twelfth Annual National Print Exhibition, 1992, Artlink

PUBLICATIONS: *Fiber Arts Design Book Five*, 1995

GUILD SOURCEBOOKS: *Designer's 14*

BEV PRECIOUS
pp. 177

Precious Design Studios, Inc.
950 North Alabama Street
Indianapolis, IN 46202
TEL/FAX 317-631-6560
E-mail: bbprec@aol.com

The artist's use of dichroic glass enables color to transform such traditional materials as stainless steel, aluminum and limestone into highly kinetic sculpture. In large-scale public art, the color is not only contained in the sculpture, but reflected onto the surroundings, integrating the piece with its environment.

RECENT PROJECTS: University of Wisconsin, Madison; Merrill Lynch, Pennington, NJ; Miami University, Middletown, OH; Charlotte County Courthouse, Punta Gorda, FL

AWARDS: Design Award, 1998, AIA Georgia

GUILD SOURCEBOOKS: *Architect's 8, 9, 10, 11, 12, 13, 14, 15*

JOHN PUGH
pp. 230

PO Box 1332
Los Gatos, CA 95031
TEL 408-353-3370
FAX 408-353-1223
Web: www.artofjohnpugh.com

John Pugh's trompe l'oeil murals transform flat walls into other "spaces." He has been awarded an array of national public art projects, and articles about John's work have appeared throughout the world. For all murals, indoor or outdoor, large or small, projects may be painted in Pugh's studio on canvas or non-woven media (outdoor material) and then site-specifically integrated. Prints are also available.

COMMISSIONS: Cities of Anchorage, Boise, Denver, Dublin, Miami, Palm Desert, Sacramento, San Jose, South San Francisco and Syracuse; University of Alaska; California State University, Chico; University of Northern Florida; Stanford University

PUBLICATIONS: *Time, Focus, Artweek, Via, Art Business News, Southwest Art, L.A. Times, New York Times, San Francisco Examiner*

MAYA RADOCZY
pp. 70

Contemporary Art Glass
PO Box 31422
Seattle, WA 98103
TEL 206-527-5022
FAX 206-524-9226
E-mail: maya@serv.net
Web: www.mayaglass.com

Maya Radoczy is known for creating cast glass collages, bas-relief images and sculpture for corporate, public and residential projects. She exhibits internationally and is included in numerous collections.

COMMISSIONS: Elliot Hotel, Seattle, WA, 2001; REI Flagship Stores, Tokyo, Japan, and Denver, CO, 2000; King St. Center, Seattle, WA, 1999; Deschutes County Library, Bend, OR, 1999

EXHIBITIONS: *International Sculpture Invitational,* Seadrift, TX, 2001; Sculpture show, Erlangen, Germany, 2000; *Northwest Women in Glass,* Tacoma, WA, 1999; *Focus on Fire: Fine Art in Architecture,* Seattle, WA, 1994

PUBLICATIONS: *Glass House,* 2002; *Seattle Homes & Lifestyles Magazine,* 2001, *Modern Masters* HGTV, 1999

TANYA RAGIR
pp. 118-119

Tanya Ragir Studio
3587 Ocean View Avenue
Los Angeles, CA 90066
TEL 310-390-5919
FAX 310-398-7965
E-mail: tanya@tanyaragir.com
Web: www.tanyaragir.com

Tanya Ragir is a figurative sculptor who works in a variety of media, including bronze, resin and clay. Her work is produced in either limited editions of nine or as unique pieces. Much of the work is inspired by the sensual relationship between landforms and human forms. By framing details of the figure, then changing the scale, the allegory becomes apparent.

"When sculpting people, I am interested in the essence of that person. I perceive beauty as authenticity, not perfection. In all the work, I have a great reverence for grace, and I attempt to find a balance between sensuality and power. In recent work I have been exploring my own conflict between my love for beauty in the physical form and my striving to go beyond the surface in the expression of that beauty. Much of the work deals with the juxtaposition of how a woman may be perceived externally, and her internal experience."

TANYA RAGIR
pp. 118-119

Tanya Ragir Studio
3587 Ocean View Avenue
Los Angeles, CA 90066
TEL 310-390-5919
FAX 310-398-7965
E-mail: tanya@tanyaragir.com
Web: www.tanyaragir.com

Tanya received a B.A. in Sculpture and Dance from the University of California at Santa Cruz in 1976. Her work has received numerous awards, has been featured in film and television productions and has been collected internationally.

Museums, collections and public commissions include *Artisans Walk*, City of Brea, CA; Rose Museum at Brandeis University; Columbia College of Dance Chicago; Total Art Museum, Seoul, Korea; Cultural Philosophic Center, Stockholm, Sweden; Frederick R. Weisman Art Foundation; Los Angeles County Museum of Art, *Art and Architecture Special Project*. Publications, reviews and media include *Mannequin,* feature film; "Two on the Town," TV magazine show; TV News Short, CBS Network, Dan Rather; *ArtScene; Los Angeles Times; Sculpture; Smithsonian Magazine; Art Business News; Glue Magazine.*

JANE RANKIN
pp. 121

19335 Greenwood Drive
Monument, CO 80132
TEL 719-488-9223
FAX 719-488-1650
E-mail: jrankin@magpiehill.com

Jane Rankin creates limited-edition bronze sculpture specializing in life-size and tabletop figures, mostly of children and child-related things.

COMMISSIONS: Harvest Community, 2002, Ft. Collins, CO; Town Hall, 1999, Cary, NC; Morse Park, 1998, Lakewood, CO

COLLECTIONS: Dogwood Festival Center, Jackson, MS; Waukegan Public Library, IL; Colorado Springs Fine Art Center, CO; Buell Children's Museum, Pueblo, CO; Lincoln Children's Museum, NE; Creative Artist Agency, Beverly Hills, CA

EXHIBITIONS: Pueblo Street Gallery, 2001-2002, Pueblo, CO; American Numismatic Association, 2002, Colorado Springs, CO

GUILD SOURCEBOOKS: *Architect's 14, 15; Architectural & Interior Art 16*

KIM CLARK RENTERIA
pp. 71

Lighthouse Glass
2409 Huldy Street
Houston, TX 77019
TEL 713-524-5945
FAX 713-522-4394
E-mail: lhglass@juno.com
Web: www.lighthouseglass.com

Before establishing Lighthouse Glass, Kim Clark Renteria worked in the field of design and lived in New York City, Toronto, Montreal and Hong Kong. She has an exceptional ability to create in a way that goes far beyond the boundaries of the conventional. Lighthouse Glass provides innovative, site-specific architectural art glass, combining the highest standards of fabrication while working both independently and in collaboration with architects, interior designers and individuals. Commissions include residential, commercial and liturgical applications. Brochure and project costs are available on request.

RECENT PROJECTS: Woman's Wellness Center, 2001, St. Joseph's Hospital, Houston, TX

GUILD SOURCEBOOKS: *Architect's 12, 14*

KIA RICCHI
pp. 179

Centerline Production, Inc.
2425 McMichael Road
St. Cloud, FL 34772
TEL/FAX 407-891-1422
E-mail: kia@gdi.net
Web: www.centerlineart.com

Kia Ricchi creates sculpture that is functional and aesthetic. Made from cement and steel, her sculptures enhance pool and garden settings. Her work can also be placed in high-traffic areas such as airports and malls, where it may provide public seating or creative signage.

RECENT PROJECTS: *Character Through Competition,* 2001, Hillsborough County, FL

COMMISSIONS: Hardin Holdings, 2001, Ft. Lauderdale, FL

EXHIBITIONS: Ann Norton Sculpture Garden, 2000, Palm Beach, FL; Orlando Museum of Art, 1999, Orlando, FL

PUBLICATIONS: *Landscape Architecture,* 2001; *Florida Design,* 2001; *Pool and Spa News,* 2001

GUILD SOURCEBOOKS: *Architectural & Interior Art 16*

CLAUDE RIEDEL
pp. 72

5133 Bryant Avenue South
Minneapolis, MN 55419
TEL 612-824-5308
FAX 651-645-2439
E-mail: riede006@umn.edu

"It belongs in this place," clients respond passionately to Claude Riedel's timeless designs, which blend ancient traditions with modern sensibilities. With sensitivity and fine craftsmanship, Claude creates ceremonial art in stained glass windows, lamps, wall reliefs and sculptures that capture the essence of his clients' visions within the architectural setting.

COMMISSIONS: *Wall of Joy,* glass, stone and wood relief sculpture, B'nai Emet Synagogue, St. Louis Park, MN; *Healing Hands,* glass sculpture, St. John's Hospital meditation room, Maplewood, MN; *Tree of Life,* ornamental glass case, Adath Jeshurun Synagogue, Minnetonka, MN; votive candleholder, blown glass, St. Elizabeth Ann Seton Catholic Church, Coral Springs, FL; *Ner Tamid,* Shir Tikva Synagogue, Minneapolis, MN and Bet Shalom Synagogue, Minnetonka, MN

KIM H. RITTER
pp. 306

www.galleryquilts.com
18727 Point Lookout
Houston, TX 77058
TEL 281-333-3224
FAX 281-333-8581
E-mail: kim@galleryquilts.com
Web: www.galleryquilts.com

Kim H. Ritter creates layered and quilted constructions in silk, incorporating surface treatments such as dyeing, painting, screen-printing and beading. Her art quilts and mixed-media works for unique spaces explore the tensions between surface and layer, both real and imagined.

COLLECTIONS: TAACCL, Houston, TX

EXHIBITONS: *Face Value: Quilts by Kim H. Ritter,* Wheelwright Museum

PUBLICATIONS: *Fiberarts Magazine,* 2002; *American Craft,* 2001; *Fiberarts Design Book 6,* 1999

GUILD SOURCEBOOKS: *Architectural & Interior Art 16*

ROB FISHER SCULPTURE
pp. 150-151

228 North Allegheny Street
Bellefonte, PA 16823
TEL 814-355-1458
FAX 814-353-9060
E-mail: glenunion@aol.com
Web: www.sculpture.org/portfolio

Lanterna and *Protos* express the dynamic relationship between contrasting, yet complementary, forms. They represent a growing body of work that parallels Rob Fisher's widely recognized suspended sculptures installed throughout the U.S., Japan and Saudi Arabia. Fabricated in stainless steel and aluminum, these artworks range in scale from floor and wall pieces, such as *Chambered Nautilus,* for private residences, to the Arrivals Hall of the Philadelphia International Airport.

GUILD SOURCEBOOKS: *Architect's 9, 11, 12, 13, 14, 15; Architectural & Interior Art 16*

ROB FISHER SCULPTURE
pp. 150-151

228 North Allegheny Street
Bellefonte, PA 16823
TEL 814-355-1458
FAX 814-353-9060
E-mail: glenunion@aol.com
Web: www.sculpture.org/portfolio

COMMISSIONS: Arrivals Hall artwork, 2002, Philadelphia International Airport, PA, light, glass and painted aluminum; monumental kinetic sculpture, 2002, Gateway Exchange, Columbia, MD, aluminum masts, stainless steel nets and rigging, and painted aluminum; suspended atrium sculpture, 2002, National Education Association headquarters, Washington, DC, painted steel, anodized aluminum and stainless steel; *Ark Doors* sculpture and *Eternal Light,* 2002, Temple Beth El, Lancaster, PA, bronze and copper; aerial sculpture, visitor center, 2002, Astra Zeneca Pharmaceuticals, Wilmington, DE

KEVIN ROBB
pp. 152

Kevin Robb Studios
7001 W. 35th Avenue
Wheat Ridge, CO 80033-6373
TEL 303-431-4758
FAX 303-425-8802
E-mail: 3d@kevinrobb.com
Web: kevinrobb.com

Kevin Robb creates individual contemporary sculptures in stainless steel or bronze, as well as limited-edition cast bronze for intimate environments and large-scale public areas. Robb brings a natural curiosity to his work, combined with the knowledge gained from an understanding of how positive and negative spaces, shadow and light work together.

RECENT PROJECTS: Macaroni Grill, Dallas, TX; Olen Properties, Newport Beach, CA

COMMISSIONS: Abrasive Technologies, Powell, OH, 2001; First Presbyterian Church, St. Paul, MN, 2001

GUILD SOURCEBOOKS: *Architect's 12, 13, 14, 15*

BERNARD J. ROBERTS
pp. 154

W1952 Roosevelt Road
Oconomowoc, WI 53066-9551
TEL 920-474-4103
E-mail: impr@gdinet.com
Web: www.bernardjroberts.com

Bernard Roberts has a broad background as a sculptor, with direction and interest towards hand-carved wood. His sculptures are finished in their natural wood or used as models for casting in bronze. Enlarged or reduced sizes are available. Roberts finds inspiration and form from the dynamics of growth and life processes, cell division and amoeboid shapes, as well as human, animal and plant forms. He is confident and productive in his artistic creations, constantly pursuing the search for new materials and forms of expression.

GUILD SOURCEBOOKS: *Designer's 11, 12, 14; Architect's 15*

PRISCILLA ROBINSON
pp. 282-283

2811 Hancock Drive
Austin, TX 78731
TEL 512-452-3516
TEL 505-758-2608
FAX 512-452-3516
E-mail: pjr@priscillarobinson.com
Web: www.priscillarobinson.com

Priscilla Robinson creates three-dimensional wall sculptures and heavily textured paintings using organic plant cellulose and space-age synthetics. These unique pieces are designed for specific locations in large corporate lobbies and intimate private residences.

RECENT PROJECTS: Charles Schwab & Co., 2001, Austin, TX; Kaiser Permanente, 2001, Orange County, CA; Morristown Memorial Hospital, 2002, Morristown, NJ

COMMISSIONS: Blue Cross Blue Shield, Shell Oil, Tokyo Electron American Headquarters

COLLECTIONS: American Airlines, Chevron Pipeline

EXHIBITIONS: Holland Paper Biennale; Museum de Corso, Rome

GUILD SOURCEBOOKS: *Designer's 14; Architectural & Interior Art 16*

ROCK COTTAGE GLASSWORKS, INC.
pp. 219

Dierk Van Keppel
6801 Farley
Merriam, KS 66203
TEL 913-262-1763
FAX 913-262-0430
E-mail: rcglass@grapevine.net

Rock Cottage Glassworks creates blown and cast glass objects and combines them with wrought iron, wood or stone to produce custom lighting for residential, restaurant and hospitality projects.

Brochure and CD-ROM of additional installations and art glass inventory available upon request.

COMMISSIONS: Union Café, Union Station, Kansas City, MO, 1999; Pierpont's, Union Station, Kansas City, MO, 1999; Lydia's, Kansas City, MO, 2000

COLLECTIONS: Northwest Airlines, Detroit, MI

ALAN ROSEN
pp. 205

Alan Rosen Furniture Makers Ltd.
3740 Legoe Bay Road
Lummi Island, WA 98262
TEL 360-758-7452
FAX 360-758-2498
E-mail: alindyrosen@earthlink.net

Since 1974 Alan Rosen has been creating distinctive original and custom furniture known for its simple elegance, uncompromising craftsmanship and attention to detail. The careful selection of woods, traditional joinery and signature hand-rubbed finish ensure enjoyment by future generations.

COMMISSIONS: William Gates III, 1999, Medina, WA; Paul Allen, 1999, Mercer Island, WA; David Usher, 1995, Carmel, CA; Sacred Heart Church, 1993, Bellevue, WA

COLLECTIONS: Grizzly Industrial Inc., Bellingham, WA, Columbus, MD and Williamsport, PA

TALLI ROSNER-KOZUCH
pp. 268

Pho-Tal Inc.
15 North Summit Street
Tenafly, NJ 07670
TEL 201-569-3199
FAX 201-569-3392
E-mail: tal@photal.com
Web: www.photal.com

Talli Rosner-Kozuch works in black and white, sepia tones, color, platinum prints, lithographs and etchings. Her areas of expertise include large-format photography. The images range in size and vary in style from architectural portraiture and documentary to landscape and still life. Using signature techniques, she achieves a unique blend of minimalism and sensuality in her work.

RECENT PROJECTS: Twenty exhibitions all over the United States, Europe and Asia working with designers and galleries on hospitals, hotels, restaurants and companies in commercial buildings.

COMMISSIONS: Restaurants, hotels, banks, corporations, building entrances, stores, Ethan Allen catalog

GUILD SOURCEBOOKS: *Designer's 13, 14, 15; Architectural & Interior Art 16*

CYBELE ROWE
pp. 153

PO Box 393
Silverado, CA 92676
TEL 714-649-3109
E-mail: cybele@cybele3.net
Web: www.cybele3.net

Bold in color and message, Cybele's work is suitable for exterior and interior placement. Each unique piece is hand-built ceramic with a dynamic and vibrant painterly approach to glazing. The hollow vessels are made in one piece and are predominantly human-size in scale. Cybele's credits include the Smithsonian Institute, Washington, DC, World Bank, Washington, DC, Bergdorf Goodman, New York, NY, The Kennedy Center, Washington, DC, Rockefeller Center, New York, NY, and galleries and collections on three continents. Please visit her website and see in detail the accomplishments of this prolific and creative artist.

BRIAN F. RUSSELL
pp. 155

Brian F. Russell Studio
10385 Long Road
Arlington, TN 38002
TEL 901-867-7300
FAX 901-867-7843
E-mail: info@brianrusselldesigns.com
Web: www.brianrusselldesigns.com

The transparency and optical nature of colored cast glass has an inherent emotional effect that enables the artist to speak quietly, yet powerfully, about his ideas on the nature of reality and the purity of form. The effect of the metal forgings, synergized by the images presented in vivid glass castings, gives life to his sculptures.

COMMISSIONS: Rhodes College, 2001, Memphis, TN

COLLECTIONS: Bell South Collection, Tennessee State Museum, Nashville, TN

PUBLICATIONS: *Direct Metal Sculpture,* 2001

JAMES THOMAS RUSSELL
pp. 156

James Russell Sculpture
1930 Lomita Boulevard
Lomita, CA 90717
TEL 310-326-0785
FAX 310-326-1470
E-mail: james@russellsculpture.com
Web: www.russellsculpture.com

James T. Russell's sculptures are ribbons of stainless steel, gracefully arching and twirling in space. He is in his fourth decade of creating worldwide commissions of innovative and durable sculpture, ranging from wall relief to gallery editions to fountain settings and monumental towers of gleaming inspiration.

COMMISSIONS: Princess Cruises, 2000, Monfalcone, Italy; City of South San Francisco, 1999, CA; AT Kearney, Inc., 1999, Chicago, IL; Motorola Corporation, 1998, Beijing, China

COLLECTIONS: Architectural Digest, CA; Riverside Art Museum, Riverside, CA; Caesar's World, Century City, CA

PUBLICATIONS: *Landscape Architect,* 2000; *Focus Santa Fe,* 2000; *Art Calendar,* 1999

GUILD SOURCEBOOKS: *Architect's 7, 8, 12, 13, 14, 15; Architectural & Interior Art 16*

SABLE STUDIOS
pp. 101

Paul Sable
2737 Rosedale Avenue
Soquel, CA 95073
TEL 800-233-7309
E-mail: paul@sablestudios.com
Web: www.sablestudios.com

Paul Sable has collaborated successfully with art consultants, architects and designers for over 35 years. His kinetic, acrylic mobiles integrate color, light and movement to create a multidimensional experience. His custom-designed sculptures harmonize into private, corporate and public spaces.

RECENT PROJECTS: Union City Senior Center, CA; Lucent Technologies, CO

COMMISSIONS: Metro Plaza building, San Jose, CA; Syntex Corporation, Hayward, CA; Berklee Performance Center, Boston, MA; Quantum Corporation; 3 Comm; Cadence Corporation

GUILD SOURCEBOOKS: *Architect's 11, 12, 13, 14, 15; Architectural & Interior Art 16*

ALEXANDRE SAFONOV
pp. 193

351 NE 163rd Street
Seattle, WA 98155
TEL/FAX 206-368-0137
E-mail: safonov@foxinternet.net
Web: www.sashasart.com

Sculptor and master wood carver Alexandre Safonov works with equal ease in wood, bronze or stone. His pieces pulse with energy and movement, yet show exquisite detail. The flawless proportions of his work and the expressive faces he sculpts give each figure a timeless beauty. His passion is to make liturgical works that glorify the Lord.

RECENT PROJECTS: *Fishermen's Memorial,* Jerisich Park, Gig Harbor, WA, *Madonna and Child,* Little Company of Mary Hospital, Torrence, CA

COLLECTIONS: Trinity Broadcasting Network, Tustin, CA; Benny Hinn Ministries, Irving, TX; Bill Gates, Redmond, WA

EXHIBITIONS: *Winter Visuals,* 2001, Gig Harbor, WA; *Potpourri of Art,* 2000, Bellingham, WA

GUILD SOURCEBOOKS: *Designer's 14, 15*

EDWINA SANDYS
pp. 178

565 Broadway #2
New York, NY 10012
TEL 212-343-7066
FAX 212-343-2979
E-mail: edwinasandys@yahoo.com
Web: www.edwinasandys.com

Edwina Sandys is a sculptor and painter, and the 1997 recipient of the United Nations' Society of Artists Award for Excellence. The art of Edwina Sandys encompasses diverse subject matter, ranging from lighthearted to profound. Her clearly recognizable style uses positive and negative forms to powerful effect. "If you have the image right, the piece will work regardless of scale or materials," she says.

Sandys' work is "people friendly" and she welcomes commissions for lively places, both public and private. She would love to create art and murals for restaurants and hotels. In 1999, her 12-foot-high *Millennium Tulips* graced New York's Park Avenue.

JOY SAVILLE
pp. 307

244 Dodds Lane
Princeton, NJ 08540
TEL/FAX 609-924-6824
E-mail: jsaville@rcn.com
Web: www.joysaville.com

Joy Saville expresses "frozen moments" in her fabric constructions by piecing cotton, linen and silk in an impressionistic, painterly manner. A colorist, she uses the inherent quality of natural fabrics to absorb or reflect light, producing a constant interplay of light, texture and color.

COMMISSIONS: Johnson & Johnson; Ortho Pharmaceutical; The Jewish Center, Princeton, NJ

COLLECTIONS: American Craft Museum; The Newark Museum; Bristol-Myers Squibb; Time-Warner, Inc.; Ropes & Gray, Boston, MA; Wilmington Trust, DE; H.J. Heinz; PepsiCo; Art in Embassies 2000 Program, Brunei

EXHIBITIONS: Solo and group exhibitions throughout North America and internationally since 1980

JOAN SCHULZE
pp. 308

808 Piper Avenue
Sunnyvale, CA 94087
TEL/FAX 408-736-7833
E-mail: joan@joan-of-arts.com
Web: www.joan-of-arts.com

Schulze's cutting-edge mixed-media quilts have helped this American art form gain worldwide recognition. Her aesthetics reflect today's world while simultaneously celebrating beauty in their detail.

COMMISSIONS: Adobe Systems, Inc., San Jose, CA; Isle of Daiichi Chapel, Tokyo, Japan; Allied Capital, MD

COLLECTIONS: American Craft Museum; Renwick Gallery, Smithsonian; Cities of Palo Alto and Sunnyvale; Allied Capital; Allstate; State Farm; Kaiser

EXHIBITIONS: Beijing International Art Tapestry Exhibition, 2000; Danish Textile Museum, 2000

PUBLICATIONS: *The Art of Joan Schulze,* 1999

GUILD SOURCEBOOKS: *THE GUILD 3, 4, 5; Designer's 8, 9, 10, 12, 13*

MARSH SCOTT
pp. 180

3275 Laguna Canyon Road
Studio M1
Laguna Beach, CA 92651
TEL 949-494-8672
FAX 949-494-8671
Email: marsh@marshscott.com
Web: www.marshscott.com

Marsh Scott works in sculptural and 2D media to create site-specific commissions for public, corporate, medical, residential and hospitality projects.

COMMISSIONS: Public Art, 2000, 1999, Brea, CA; Laguna Beach, CA, 2001, 2000; Los Angeles, CA, 2001; Associated Television International, CA; Baxter Labs, CA; Canal Plus US, CA; Discovery Museum, CA; Edison Co., NV and CA; Four Seasons, NV; Regency Hotel, Guam; Orange County Airport, CA; Torrance Memorial Hospital, CA; Verizon, CA; Viking Components, CA; Waterfront Hilton, CA

SCULPTURE BY TIMOTHY P. SCHMALZ, INC.
pp. 122-123, 194-195

PO Box 424
Kitchener, ON N2G 3Y9
Canada
TEL 800-590-3264
FAX 519-742-1273
E-mail: tony@sculpturebytps.com
Web: www.sculpturebytps.com

Inspiring Christian and contemporary figurative sculpture by one of the world's leading artists. Timothy is a master of the human form and expression. Most of his work is cast in bronze with some smaller pieces cast in resin stone. His work for the general public ranges in size from monumental to miniature.

RECENT PROJECTS: *One Body,* Vatican Gardens, Rome, Italy; *St. Francis,* Assisi, Italy; *Our Lady Queen of Peace,* 23 bronze sculptures, Gainesville, FL; *Open Your Heart,* St. Paul the Apostle, New Middleton, OH; Mining monument, Bell Park, Sudbury, ON, Canada

COLLECTIONS: Mother Teresa Memorial, National Museum of Catholic Art & History, New York, NY

PUBLICATIONS: *Environment & Art,* 2001; *Ministry & Liturgy,* 2001; *Celebrations,* 2001

MAUREEN A. SEAMONDS
pp. 181

The Produce Station Studios
723 Seneca Street
Webster City, IA 50595
TEL 515-832-5120
FAX 515-832-4851
E-mail: seamonds@wmtel.net
Web: www.wmtel.net/~seamonds

Maureen Seamonds' sculptural works relate the rhythms of the land to the gestural expression of the human spirit. Her sculptures often incorporate water and light to create a dynamic integration of space and form. Seamonds will work with architects and designers to create site-specific sculpture and fountains; prices start at $8,000.

RECENT PROJECTS: Main Street, Ames, IA; Blanden Museum (commission), Fort Dodge, IA; Drake University, Des Moines, IA

COLLECTIONS: Ocean Sports Medicine Clinic, Myrtle Beach, SC; Art on Main Street, Ames, IA (purchase award)

PUBLICATIONS: *Lifework: Portraits of Women Artists,* 1998; *Iowa Women Artists Archives,* 1998; *Craft in America: Celebrating the Creative Work of the Hand,* 1998

GERALD SICILIANO
pp. 182

Studio Design Associates
9 Garfield Place
Brooklyn, NY 11215-1903
TEL/FAX 718-636-4561
E-mail: gsstudio@concentric.net
Web: www.geraldsicilianostudio.com

Classical figurative and non-representational sculptures, meticulously crafted in elegant and durable materials, are the hallmarks of Gerald Siciliano's work. From the intimate to the monumental, studio and commission-based sculptures are created for discerning collectors, architects, designers and corporations worldwide. We invite your inquiries via telephone, e-mail or the internet.

COMMISSIONS/COLLECTIONS: American Airlines; Bristol-Myers Squibb; The Brooklyn Museum; American Axle & Manufacturing Co.; The John Templeton Foundation; Canon USA; The Mozart Companies; Sparks Exhibits & Environments Co.; Dong Baek Art Center, Pusan, Korea; Pusan International Sculpture Symposium; Olympic Park, Pusan, Korea; Kyongnam International Sculpture Symposium

JEFF G. SMITH
pp. 75

Architectural Stained Glass, Inc.
PO Box 1126
Fort Davis, TX 79734-1126
TEL 915-426-3311
FAX 915-426-3366
E-mail: asg@overland.net
Web: www.overland.net/~asg

Since 1978, Smith has developed the ability to weave varied perspectives into glass tapestries that are meaningful to all. Smith was again recognized by the AIA's Interfaith Forum on Religion, Art and Architecture with a 2001 Honor Award for St. Albert Catholic Church in Austin, TX. Refer to previous GUILD sourcebooks for additional examples of both liturgical and secular work.

RECENT PROJECTS: St. Bridget Catholic Church, Seattle, WA; Wilcox Interdenominational Chapel, Lihue, HI; Washington (DC) Hebrew Congregation; US Courthouse, Fargo, ND; American Airlines Admirals Club, Dallas-Fort Worth, TX; University of Alaska, Fairbanks, AK

GUILD SOURCEBOOKS: *THE GUILD 4, 5; Architect's 7, 8, 9, 10, 11, 12, 13, 14, 15; Architectural & Interior Art 16*

CYNTHIA SPARRENBERGER
pp. 124

Sparrenberger Studio
5975 East Otero Drive
Englewood, CO 80112
TEL 303-741-3031 (studio)
TEL 303-618-8974 (cell)
E-mail: cynthia6@mac.com
Web: www.sparrenbergerstudio.com

Cynthia Sparrenberger's work is figurative with a loose, impressionistic quality. Because of her dance background, she is passionate about gesture, line and movement, for it is these very elements that bring a sculpture to life.

RECENT PROJECTS: Life-size sculpture for Mynelle Gardens, Jackson, MS

COMMISSIONS: Canine portrait, 2002, Sedalia, CO; private portrait, 2000, Parker, CO

COLLECTIONS: Mynelle Gardens, Jackson, MS; The Washington Ballet, Washington, DC

EXHIBITIONS: *The Renaissance Sale,* 2001, Houston, TX; *The American Art Classic,* 2001, Houston, TX; *Sculpture in the Park,* 2000, Loveland, CO

PUBLICATIONS: *The Hilton Head Monthly,* 2001; *The Clarion Ledger,* 2001

ARTHUR STERN
pp. 76-77, 196-197

Arthur Stern Studios
1075 Jackson Street
Benicia, CA 94510
TEL/FAX 707-745-8480
E-mail: arthur@arthurstern.com
Web: www.arthurstern.com

Arthur Stern Studios creates site-specific architectural glass installations, primarily in leaded glass. Specializing in the collaboration with design professionals and clients, the studio currently has installations in 36 states, as well as Japan. Commissions range from residential work to large public art projects and churches. Arthur Stern has been widely published and has won numerous awards, including several American Institute of Architects design awards, as well as honors from the Interfaith Forum on Religion, Art & Architecture, The Construction Specifications Institute and *Ministry and Liturgy* magazine's BENE Awards.

ARTHUR STERN
pp. 76-77, 196-197

Arthur Stern Studios
1075 Jackson Street
Benicia, CA 94510
TEL/FAX 707-745-8480
E-mail: arthur@arthurstern.com
Web: www.arthurstern.com

Arthur Stern is an award-winning architectural glass artist who offers complete art glass services, beginning with the design process and professional renderings, expert fabrication and following through to installation. The studio can accommodate projects of any scale. Stern considers himself a designer first and an artist second, creating each installation with sensitivity to its environment and the project's design criteria. Each project undertaken receives the same thorough attention to detail and fine craftsmanship. Arthur Stern also works in other media, including wood and glass bas-relief sculpture, mixed media works on canvas and works on paper.

ARTHUR STERN
pp. 76-77, 196-197

Arthur Stern Studios
1075 Jackson Street
Benicia, CA 94510
TEL/FAX 707-745-8480
E-mail: arthur@arthurstern.com
Web: www.arthurstern.com

RECENT PROJECTS: Pasao Colorado, Pasadena, CA; St. Luke Lutheran Church, Ann Arbor, MI; First Baptist Church, Davis, CA; Christ Church Episcopal, Portola Valley, CA; Sorenson residence, Wausau, WI; Meitus residence, Santa Fe, NM; McLaughlin Youth Center, Anchorage, AK; Pearson residence, Mill Valley, CA; Peace Health Medical Center, Longview, WA; Shell Ridge Community Church, Walnut Creek, CA; Creasman residence, Monte Serena, CA; Dobbs residence, New York, NY; Carneros Creek Winery, Napa, CA; Lilienfeld residence, Hillsborough, NJ; Koski residence, San Francisco, CA; Baalman residence, Richland, WA; Bell residence, Los Altos, CA; Bradshaw residence, Havana, FL; Dr. Hoyt office, Modesto, CA; Eberhard residence, Washington, DC

ARTHUR STERN
pp. 76-77, 196-197

Arthur Stern Studios
1075 Jackson Street
Benicia, CA 94510
TEL/FAX 707-745-8480
E-mail: arthur@arthurstern.com
Web: www.arthurstern.com

AWARDS: Bene Award, 2001 and 2000, *Ministry and Liturgy* magazine; Millennium Design Award in "Art in Architecture," 2000, American Institute of Architects and the Interfaith Forum on Religion, Art and Architecture; "Colleague Award"/AIA East Bay Chapter Award, 1999, American Institute of Architects; Design Award, 1996, American Institute of Architects; San Francisco Chapter Award, 1995, The Construction Specifications Institute; *Architectural Record* magazine Award, 1995; Gold Award, 1994, *Art of California* magazine Discovery Awards; Dichroic Glass in Architecture Award, 1993, Optical Coatings Laboratory, Inc.; Award in "Art in Architecture," 1990, Interfaith Forum on Religion, Art and Architecture (an affiliate of the American Institute of Architects)

JANE STERRETT
pp. 231

Jane Sterrett Studio
160 Fifth Avenue
New York, NY 10010
TEL 212-929-2566
FAX 212-929-0924
E-mail: sterjak@ix.netcom.com
Web: www.janesterrett.com

Jane Sterrett's art is available as digital reproductions printed with archival inks, ranging in size from original dimensions to mural enlargements. These collages use imagery that often includes her original photography. Her art has been commissioned by corporate and private clients and has been exhibited internationally.

RECENT PROJECTS: Children's Hospital, Montefiore Medical Center, Bronx, NY; Opus One restaurant, Naples, FL; Chase Metrotech Cafeteria, Brooklyn, NY

COLLECTIONS: Trigon, Richmond, VA; Hymmen Group, Bielefeld, Germany; New York Life Insurance, NY; Eli Lilly, Indianapolis, IN

PUBLICATIONS: *Object Lessons*, 2001

GUILD SOURCEBOOKS: *Designer's 14, 15; Architectural & Interior Art 16*

MARTIN STURMAN
pp. 281

Martin Sturman Sculptures
416 Cricketfield Court
Westlake Village, CA 91361
TEL 805-381-0032
FAX 805-381-1116
E-mail: mlsturman@aol.com
Web: www.steelsculptures.com

Martin Sturman creates original contemporary sculptures and furniture in carbon steel or stainless steel. His work is suitable for indoor or outdoor placement. Stainless steel surfaces are burnished to achieve a beautiful shimmering effect. Carbon steel sculptures are painted with acrylic and coated with polyurethane to preserve color vitality. Sturman encourages site-specific and collaborative efforts.

COMMISSIONS: Hyatt Westlake Plaza Hotel, Westlake Village, CA; Tesoro Galleries, Beverly Hills, CA; Manhattan Beach Car Wash, Manhattan Beach, CA

COLLECTIONS: McDonald's Corporate Art Collection, Oakbrook, IL; McGraw-Hill Publishing Company, Columbus, OH

GUILD SOURCEBOOKS: *Architect's 12, 14; Designer's 7, 8, 9, 10, 11, 12, 13, 14, 15; Architectural & Interior Art 16*

CHARLES P. STURROCK
pp. 157

Free Form Fabrication, Inc.
875 Van Gordon Street
Golden, CO 80401
TEL 303-237-4590
E-mail: freeformfab@aol.com

The work created by Charles Sturrock has been described as mesmerizing. His sculptures have a celestial quality; their motion is similar to that of satellites effortlessly rotating in space. Scale ranges from monumental to tabletop. His sculptures are unique and have captured the imaginations of numerous private collectors across the United States, Canada and Mexico.

COMMISSIONS: Lamar Community College, 2001, Lamar, CO

COLLECTIONS: Art in Public Places, State of Colorado; Art on the Corner, Grand Junction, CO; City of Greeley, CO; Catholic Archdioceses of Denver, CO

DAVID SWAGEL
pp. 206

Thunder Diamonds and Steel Woodcarving
2700 North Hayden Road #3001
Scottsdale, AZ 85257
TEL/FAX 480-945-5717
CELL 480-628-6820
E-mail: daveswagel@aol.com
Web: www.geocities.com/DiamondDave 85257/SwagelArtMusic.html

David Swagel has studied the ancient trade of timber framing, and the use of joinery derived from this trade pervades his work. Although known for his carving, inlay and joinery, Swagel has also completed some very involved turning and finishing projects. His work tends to be bold, unusual and often whimsical.

RECENT PROJECTS: Bahar private collection; Cottrell private collection, Scottsdale/Paradise Valley, AZ

COMMISSIONS: Parrish collection, 1998, Scottsdale/Paradise Valley, AZ; Timbanard collection, 1997, Paradise Valley, AZ

EXHIBITIONS: L'Asietique Gallery, 2002, Scottsdale, AZ; Kismet Gallery, 2002, Scottsdale, AZ; Toklat Gallery, 2002, Aspen, CO; Ra Fine Art, 2000, Scottsdale, AZ; Life Forms Interiors, 2000, Aspen, CO

T. DELANEY INC./SEAM STUDIO
pp. 83

Topher Delaney
156 South Park
San Francisco, CA 94107
TEL 415-896-2998
FAX 415-896-2995
E-mail: tdelaney@tdelaney.com
Web: www.tdelaney.com

Topher Delaney majored in cultural anthropology and philosophy with an ultimate degree in landscape architecture. This combination of disciplines has created a framework for their studio, a collaborative team that has extensive training in engineering, science, drawing and sculpture to integrate the dream with the reality. Seam Studio, as the name implies, is a venue for the investigation of a wide range of media seamed together to form unique sculptures, as well as complex dynamic installations. Seam Studio has explored the boundaries of site installations for 27 years. Their team is composed of four full-time artists and 12 fabricators of colored concrete, mosaic, metal and stone. Studios located in San Francisco and New York offer public galleries that feature the studio's work, as well as installations by fellow artists.

NAOMI TAGINI
pp. 284

1902 Comstock Avenue
Los Angeles, CA 90025
TEL 310-552-1877
FAX 310-552-2679
FAX 310-277-5329
E-mail: naomi@naomitagini.com
Web: www.naomitagini.com

Naomi Tagini creates moveable blocks of color for positioning practically anywhere in an environment — down a hallway, up a staircase or around a corner.

She creates her graphic art for the wall using several coats of paint that are brushed, rolled or sprayed on; she frequently applies a crackle finish at the end of her design process. Each completed piece proves that color, texture, clean lines and asymmetry can all be achieved through the versatility of wood.

Tagini's work is created in pieces that are meant to be interchangeable. She wants the owner to have fun with the work — to rearrange it on a whim and participate with it.

Larger format work and custom colors are available.

GLENN TERRY
pp. 125

22800 Sandy Drive NE
East Bethel, MN 55005
TEL/FAX 763-413-1991
E-mail: greatart@skypoint.com
Web: www.glennterryart.com

Glenn Terry's figurative sculpture, fountains and murals express a refined sense of beauty, harmony and unity. They are distinctly American, yet profoundly timeless. He enjoys creating works that uplift and inspire others. Personalities rendered reveal their inner spirit and innate goodness. Allegorical works are visionary, anticipating a golden age of high ideals. A background in architecture, construction management and mural painting — in addition to sculpture — brings intelligent, graceful solutions to Glenn's incorporation of art with architecture. His broad range of interests and ability to work in all media are combined with an intuitive ability to understand a client's needs and aspirations. Expect an enjoyable experience.

COMMISSIONS: Cathedral of Saint Paul, Fort Snelling National Cemetery, United States Hockey League, Maple Hills Office Center, American Family Insurance, churches, offices, private residences, restaurants, gardens

MARJORIE TOMCHUK
pp. 293

44 Horton Lane
New Canaan, CT 06840
TEL 203-972-0137
FAX 203-972-3182
E-mail: mtomchuk@aol.com
Web: www.mtomchuk.com

Known for limited editions and her own handmade paper, the artist's work displays embossing with bold designs. Vibrant color is achieved with the use of an airbrush. An artist for 35 years, she has art in over 200 corporations and in 22 museums.

COLLECTIONS: Library of Congress Print Collection, Washington, DC; Art in Embassies, State Department, Washington, DC; American Museum of Papermaking, Atlanta, GA; Istanbul Ebri Evi, Uskadar, Turkey; Minato Mirai Concert Hall, Yokahama, Japan

EXHIBITIONS: American Museum of Papermaking, 2001, Atlanta, GA; Art Expo, 1979-2001, New York, NY

PUBLICATIONS: *Art Trends,* August 2000; *Journal of the Print World,* 1996, 1994, 1991

GUILD SOURCEBOOKS: *THE GUILD 5; Designer's 6, 7, 8, 9*

LUIS TORRUELLA
pp. 159

Cond. Tenerife, Apartment 1201
Ashford Avenue 1507
San Juan, PR 00911
TEL/FAX 787-722-8728
TEL 787-268-4977
E-mail: luistorruella@aol.com
Web: www.luistorruella.com

Luis Torruella, a Puerto Rican sculptor, designs in a contemporary, abstract context. His Caribbean heritage is reflected in his work's color, rhythm and movement. Torruella collaborates with architects, designers and developers in public and private commissions.

COLLECTIONS: Museo de Arte de Puerto Rico, San Juan; Mead Art Museum, Amherst, MA; Performing Arts Center, San Juan, PR; Skokie Sculpture Park, IL

EXHIBITIONS: Palma de Mallorca, 2001, Spain; Galeria Botello, 2002, 1997, 1994, 1992, San Juan, PR; Theatrical Institute, 1992, Moscow; World Expo, 1992, Seville, Spain; numerous private exhibitions

GUILD SOURCEBOOKS: *Architect's 14, 15; Architectural & Interior Art 16*

TRAVIS TUCK, METAL SCULPTOR
pp. 87

Travis Tuck
7 Beach Street
Martha's Vineyard, MA 02568
TEL/FAX 508-693-3914
E-mail: travis@travistuck.com
Web: www.travistuck.com

Travis Tuck is world renowned for the finest in custom weathervanes. Themes can also be executed as wall or free-standing sculptures. Each heirloom-quality piece is a three-dimensional sculpture, constructed in the pre-1800s repoussé method from copper and 23K gold leaf. Tuck creates work that complements any architectural style or depicts any personal interest, business symbol or logo.

RECENT PROJECTS: Nittany Lion weathervane, Penn State Beaver Stadium, State College, PA, 10.25' x 5'. Largest sculpted weathervane in the world.

GUILD SOURCEBOOKS: *Architect's 8, 10, 11, 12, 13, 14, 15; Architectural & Interior Art 16*

ANGELIKA TRAYLOR
pp. 73

100 Poinciana Drive
Indian Harbour Beach, FL 32937-4437
TEL 321-773-7640
FAX 321-779-3612
E-mail: angtraylor@earthlink.net
Web: www.angelikatraylor.com

Angelika Traylor specializes in one-of-a-kind architectural designs, autonomous panels and lamps which are easily recognized by their intricate and jewel-like compositions.

Often referred to as having painterly qualities, her works — such as the installation at Holmes Regional Medical Center shown in this book — reflect an original and intensive design process, implemented with meticulous craftsmanship and an unusually beautiful selection of glass.

She has received many awards, and her work has been featured in numerous publications.

COMMISSIONS: Holmes Regional Medical Center, Melbourne, FL, 1998; White House Christmas ornament collection, 1997, 1993; other corporate and private collections

GUILD SOURCEBOOKS: *THE GUILD 2, 3, 4, 5; Architect's 6; Designer's 7, 8, 9, 10, 11, 12, 13, 14, 15; Architectural & Interior Art 16*

TRIO DESIGN GLASSWARE
pp. 88

Renato Foti
253 Queen Street South
Kitchener, ON N2G 1W4
Canada
TEL 519-749-2814
FAX 519-749-6319
E-mail: renatofoti@rogers.com
Web: www.triodesignglassware.com

Contemporary designs and bold colors exemplify Renato's work. His main focus is to add structure, balance, color and simplicity to home and work environments. Balance is of critical importance to the designed spaces; it is a reflection of Renato's personal philosophy in life and in his art. These fused and slumped glass products range from small coasters to very large decorative wall sculptures, panels and sinks.

EXHIBITIONS: *One of a Kind,* Chicago, IL, 2001; *Retro Material Matters,* Toronto, ON, 2001; *The Masks We Wear,* Sandra Ainsley Gallery and Sculpture Society of Canada, Toronto, ON, 1998

PUBLICATIONS: *Canadian House & Home,* Dec/Jan, 2001-2002; *Glass Craftsman,* 2000

LAUREL TRUE
pp. 37

True Mosaics
Oakland, CA
TEL 415-584-9594
E-mail: truemosaics@hotmail.com
Web: www.truemosaics.com

Laurel True has been using ceramic tile, glass, mirror and stone to create architectural, sculptural and public art mosaics for over a decade. Her durable and beautiful mosaics adorn parks, hospitals, schools, restaurants, shops and private residences. True gracefully combines her materials, using skilled setting techniques and reflective materials to enhance the beauty and depth of a piece, adding an element of movement and change depending on the lighting and the position of the viewer.

GUILD SOURCEBOOKS: *Architect's 11, Designer's 10*

TUSKA INC.
pp. 207

Seth Tuska
147 Old Park Avenue
Lexington, KY 40502
TEL 859-255-1379
FAX 859-253-3199
Web: www.tuskastudio.com

Tuska Inc. represents the work of fine artist John R. Tuska (1931-1998). The studio offers reproductions of one of the artist's most engaging works: *Illuminates,* cutworks of the human form engaged in the motion of dance, suspended on open screens.

Each screen is assembled by hand to order in custom dimensions and materials, ranging from natural materials such as woods, steel, aluminum or bronze to contemporary polymers.

Each screen is meticulously executed and rendered in exceeding detail. True craftsman quality makes them ideal for use as window or wall hangings, room dividers, gates, shutters, landscape decorations or other custom applications.

KAREN URBANEK
pp. 309

314 Blair Avenue
Piedmont, CA 94611-4004
TEL 510-654-0685
FAX 510-654-2790
E-mail: KrnUrbanek@aol.com

Karen Urbanek builds painterly images and forms from complex color layers of dyed fibers compacted and coated for strength. Pieces can be two-sided, multi-layered, encompass areas of openwork, translucence, density and texture.

Works range from intimate to grand in scale, include wall pieces, standing and hanging sculptures, are strong rather than delicate, need not be framed and may be easily cleaned.

Commissions accepted. Visuals/pricing available upon request.

GUILD SOURCEBOOKS: *Designer's 13, 14, 15; Architectural & Interior Art 16*

ALICE VAN LEUNEN
pp. 295

Van Leunen Studios
9025 Southeast Terrace View Court
Amity, OR 97101
TEL 503-538-7789
TEL 503-349-7777
FAX 503-538-7704
E-mail: avanleunen@msn.com

Alice Van Leunen specializes in mixed-media wall treatments using paper, fabric, fibers, paint, metals, metallic foil, acrylic and glass – especially dichroic glass. Works range in size from small, intimate pieces to major architectural installations. The artist has had extensive experience collaborating with designers and architects to create site-specific works designed to meet the client's needs, and she is available to supervise installations of major works. Van Leunen's work is represented in numerous public, corporate and private collections. Commissions are welcome. Prices, slides and further information are available upon request.

SUSAN VENABLE
pp. 285

Venable Studio
2323 Foothill Lane
Santa Barbara, CA 93105
TEL 805-884-4963
FAX 805-884-4983
E-mail: susan@venablestudio.com
Web: www.venablestudio.com

Susan Venable's work is an exploration of surface and structure. Her reliefs are constructed of steel grids and copper wire, while the paintings are encaustic and oil. The physicality of the materials is expressed in the rich and complex surfaces.

Venable's work has been installed in public spaces, homes, corporations and museums in the United States, Europe, Asia, Mexico and Australia. These expressive and luminous pieces are low maintenance. They inspire both public and private spaces.

GUILD SOURCEBOOKS: *Architect's 12; Designer's 9, 10, 11, 12, 14, 15; Architectural & Interior Art 16*

RONNY WALKER
pp. 126

Ronny Sculpture Studios
PO Box 102684
Denver, CO 80250
TEL 303-810-5762
FAX 719-488-1563
E-mail: ronnysculpt@earthlink.net
Web: www.home.earthlink.net/~ronnysculpt

Ronny's bronze sculptures are an impressionistic rendering of the spiritual essence of her subjects. Versatile themes of music, religion, romance and more capture "moments in time." Her European and American training in the fine arts gives Ronny's sculpture a unique essence.

COMMISSIONS: St. Michael's Hospital, Oklahoma City, OK

PUBLICATIONS: *Sculpture Magazine*, 1998

WANNER SCULPTURE STUDIO
pp. 127

David M. Wanner
Jordan M. Wanner
5828 North 97th Street
Milwaukee, WI 53225
TEL/FAX 414-462-3569
E-mail: jwanner@execpc.com

For over 35 years, the Wanner Sculpture Studio has worked successfully with architects, designers and committees to complete sculptures for over 200 architectural settings throughout the U.S., including civic and private institutions, numerous cathedrals, hospitals and churches, and corporations such as American Family Insurance International Headquarters, State Bar of Wisconsin and the City of Milwaukee. The studio has its own art foundry and produces small to heroic-size bronzes.

WAYNE WILLIAMS STUDIO
pp. 269

Wayne Williams
15423 Sutton Street
Sherman Oaks, CA 91403
TEL 818-905-8097
FAX 818-995-6888
E-mail: wwclick@earthlink.net
Web: www.WayneWilliamsStudio.com

"Imagine a world without pollution, trash or development. No, it's not a John Lennon ballad, but the work of Wayne Williams."

The Los Angeles Times

Wayne Williams creates powerfully serene, unique images, capturing on film the singular, magic moments nature provides. Commissions are accepted.

COMMISSIONS: The Capital Group

COLLECTIONS: Kaiser, General Electric

EXHIBITIONS: International Photography Hall of Fame, 2001, Oklahoma City, OK

PUBLICATIONS: *America's Vanishing Landscapes: The Western States*

GUILD SOURCEBOOKS: *Architectural & Interior Art 16*

RED WOLF
pp. 89

Red Wolf Fine Art
PO Box 396
Laytonville, CA 95454
TEL 707-984-7003
FAX 707-984-9377
E-mail: redwolf@redwolffineart.com
Web: www.redwolffineart.com

Red Wolf incorporates modern industrial materials in a thin film-layering process that enables him to create elements of structural color within his painted artwork. Structural color in nature is observed in hummingbird feathers, tropical fish and opals. These effects have never been produceable in traditional pigmented paintings. Artwork is painted upon sandwiched honeycomb aluminum aerospace panels that are lightweight, rigid and nonflammable. Panels can be cut to conform to any configuration or any scale.

COMMISSIONS: Bahrain Sheraton night club, 2002, Manama, Bahrain; Nagoya Marriott Associa Hotel, 2000, Nagoya, Japan; Lockheed Space and Exhibition Center lobby, 1997, Sunnyvale, CA

PUBLICATIONS: *Designer's Workshop,* August 2000, Japan

BRUCE WOLFE
pp. 128-129

Bruce Wolfe Ltd.
206 El Cerrito Avenue
Piedmont, CA 94611
TEL 510-655-7871
FAX 510-601-7200
E-mail: landbwolfe@earthlink.net
Web: www.brucewolfe.com

Bruce Wolfe is a master of movement and contemporary figurative sculpture. He has 35 years of experience doing portraits, both bronzes and oils. He is able to capture likeness and personality in his pieces, bringing the subject to life in bronze. His tabletop nude bronzes have nuances of the figure and equally subtle patinas. Wolfe's pieces are collected by architects, corporations, designers, churches and individuals.

RECENT PROJECTS: Life-size bronze of Barbara Jordan for the Austin, TX, airport

PUBLICATIONS: *The Artists Magazine,* April 2000; *International Artist,* December/January 2000; *Sculpture Review,* Summer/Spring 2000 and Winter/Fall 1999

BRUCE WOLFE
pp. 128-129

Bruce Wolfe Ltd.
206 El Cerrito Avenue
Piedmont, CA 94611
TEL 510-655-7871
FAX 510-601-7200
E-mail: landbwolfe@earthlink.net
Web: www.brucewolfe.com

COMMISSIONS: Santa Barbara Mission, CA, 2001; Asian Art Museum, San Francisco, CA, 2000; Fratilli Della Scuole Cristiane, Rome, Italy, 1999; Steve Silver Productions, San Francisco, CA, 1999; Hazelton Moffit Braddock School, Hazelton, ND, 1998; Foster Enterprises, Foster City, CA, 1998; San Francisco Medical Center, San Francisco, CA, 1997; Bohemian Club, San Francisco, CA, 1996; Hebrew University, Jerusalem, Israel, 1996; Hoover Institute, Stanford University, CA, 1996; St. Mary's College, Moraca, CA, 1992-2000; San Francisco Opera House, San Francisco, CA, 1967

GUILD SOURCEBOOKS: *Architect's 11, 12, 13, 14, 15; Architectural & Interior Art 16*

DAVID WOODRUFF
pp. 211

Woodruff Woods
192 Sonata Drive
Lewisville, NC 27023
TEL 866-739-6637 (toll free)
E-mail: pdwoods@triad.rr.com
Web: www.pdwoods.com

David Woodruff creates one-of-a-kind hollow-formed vessels and other art objects from woods that possess great character as a result of trauma in the growing environment. This combination of genetic and environmental forces provides the raw materials for the multidimensional beauty found in Woodruff's art objects. The artist, using a wood lathe and museum-quality lacquer, creates art pieces that reveal the beauty of the variety in nature.

COMMISSIONS: Weaver-Cooke Construction, Greensboro, NC; Novant Healthcare, Winston-Salem, NC

EXHIBITIONS & AWARDS: Top score, Krasl Art Fair, St. Joseph, MI; top score, Tennessee Association of Craft Artists Crafts Fair, Chattanooga, TN; Piedmont Craftsman Guild, NC

GUILD SOURCEBOOKS: *Designer's 15; Architectural & Interior Art 16*

LARRY YOUNG
pp. 183

Larry Young Sculpture
8700 North Millsite Road
Columbia, MO 65201
TEL 573-449-6810
FAX 573-449-4759
E-mail: nexus@socket.net
Web: www.youngsculpture.com

From maquette to monumental, Young's work blends contemporary forms with classical themes and compositions that capture the human spirit. Refined forms, fluidity, movement and innovative use of negative space characterize Young's uniquely recognizable style.

COMMISSIONS: Stower's Institute for Medical Research, 2001, Kansas City, MO; Grand Bohemian Hotel, 2000, Orlando, FL; Matto City Museum, 1988, Japan

COLLECTIONS: Grounds for Sculpture, Hamilton, NJ; Museum of Art and Archaeology, Columbia, MO; Wandell Sculpture Garden, Urbana, IL; Methodist Hospital, Houston, TX

DANA ZED
pp. 78

5551 Masonic Avenue
Oakland, CA 94618
TEL 510-655-0289
FAX 510-428-2705
E-mail: studio@danazed.com
Web: www.danazed.com

Since 1981, Dana Zed has been fusing metal into glass. Site-specific projects include windows, doors, lamps, stairs, fireplaces, countertops, tables and walls. With a background in fine art, Dana is highly innovative and able to manifest ideas with the finest workmanship available.

COMMISSIONS: Pacific Gas and Electric Co. Executive Offices, San Francisco, CA

COLLECTIONS: Oakland Museum, Oakland, CA; Corning Museum of Glass, Corning, NY

EXHIBITIONS: Braunstein/Quay Gallery, San Francisco, CA

PUBLICATIONS: *Object Lessons,* 2001; *American Craft,* 1999, 1996; *Glass Art* magazine, 1996, 1994

LARRY ZGODA
pp. 79

Larry Zgoda Studio
2117 W. Irving Park Road
Chicago, IL 60618
TEL 773-463-3970
FAX 773-463-3978
E-mail: lz@larryzgodastudio.com
Web: www.larryzgodastudio.com

Larry Zgoda has been an artist of stained glass for nearly 30 years. Designs that reflect the essence of place, material innovations, and a reflective consideration of the total environment root Larry Zgoda's stained glass installations prominently in the architectural ornament tradition.

RECENT PROJECTS: Our Lady of the Angels Chapel, Marian Village Retirement Community, Lockport, IL

COMMISSIONS: Woodfin Suites, Emeryville, CA; TCF Tower, Minneapolis, MN; AARP, Washington, DC

PUBLICATIONS: *The Art of Stained Glass,* 1998; *Beautiful Things,* 2000; *Stained Glass Quarterly,* Fall 2001

GUILD SOURCEBOOKS: *THE GUILD 1, 2, 3, 4, 5; Architect's 6, 7, 8, 9, 10, 11, 12, 13, 14, 15*

BARBARA ZINKEL
pp. 256

Barbara Zinkel Editions
333 Pilgrim
Birmingham, MI 48009
TEL 248-642-9789
FAX 248-642-8374

Barbara Zinkel is known for her dramatic use of color in her limited-edition silkscreen prints and in her professionally hand-tufted and hand-carved custom wool rugs for residential and corporate interiors. Zinkel's work has been featured in decorators' show houses in Detroit and Columbus, on several television sets, and in the *Detroit News* (1994), *Hour Detroit* magazine (1999), and *Better Homes and Gardens Decorating* magazine (1987). While featured in various collections in the Netherlands, Hong Kong, Venezuela and Spain, Zinkel's domestic collection placements include General Motors, DaimlerChrysler Corporation Headquarters, Ford, Dupont, Steelcase, CBS, Chase Manhattan Bank, Texas Instruments, Honeywell, Ericcson and Verisign.

GUILD SOURCEBOOKS: *Designer's 15*

ARIZONA

ARKANSAS

CALIFORNIA

COLORADO

INDEX OF ARTISTS & COMPANIES